Fodor's InFocus

FLORIDA
KEYS

W9-BTM-532

14

TOP EXPERIENCES

The Florida Keys offer terrific experiences that should be on every traveler's list. Here are Fodor's top picks for a memorable trip.

1 Key West Architecture

Built on stilts to keep things cool, Key West's clapboard Conch houses feature porches with gingerbread trim. Many have been converted into atmospheric bed-and-breakfasts. *(Ch. 5)*

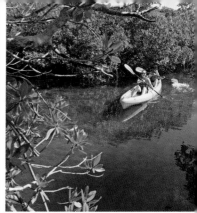

2 Kayaking and Canoeing

Whether you prefer sea kayaking, canoeing through calm and wildlife-rich mangrove waters, or stand-up paddleboarding, the Keys provide the setting and the perfect outfitters. *(Ch. 2)*

3 Key Lime Pie

You're going to need a lot of time and appetite, because key lime pie is everywhere, and everyone claims to make the best. *(Ch. 5)*

4 Dolphin Adventures

From watching them in the wild or captivity, to getting in the water to swim and interact with them, experiencing dolphins is a classic Keys adventure. *(Ch. 2)*

5 The Cuba Connection

Cuba looms large in Key West, which was settled by cigar-making immigrants. El Meson Pepe and El Siboney are two restaurants that serve Cuban delicacies. *(Ch. 5)*

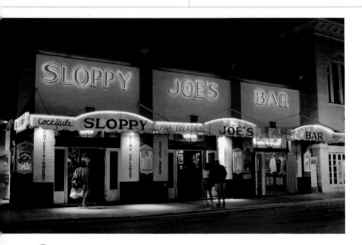

6 Duval Street

Do the Duval Crawl in Key West. There are no rules: stop for a drink, simply wander, or shop instead of drink. But you aren't allowed to go fun-free. *(Ch. 5)*

7 Key Largo's Christ of the Deep

Just outside of John Pennecamp Coral Reef State Park on Key Largo, this submerged 9-foot-tall statue makes a divine underwater sight. *(Ch. 2)*

8 Ernest Hemingway's Home

You'll see his name all over Key West, but the best place to start is his historic home, where descendants of his six-toed cats still prowl. *(Ch. 5)*

9 Highway 1

Despite the traffic, the Overseas Highway (aka U.S. 1) is an engineering marvel and the only way to reach the southernmost point in the U.S. *(Ch. 2)*

10 Beaches

Keys beaches, including Bahia Honda State Park, Marathon's Sombrero Beach, and Key West's Fort Zachary Taylor Historic State Park, can be beautiful. *(Ch. 4, 3, 5)*

11 The Dry Tortugas

Seaplanes and fast ferries deliver you to Dry Tortugas National Park, known for its birding, snorkeling, and historic Fort Jefferson. *(Ch. 5)*

12 Fresh Seafood

You don't have to catch your own to relish the lobster, yellowtail snapper, hogfish, and mahi-mahi that are signatures of the Florida Keys. You'll find fresh seafood everywhere. *(Ch. 3)*

13 Fishing

Jump on a party or charter boat for offshore or back-bay fishing. Or cast a line from one of the Keys' many bridges. *(Ch. 4)*

14 Sunset at Key West's Mallory Square

Not only does the setting sun put on a fabulous show, but local musicians, magicians, and performance artists also join the act every evening. *(Ch. 5)*

CONTENTS

ABOUT THIS GUIDE

Fodor's Ratings

Everything in this guide is worth doing—we don't cover what isn't—but exceptional sights, hotels, and restaurants are recognized with additional accolades. Fodor'sChoice★ indicates our top recommendations; ★ highlights places we deem highly recommended. Care to nominate a new place? Visit Fodors.com/contact-us.

Trip Costs

We list prices wherever possible to help you budget well. Hotel and restaurant price categories from $ to $$$$ are noted alongside each recommendation. For hotels, we include the lowest cost of a standard double room in high season. For restaurants, we cite the average price of a main course at dinner or, if dinner isn't served, at lunch. For attractions, we always list adult admission fees; discounts are usually available for children, students, and senior citizens.

Hotels

Our local writers vet every hotel to recommend the best overnights in each price category, from budget to expensive. Unless otherwise specified, you can expect private bath, phone, and TV in your room. For expanded hotel reviews, facilities, and deals, visit Fodors.com.

Restaurants

Unless we state otherwise, restaurants are open for lunch and dinner daily. We mention dress code only when there's a specific requirement and reservations only when they're essential or not accepted. To make restaurant reservations, visit Fodors.com.

Credit Cards

The hotels and restaurants in this guide typically accept credit cards. If not, we'll say so.

Top Picks
★ Fodor'sChoice

Listings
⊠ Address
⊠ Branch address
🕮 Mailing address
☏ Telephone
🖶 Fax
⊕ Website
✉ E-mail

🎫 Admission fee
🕓 Open/closed times
Ⓜ Subway
⊹ Directions or Map coordinates

Hotels & Restaurants
🏨 Hotel
🛏 Number of rooms
🍴 Meal plans

✗ Restaurant
🍴 Reservations
👔 Dress code
⊟ No credit cards
💲 Price

Other
⇨ See also
☞ Take note
⛳ Golf facilities

EXPERIENCE THE FLORIDA KEYS

WHAT'S WHERE

Gulf of Mexico

National Key
Deer Refuge

4
Key West

Boca Chica Key

Saddlebunch Keys

3

Cudjoe Key

Summerland Key

No Name Key

Pigeon Key

Marathon Airport

Seven Mile
Bridge

2

**Key West
International
Airport**

Stock Island

Big Coppit Key

Sugarloaf Key

Ramrod Key

Little Torch Key

Big Pine Key

Bahia Honda

Little Duck Key

Marathon

Vaca Key

|0   20 miles|
|0   30 km|

■ **The Upper Keys. As the doorstep** to the islands' coral reefs and blithe spirit, the Upper Keys introduce all that is sporting and sea-oriented about the Keys. They stretch from Key Largo to the Long Key Channel (MM 106–65).

■ **The Middle Keys. Centered** around the town of Marathon, the Middle Keys hold most of the chain's historic and natural attractions outside of Key West. They go from Conch (pronounced *konk*) Key through Marathon to the south side of the Seven Mile Bridge, including Pigeon Key (MM 65–40).

3 The Lower Keys. Pressure drops another notch in this laid-back part of the region, where wildlife and the fishing lifestyle peak. The Lower Keys go from Little Duck Key south through Big Coppitt Key (MM 40–9).

4 Key West. The ultimate in Florida Keys craziness, the party town Key West isn't the place for those seeking a quiet retreat. The Key West area encompasses MM 9–0.

FLORIDA KEYS PLANNER

Activities	Logistics
The Keys are all about being on and in the water. **Diving** in particular draws water sports' enthusiasts to explore the clear waters, vibrant reefs, and sea life. Dive shops up and down Overseas Highway sell dive trips, instruction, and equipment. **Fishing**, too, is spectacular, bringing the rod-and-reel crowd in search of big game such as marlin, tarpon, and mahimahi as well as flats dwellers, most notably the easily spooked bonefish. On land, exploring **Key West** is the most popular pastime. Visitors do the "Duval Crawl" through the pubs and bars of Old Town. On its fringes, the island holds some of the Keys' best beaches, although they are all man-made. For a more serious crowd, plenty of museums, galleries, and historic sites offer cultural stimulation.	**Getting to the Islands:** You can fly into Key West, but because flights are few, many prefer flying into Miami International Airport (MIA) and driving the 110-mile Overseas Highway (aka U.S. 1). Marathon has an airport, but it's served only by charter flights. There's also ferry service from Marco Island and Fort Myers Beach. **Hassle Factor:** Medium to high, depending on how far you have to drive. **Nonstops:** You can fly nonstop to Key West from Atlanta (Delta), Fort Lauderdale (United), Miami (American), Tampa (American, United), or Fort Myers (Cape Air). **On the Ground:** There are both bus and shuttle services from the Miami airport to the Keys; the Lower Keys Shuttle runs between Key West and Marathon, offering cheap service and multiple stops. **Renting a Car:** It's possible to get by without a car in Key West, but you'll need one virtually everywhere else. It's usually cheaper to rent in either Fort Lauderdale or Miami if you are driving down from one of those airports. There are substantial drop-off charges if you rent in Key West but drop off your car in Miami.

Where to Stay

The Keys offer accommodations for every type of vacationer, from fishing lodges to luxury hotels to the famed historic B&Bs of Key West.

Resorts: Name-brand destination resorts such as Westin and Marriott take care of guests' every need with swimming pools, beaches, spas, restaurants, and concierges who will arrange tours and activities. Smaller resorts have a mom-and-pop feel— some every bit as luxurious as the big guys, others ultracasual.

B&Bs: Government incentives to turn headed-for-decrepit historic homes into lodgings have led to Key West's abundance of guesthouses and B&Bs. They range from all-male gay properties and little bohemian enclaves to elegantly turned-out mansions with no luxury spared. Other Keys have a few more fine choices away from the Key West crowds and clamor.

Fishing Lodges: It's easy to find a fishing lodge in the Keys, outside of Key West. Some are simple and some more luxurious, with marina facilities on-site or close by.

Hotel and Restaurant Costs

Prices in the restaurant reviews are the average cost of a main course at dinner or, if dinner is not served, at lunch; taxes and service charges are generally included. Prices in the hotel reviews are the lowest cost of a standard double room in high season, excluding taxes, service charges, and meal plans (except at all-inclusives). Prices for rentals are the lowest per-night cost for a one-bedroom unit in high season.

Pick the Right Key

Key Largo is great for diving and luxurious resorts and condo rentals; its proximity to the Everglades also makes it a destination for birders.

Islamorada is known for sportfishing (and at times celebrity spotting, particularly for those celebs who like game fishing).

Big Pine Key is great for fishing on a smaller scale or for kayaking.

Key West is known for cultural attractions, nightlife, dining, and great B&Bs; it's also the most popular gay destination in the Keys.

Marathon, while not bucolic or beautiful, has lots of midrange accommodations, pretty good food, and great access to water sports.

Bahia Honda Key has the best beach in the Keys, hands down.

IF YOU LIKE ...

Water Sports

Fishing, snorkeling, scuba diving, and glass-bottom-boat tours top the list of Keys activities, but you'll find all manner of water sports from kayaking and stand-up paddleboarding to swimming and sailing.

Bahia Honda State Park, Bahia Honda Key. Not only does this state park boast the Keys' best white-sand beach, it's also the place to go snorkeling and kayaking.

Dry Tortugas National Park. A fast ferry makes the 2¼-hour trip each way from Key West to the reefs and historic fort on Garden Key. Once there, the snorkeling is fabulous.

Fishing trips. Party boats and charter captains in all the major Keys take you where the fish are biting. You have your choice of back-bay (known by locals as backcountry) and deep-sea excursions.

John Pennekamp Coral Reef State Park, Key Largo. One of the most popular stops for snorkelers and divers, it also offers glass-bottom-boat tours to the reef that rims it.

Looe Key Reef, Lower Keys. One of the most stunning stretches of reef and marine life in the Keys, it is also the setting for the annual Underwater Music Festival.

Seafood

You don't have to eat seafood in the Keys, but it's so fresh that it's hard to resist. Talented chefs, however, prepare a variety of cuisines besides the trademark fish-heavy Keys style.

Ambrosia, Key West. The undisputed master of sushi in these parts, it makes the ultimate use of local fresh fish.

B.O.'s Fish Wagon, Key West. It doesn't get any funkier than this broken-down food truck that has grown into a junkyard-chic restaurant.

El Meson de Pepe, Key West. Authentic Cuban cuisine is easy to find in Key West, but this one has the best setting for watching the sunset at Mallory Square.

The Fish House, Key Largo. The very definition of Keys dining, it sports an old-island look, casual appeal, and focus on what's fresh from the deep.

Little Palm Island Restaurant. This top-of-the-toque dining experience includes a boat ride to a South Seas–style resort, gourmet food with island flair, and candlelight dining waterside.

Pierre's, Islamorada. Here is one fine example of how Keys' chefs know their way around fine Continental cuisine.

Nightlife

You don't have to wait for nightfall to get started on Key West's celebrated party scene. The other Keys, too, claim their favorite watering holes—usually (and appropriately) on the water.

The Garden of Eden, Key West. Bare it all at this upstairs clothing-optional spot.

Green Parrot Bar, Key West. Another Key West classic—in fact, the town's oldest bar—it hosts live entertainment nightly at mile marker 0.

La Te Da Bar, Key West. For purely Keys-style entertainment, catch the hilarious drag shows here.

Lorelei Cabana Bar, Islamorada. Teetering at the edge of a marina, its sunset entertainment draws the fishing and party crowds.

Sloppy Joe's, Key West. The first name in nightlife in Old Town, it jams day and night with live music.

Snapper's, Key Largo. Live bands play daily at this marina-side spot, where the food is as good as the cocktails.

Culture

Don't discount the Keys' serious side. The islands offer both history and arts in the most surprising places.

Ernest Hemingway Home and Museum, Key West. The unofficial patron saint of Key West, Nobel Prize–winning author Ernest Hemingway lived, fished, and wrote in Key West for more than ten years—one of several celebrated writers who migrated here.

History of Diving Museum, Islamorada. It peeks into the development of scuba diving with 13 galleries of hands-on exhibits.

Key West Forts. Explore Fort Zachary Taylor Historic State Park and East and West Martello Towers to learn Key West's military importance in times past.

Key West Museum of Art and History, Key West. Housed in the late-19th-century customs house, the museum hosts changing art exhibits and permanent displays about island bygones.

Pigeon Key, Marathon. Take a ferryboat to this five-acre key that once held the Keys' railroading operations and housed its workers. Check out the railroad museum and Bahamian architecture.

WHEN TO GO

In high season, from mid-December through mid-April, traffic is inevitably heavy. From November to mid-December, crowds are thinner, the weather is superlative, and hotels and shops drastically reduce their prices. Summer is a second high season, especially among families, Europeans, bargain-seekers, and lobster divers.

Florida is rightly called the Sunshine State, but it could also be dubbed the "Humidity State." From June through September, 90% humidity levels are not uncommon. Thankfully, the weather in the Keys is more moderate than in mainland Florida. Temperatures can be 10°F cooler during the summer and up to 10°F warmer during the winter. The Keys also get substantially less rain than mainland Florida, mostly in quick downpours on summer afternoons. In hurricane season, June through November, the Keys get their fair share of warnings; pay heed, and evacuate earlier rather than later, when flights and automobile traffic get backed up.

Festivals and Events

Many of the Keys' biggest events have to do with fishing, diving, and being water-bound. Fishing tournaments start in December with the **Islamorada Fishing Club Sailfish Tournament** in the so-called Sportsfishing Capital of the World. Come spring and summer, different target fish inspire the **Islamorada All-Tackle Spring Bonefish Tournament** in April and **Big Pine & Lower Keys Dolphin Tournament** in June. (Mahimahi is the catch of the latter.)

Key Largo celebrates Easter Keys-style during its **Underwater Easter Egg Hunt** followed in July by another signature below-the-surface tradition, the **Underwater Music Festival** on Looe Key Reef.

Next in importance comes seafood. Four biggies take place during the winter season, starting in late January with the **Key West Wine and Food Festival** and the **Florida Keys Seafood Festival** in Key West, as well as the **Key Largo Stone Crab & Seafood Festival.** In March, the **Original Marathon Seafood Festival** has been happening since the 1970s. To celebrate lobster season, Key West throws its **Lobsterfest** each August.

Finally, the islands celebrate their culture and heritage at such hallmark events as **Sculpture Key West**, a winter-long outdoor exhibition; Marathon's annual **Pigeon Key Art Festival** in February; and the 10-day **Conch Republic Independence Celebration** in Key West every April. Two of Key West's most publicized events include the **Hemingway Days** in July, with its highly competitive Hemingway look-alike contest, and October's manic **Fantasy Fest.**

KIDS AND FAMILIES

Families who love beaches, snorkeling, kayaking, and sea creatures will revel in the Keys. Although many smaller resorts and B&Bs discourage children, plenty of family resorts have kids programs and activities. Key West's wild party scene may seem the least attractive to families, yet it, too, boasts family resorts, beaches, and age-appropriate attractions.

Upper Keys

The **Hilton Key Largo Resort** and **Marriott's Key Largo Bay Beach Resort** offer the best family amenities in a beachfront destination resort setting with planned activities. **John Pennekamp Coral Reef Resort** also provides snorkel and glass-bottom-boat tours, kayak rentals, and safe beaches. In Islamorada to the south, the climate is more upscale, but **Cheeca Lodge** has always been a family favorite, given its private beach and eco-educational Camp Cheeca.

Take the kids to **Robbie's Marina** in Islamorada, and have lunch at **Hungry Tarpon** before you feed sardines to the truly hungry tarpon. **Theater of the Sea** entails more marine life interaction, including rays, dolphin, and sea lions.

Middle Keys

Hawk's Cay, north of Marathon, is a perfect match for families with its villas, pirate-themed pool, kids program, and dolphin encounters. For more dolphin interactions, check out **Dolphin Research Center** or **Dolphin Cove**. Families will also feel at home at **Tranquility Bay** in Marathon, where they can play on the beach and spread out in a townhouse behind picket fences. Don't miss **Crane Point Museum, Nature Center & Historic Site** and **Pigeon Key** for easy-to-absorb lessons in history and the environment.

Lower Keys and Key West

Budget at least a half day to spend beaching, snorkeling, kayaking, and hiking at **Bahia Honda State Park**. It's also a good place to rent a cabin (if you reserve early). Go in the morning or evening to try to spot the tiny deer at **National Key Deer Refuge** on Big Pine Key. In Key West, family lodging choices include the **Hyatt Key West Resort**, **Southernmost Hotel**, and **The Reach Resort**—all boast beach access and distance from the Duval Street hubbub. Casual seafood restaurants such as the **Half Shell Raw Bar** welcome children, and the **Key West Butterfly & Nature Conservatory**, **Key West Aquarium**, **Conch Train**, beaches, and **Eco-Discovery Center** give families many days' worth of entertainment and enlightenment.

GREAT ITINERARIES

If You Have 3 Days

Spend your first morning diving or snorkeling at John Pennekamp Coral Reef State Park in **Key Largo.** Celebrate sunset with dinner at a waterside restaurant. On Day 2 savor the breathtaking views on the two-hour drive to Key West. Along the way, stop at Crane Point Museum, Nature Center and Historic Site in **Marathon.** Another worthwhile detour is Bahia Honda Key State Park on **Bahia Honda Key,** where you can stretch your legs on a nature trail or snorkel on an offshore reef. Once you arrive in **Key West,** watch the sunset at the Mallory Square celebration. The next day, take a trolley tour of Old Town, stroll Duval Street and visit a museum or two, or spend some beach time at Fort Zachary Taylor Historic State Park.

If You Have 7 Days

Spend your first day as you would in the above itinerary, but stay both the second and third nights in **Islamorada,** fitting in some fishing, boating, or kayaking excursions from Robbie's Marina and a visit to Theater of the Sea. On the fourth morning head to **Marathon.** Visit Crane Point Museum, Nature Center and Historic Site and walk out on the Old Seven Mile Bridge or take the ferry to Pigeon Key. Spend the night and head the next morning to Bahia Honda State Park on **Bahia Honda Key** for snorkeling, kayaking, fishing, hiking, and beaching. Spend the night in a waterfront cabin or in the campground. On your sixth day, continue to **Key West,** and get in a little sightseeing before watching the sun set at Mallory Square, and spend the night and your last day visiting the sites, shops, restaurants, and bars in one of America's most lauded vacation spots.

If You Have 10 Days

To the seven-day itinerary add a few hours on Sombrero Beach in **Marathon** on Day 4, and spend the night in a local resort. Devote Day 6 to either snorkeling or diving at Looe Key Reef and a visit to the National Key Deer Refuge on **Big Pine Key.** Spend the night in the Lower Keys before heading to **Key West.** On Day 7, take a break from driving at Fort Zachary Taylor Historic State Park beach. Explore the fort and nearby Eco-Discovery Center. Book ferry passage to **Dry Tortugas National Park** for Day 8 to snorkel and explore the fort. Spend the remaining couple of nights and days sampling Key West's attractions and nightlife.

THE TARPON
KEL BOAT
RESTAURANT
RENT
BOATS
RESTROOM
CHARTER FISHING
KAYAKS
INFORMATION

THE UPPER KEYS

By Jill
Martin

DIVING AND SNORKELING RULE IN THE UPPER KEYS,
thanks to the tropical coral reef that runs a few miles off the
Atlantic coast. Divers of all skill levels benefit from accessible dive sites and an established tourism infrastructure.
Fishing is another huge draw, especially around Islamorada,
known for its sportfishing in both deep offshore waters
and in the backcountry. Offshore islands accessible only
by boat are popular destinations for kayakers. In short, if
you don't like the water you might get bored here.

Other nature lovers won't feel shortchanged. Within 1½
miles of the bay coast lie the mangrove trees and sandy
shores of Everglades National Park, where naturalists lead
tours of one of the world's few saltwater forests. Here
you'll see endangered manatees, curious dolphins, and
other marine creatures. Although the number of birds has
dwindled since John James Audubon captured their beauty
on canvas, bird-watchers will find plenty to see, including
the rare Everglades snail kite, bald eagles, ospreys, and a
colorful array of egrets and herons. At sunset flocks take
flight as they gather to find their night's roost, adding a
swirl of activity to an otherwise quiet time of day.

ORIENTATION AND PLANNING

GETTING ORIENTED

The best way to explore this stretch, or any stretch, of the
Florida Keys is by boat. As soon as possible you should
jump on any seaworthy vessel to see the view of and from
the water. And make sure you veer off the main drag of U.S.
1. Head toward the water, where you'll often find the kind
of laid-back restaurants and hotels that define the Keys.
John Pennekamp Coral Reef State Park is the region's most
popular destination, but it's certainly not the only place to
get in touch with nature.

PLANNING

GETTING HERE AND AROUND

Airporter operates scheduled van and bus pickup service
from all Miami International Airport (MIA) baggage areas
to wherever you want to go in Key Largo ($50) and Islamo-
rada ($55). Groups of three or more passengers receive
discounts. There are three departures daily; reservations are
preferred 48 hours in advance. Both Greyhound (approx.
$25 per person) and Keys Shuttle (approx. $60 per person)

TOP REASONS TO GO

■ **Snorkeling.** The best snorkeling spots in these parts are to be found around the awe-inspiring Christ of the Abyss east of John Pennekamp Coral Reef State Park in the Florida Keys National Marine Sanctuary.

■ **Sunsets.** Find a comfortable place to watch the sunset, keeping an eye out for the elusive green flash.

■ **Aquatic Mammals.** Get up close and personal with a dolphin or sea lion at Theater of the Sea or a number of other dolphin attractions.

■ **Boating.** Start with a visit to Robbie's Marina on Lower Matecumbe Key in Islamorada, a salty spot to find everything from fishing charters to kayak rentals.

■ **Nightlife.** It's not a disco, but you can dance the night away to music by local bands at Lorelei's Cabana Bar.

also offer shared-ride transportation to the Keys with various stops. The SuperShuttle charges about $160 for up to 10 passengers for nonstop trips from Miami International Airport to the Upper Keys. Shared-ride trips are also available. For trips to the airport, place your request 24 hours in advance. *See Air Travel in Travel Smart for details.*

HOTELS

In the Upper Keys the accommodations are as varied as they are plentiful. Most lodgings are in small, narrow waterfront complexes with efficiencies and one- or two-bedroom units. These places offer dockage and often arrange boating, diving, and fishing excursions. There are also full-scale resorts with every type of activity imaginable and smaller boutique hotels where the attraction is personalized service. Depending on which way the wind blows and how close the property is to the highway, there may be some noise from U.S. 1. If this is an annoyance for you, ask for a room as far away from the traffic as possible. Some properties require two- or three-day minimum stays during holiday and high-season weekends. Conversely, discounts apply for midweek, weekly, and monthly stays.

Hotel reviews have been shortened. For full information, visit Fodors.com.

RESTAURANTS

The Upper Keys are full of low-key eateries where the owner is also the chef and the food is tasty and never too fussy. The one exception is Islamorada, where you'll find more upscale restaurants. Restaurants may close for a two- to four-week vacation during the slow season between early September and mid-November.

WHAT IT COSTS				
	$	$$	$$$	$$$$
Restaurants	Under $15	$16–$20	$21–$30	Over $30
Hotels	Under $200	$201–$300	$301–$400	Over $400

Prices in the restaurant reviews are the average cost of a main course at dinner or, if dinner isn't served, at lunch. Prices in the hotel reviews are the lowest cost of a standard double room in high season. Prices don't include taxes (6%, more in some counties, and 1%–5% tourist tax for hotel rooms).

KEY LARGO

56 miles south of Miami International Airport.

The first of the Upper Keys reachable by car, 30-mile-long Key Largo is the largest island in the chain. Key Largo—named Cayo Largo ("Long Key") by the Spanish—makes a great introduction to the region. This is the gateway to the Keys, and an evening of fresh seafood and views of the sunset on the water will get you in the right state of mind.

The history of Largo reads similar to that of the rest of the Keys: a succession of native people, pirates, wreckers, and developers. The first settlement on Key Largo was named Planter, back in the days of pineapple and later key lime plantations. For a time it was a convenient shipping port, but when the railroad arrived Planter died on the vine. Today three communities—North Key Largo and Key Largo as well as the separately incorporated city of Tavernier—make up the whole of Key Largo.

What's there to do on Key Largo besides gaze at the sunset? Not much if you're not into diving or snorkeling. Nobody comes to Key Largo without visiting John Pennekamp Coral Reef State Park, one of the jewels of the state park system. Water-sports enthusiasts head to the adjacent Key Largo

Lime Tree
Bay Resort

The Upper
Keys

National Marine Sanctuary, which encompasses about 190
square miles of coral reefs, sea-grass beds, and mangrove
estuaries. If you've never tried diving, Key Largo is the
perfect place to learn. Dozens of companies will be more
than happy to show you the ropes.

Fishing is the other big draw, and world records are broken
regularly in the waters around the Upper Keys. There are
plenty of charter companies to help you find the big ones
and teach you how to hook the elusive bonefish, sometimes
known as the ghost fish.

On land, Key Largo provides all the conveniences of a
major resort town, including restaurants that will cook
your catch or prepare their own creations with inimitable
style. You'll notice that some unusual specialties pop up on
the menu, such as cracked conch, spiny lobster, and stone
crab. Don't pass up a chance to try the local delicacies,
especially the key lime pie.

Most businesses are lined up along U.S. 1, the four-lane
highway that runs down the middle of the island. Cars whiz
past at all hours—something to remember when you're
booking a room. Most lodgings are on the highway, so

you'll want to be as far back as possible. Look at MM 95 for the mural painted in 2011 to commemorate the 100th anniversary of the railroad to the Keys.

GETTING HERE AND AROUND

Key Largo is 56 miles south of Miami International Airport, the mile markers ranging from 106 to 91. The island runs northeast–southwest, with the Overseas Highway, divided by a median most of the way, running down the center. If the highway is your only glimpse of the island, you're likely to feel barraged by its tacky commercial side. Make a point of driving Route 905 in North Key Largo and down side streets to get a better feel for it.

VISITOR INFORMATION

Contacts **Florida Keys National Marine Sanctuary** ☎ *305/809–4700* ⊕ *floridakeys.noaa.gov.* **Key Largo Chamber of Commerce.** Stop in for brochures, directions, recommendations, or some colorful Key Largo T-shirts and gifts. ⊠ *MM 106 BS, 10600 Overseas Hwy.* ☎ *305/451–4747, 800/822–1088* ⊕ *www.keylargochamber.org.*

EXPLORING

Dagny Johnson Key Largo Hammock Botanical State Park. American crocodiles, mangrove cuckoos, white-crowned pigeons, Schaus swallowtail butterflies, mahogany mistletoe, wild cotton, and 100 other rare critters and plants inhabit these 2,400 acres, sandwiched between Crocodile Lake National Wildlife Refuge and Pennekamp Coral Reef State Park. The park is also a user-friendly place to explore the largest remaining stand of the vast West Indian tropical hardwood hammock and mangrove wetland that once covered most of the Keys' upland areas. Interpretive signs describe many of the tropical tree species along a wide 1-mile paved road (2-mile round-trip) that invites walking and biking. There are also more than 6 miles of nature trails accessible to bikes and wheelchairs. Pets are welcome if on a leash no longer than 6 feet. You'll also find restrooms, information kiosks, and picnic tables. ■TIP→ **Rangers recommend not visiting when it's raining, as the trees can drip poisonous sap.** ⊠ *Rte. 905 OS, 0.5 mile north of Overseas Hwy., North Key Largo* ☎ *305/451–1202* ⊕ *www.floridastateparks.org/ keylargohammock* ⊜ *$2.50 (exact change needed)* ☉ *Daily 8–sundown.*

FAMILY **Dolphin Cove.** This educational program begins at the facility's bayside lagoon with a get-acquainted session from a

Key Largo

KEY

- **1** Restaurants
- **1** Hotels
- Dive Site
- Boat Launch

Restaurants

Alabama Jack's, **1**

Ballyhoo's, **9**

Buzzard's Roost Grill and Pub, **2**

Chad's Deli & Bakery, **12**

The Fish House, **5**

The Fish House Encore, **6**

Harriette's Restaurant, **10**

Jimmy Johnson's Big Chill, **4**

Key Largo Conch House, **7**

Mrs. Mac's Kitchen, **8**

Snapper's, **11**

Sundowners, **3**

Hotels

Amy Slate's Amoray Dive Resort, **2**

Azul Del Mar, **1**

Coconut Bay Resort & Bay Harbor Lodge, **6**

Coconut Palm Inn, **13**

Dove Creek Lodge, **11**

Hilton Key Largo Resort, **9**

Island Bay Resort, **12**

Jules' Undersea Lodge, **4**

Kona Kai Resort, Gallery, & Botanic Gardens, **8**

Marriott's Key Largo Bay Beach Resort, **3**

The Pelican, **5**

Popp's Motel, **10**

Seafarer Resort and Beach, **7**

platform. After that, you slip into the water for some frolicking with your new dolphin pals. Options range from a sea lion swim (new at this location), to a shallow-water swim with a dolphin, to a hands-on structured swim with a dolphin. You can also spend the day shadowing a trainer for a hefty $670 fee. ⊠ *MM 101.9 BS, 101900 Overseas Hwy.* ☎ *305/451–4060, 877/365–2683* ⊕ *www.dolphinscove.com* ✉ *$10 admission only; interactive programs from $140* ⊙ *Daily 8–5.*

FAMILY **Dolphins Plus.** A sister property to Dolphin Cove, Dolphins Plus offers some of the same programs and the age requirement is lower. The cheapest option, a Natural Swim program, begins with a one-hour briefing; then you enter the water to become totally immersed in the dolphins' world. In this visual orientation, participants can snorkel but are not allowed to touch the dolphins. For tactile interaction (kissing, fin tows, etc.), sign up for the Structured Swim program, which is more expensive. ⊠ *MM 99, 31 Corrine Pl.* ☎ *305/451–1993, 866/860–7946* ⊕ *www.dolphinsplus. com* ✉ *Programs from $165* ⊙ *Daily 8–5.*

Key Largo and the Movies. The 1948 film noir classic *Key Largo,* starring Humphrey Bogart and Lauren Bacall, was the most famous movie filmed in the Florida Keys, but not the only one. Others have included *Beneath the Twelve Mile Reef, PT 109, License to Kill, True Lies, Speed 2,* and *Red Dragon.* Key Largo is also where the steamboat used in the film *The African Queen* came to live in 1983. On display at MM 100, it even underwent a $60,000 restoration to enable it to do tours.

Florida Keys Wild Bird Center. Have a nose-to-beak encounter with ospreys, hawks, herons, and other unreleasable birds at this bird rehabilitation center. The birds live in spacious, screened enclosures along a boardwalk running through some of the best waterfront real estate in the Keys. Rehabilitated birds are set free, whereas about 30 have become permanent residents. Free birds—especially pelicans and egrets—come to visit every day for a free lunch from the center's staff. A short nature trail runs into the mangrove forest (bring bug spray May to October). ⊠ *MM 93.6 BS, 93600 Overseas Hwy., Tavernier* ☎ *305/852–4486* ⊕ *www.fkwbc.org* ✉ *Free, donations accepted* ⊙ *Daily sunrise–sunset.*

FAMILY **Jacobs Aquatic Center.** Take the plunge at one of three swimming pools: an 8-lane, 25-meter lap pool with two diving boards; a 3- to 4-foot-deep pool accessible to people with mobility challenges; and an interactive children's play pool with a waterslide, pirate ship, waterfall, and sloping zero entry instead of steps. Because so few of the motels in Key Largo have pools, it remains a popular destination for visiting families. ⊠ *Key Largo Community Park, 320 Laguna Ave., at St. Croix Pl.* ☎ *305/453–7946* ⊕ *www. jacobsaquaticcenter.org* ☎ *$12 ($2 discount weekdays)* ⊙ *Daily 10–6 (10–7 in summer).*

FAMILY Fodor'sChoice **John Pennekamp Coral Reef State Park.** This state
★ park is on everyone's list for easy access to the best diving and snorkeling in Florida. The underwater treasure encompasses 78 square miles of coral reefs and sea-grass beds. It lies adjacent to the Florida Keys National Marine Sanctuary, which contains 40 of the 52 species of coral in the Atlantic Reef System and nearly 600 varieties of fish, from the colorful parrot fish to the demure cocoa damselfish. Whatever you do, get in the water. Snorkeling and diving trips ($30 and $55, respectively, equipment extra) and glass-bottom-boat rides to the reef ($24) are available, weather permitting. One of the most popular snorkel trips is to see *Christ of the Deep*, the 2-ton underwater statue of Jesus. The park also has nature trails, two man-made beaches, picnic shelters, a snack bar, and a campground. **Amenities:** food and drink; parking (fee); showers; toilets; water sports. **Best for:** snorkeling; swimming. ⊠ *MM 102.5 OS, 102601 Overseas Hwy.* ☎ *305/451–1202 for park, 305/451–6300 for excursions* ⊕ *www.pennekamppark. com, www.floridastateparks.org/pennekamp* ☎ *$4.50 for 1 person in vehicle, $8 for 2–8 people, $2 for pedestrians and cyclists or extra people (plus a 50¢ per-person county surcharge)* ⊙ *Daily 8–sunset.*

WHERE TO EAT

$ ✕ **Alabama Jack's.** *Seafood.* Calories be damned—the conch fritters here are heaven on a plate. Don't expect the traditional, golf-ball-sized balls of dough; these are an unusual, mountainous freeform creation of fried, loaded-with-flavor perfection. The crab cakes, made from local blue crabs, earn hallelujahs, too. The conch salad is as good as any you'll find in the Bahamas. This weathered, circa-1950 restaurant floats on two roadside barges in an old fishing community. Regulars include motorcyclists, families, boaters, and the upscale crowd from nearby Ocean Reef Club, including Kathie Lee Gifford, who all come not only for the food but to admire tropical birds in the nearby mangroves, the occasional crocodile in the canal, and to jam with the bands playing each weekend afternoon. Dinner has to be early here; Jack's closes by 7, when the mosquitoes start biting. ■TIP→ **It's about a half-hour drive from Key Largo, so you may want to plan a visit for your drive in or out.** ⑤ *Average main: $11 ⊠ 58000 Card Sound Rd.* ☎ *305/248–8741* ⚑ *Reservations not accepted.*

$$$ ╳ **Ballyhoo's.** *Seafood.* Occupying a 1930s Conch house with outdoor seating right alongside U.S. 1 under the sea grape trees, this local favorite is all about the fish (including the nautical decor). Yellowtail snapper, one of the moistest, most flavorful local fish, is served ten different ways on the all-day menu, including blackened, stuffed with crab, and Parmesan-crusted. During stone-crab season (mid-October to mid-May) get in on the all-you-can-eat special. Every Friday night, locals flock for the all-you-can-eat mojo-marinated and fried fish dinner deals. ⑤ *Average main: $21 ⊠ MM 97.8 median, 97800 Overseas Hwy.* ☎ *305/852–0822* ⊕ *www.ballyhoosrestaurant.com* ⚑ *Reservations not accepted.*

★ Fodor'sChoice ╳ **Buzzard's Roost Grill and Pub.** *Seafood.* The
$$$ views are nice at this waterfront restaurant but the food is what gets your attention. Burgers, fish tacos, and seafood baskets are lunch faves. Dinner is about seafood and steaks, any way you like them. Try the smoked-fish dip, served with Armenian heart-shaped lavash crackers. Look for the big signs on U.S. 1 that direct you where to turn—it's worth finding. ⑤ *Average main: $21 ⊠ Garden Cove Marina, 21 Garden Cove Dr., Northernmost Key Largo* ☎ *305/453–3746* ⊕ *www.buzzardsroostkeylargo.com.*

$ ╳ **Chad's Deli & Bakery.** *American.* It's a deli! It's a bakery! It's a pasta place! It's also where the locals go. By day, Chad's serves monster sandwiches in pita wraps, rolls, or subs. It also offers pizza (try the seafood pizza with rosada sauce), pasta dishes, quesadillas, vegetarian meals, salads, burgers, and breakfast. Everyone loves the homemade soups and chowders, and there's a good selection of beer and wine to wash it all down. Of course, you may bypass all this and make a meal out of one of Chad's eight varieties of cookies, approximately the size of your head, including white-chocolate macadamia-nut and chocolate-chip. ⑤ *Average main: $10 ⊠ MM 92.3 BS, 92330 Overseas Hwy., Tavernier* ☎ *305/853–5566* ⊕ *www.chadsdeli.com* ⚑ *Reservations not accepted.*

2

$$$ ✕**The Fish House.** *Seafood.* Restaurants not on the water have to produce the highest quality food to survive in the Keys. That's how the Fish House has succeeded since the 1980s—so much so that it built the Fish House Encore (a fancier version) next door to accommodate fans. The pan-sautéed catch of the day is a long-standing favorite, as is the "Matecumbe style" preparation—baked with tomatoes, capers, olive oil, and lemon juice, it will make you moan with pleasure. Prefer shellfish? Choose from shrimp, lobster, and (mid-October to mid-May) stone crab. The smoked fish chunks are the best in the Keys. The only thing bland is their side dishes: simple boiled red potatoes, a hunk of corn on the cob, or black beans and rice. For a sweet ending, the homemade key lime pie is award winning. ⑤ *Average main: $21* ⊠ *MM 102.4 OS, 102341 Overseas Hwy.* ☎ *305/451–4665* ⊕ *www.fishhouse.com* ⌂ *Reservations not accepted* ⊗ *Closed Sept.* ⌖ *American Express not accepted.*

$$$ ✕**The Fish House Encore.** *Seafood.* To accommodate the crowds that gather at the Fish House, the owners opened this place with similar but more refined cuisine ranging from sushi to steak. It's come into its own as a more formal dining venue than its sister establishment. In the off-season you can get your money's worth with all-you-can-eat specials such as mahimahi, snow crab, and peel 'n' eat shrimp. The favorite, more casual place to dine is on the patio near the trickling fountain. Live piano music entertains Thursday through Sunday. ⑤ *Average main: $27* ⊠ *MM 102.3 OS, 102341 Overseas Hwy.* ☎ *305/451–4665, 305/451–0650* ⊕ *www.fishhouse.com* ⌂ *Reservations not accepted* ⊗ *No lunch. Closed Tues. and Oct.*

$ ✕**Harriette's Restaurant.** *American.* If you're looking for comfort food—like melt-in-your-mouth biscuits the size of a salad plate—try this refreshing throwback. The kitchen makes muffins daily in 13 different flavors like mango, coconut, and key lime. Since the early 1980s, owner Harriette Mattson has been here to personally greet guests who come for the to-die-for omelets and old-fashioned hotcakes with sausage or bacon. For something unique, try the conch burger and eggs. At lunch, Harriette shines in the burger department, and her soups—from garlic tomato to chili—are homemade. ⑤ *Average main: $8* ⊠ *MM 95.7 BS, 95710 Overseas Hwy.* ☎ *305/852–8689* ⌂ *Reservations not accepted* ⊗ *No dinner* ⌖ *American Express not accepted.*

$$ ✕**Jimmy Johnson's Big Chill.** *Seafood.* Owned by former NFL coach, Jimmy Johnson, this waterfront establishment offers three entertaining experiences, and all are big winners.

You'll find the best sports bar in the Upper Keys complete with the coach's Super Bowl trophies, a main restaurant with all-glass indoor seating and a waterfront deck, and an enormous outdoor tiki bar with entertainment seven nights a week. There's even a pool and cabana club where (for an entrance fee) you can spend the day sunning. Menu favorites are the Parmesan-crusted snapper and brick-oven roasted chicken wings, but don't miss the tuna nachos—as delicious as they are artfully presented. As the sun sets over the bay, enjoy the views and a slice of white chocolate–macadamia cheesecake. ⑤ *Average main: $16* ✉ *MM104 BS, 104000 Overseas Hwy.* ☎ *305/453–9066* ⊕ *www.jjs-bigchill.com.*

$ ✕ **Key Largo Conch House.** *American.* Tucked into the trees along the Overseas Highway, this Victorian-style home (family-owned since 2004) and its true-to-the-Keys style of cooking is worth seeking out—at least the Food Network and the Travel Channel have thought so in the past. The Old South veranda and patio seating are ideal for winter dining, but indoors the seating is tighter. Raisin pecan French toast and seven varieties of Benedicts, including conch, are reason enough to rise early to get your fresh coffee fix. Lunch and dinner menus cover all bases, from a conch chowder bread bowl and vegetarian wraps to lobster and conch seviche. Lionfish is proudly served when available, as is local yellowtail snapper. Interesting fact: the restaurant's "loo" was voted "Best of" for local restaurants. ⑤ *Average main: $15* ✉ *MM 100.2, 100211 Overseas Hwy.* ☎ *305/453–4844* ⊕ *www.keylargoconchhouse.com* ⬧ *Reservations essential.*

$ ✕ **Mrs. Mac's Kitchen.** *Seafood.* Townies pack the counters and booths at this tiny eatery, where license plates are stuck on the walls and made into chandeliers, for everything from blackened prime rib to crab cakes. Every night is themed including Meatloaf Mondays, Italian Wednesdays, and Seafood Sensation (offered Friday and Saturday). There's also a Champagne breakfast (at this original location) and an assortment of tasty Angus beef burgers, sandwiches, a famous chili, and key lime freeze (a tangy concoction somewhere between a shake and a float). In season, ask about the hogfish special du jour. A second location, Mrs. Mac's Kitchen 2, is located half a mile south on the Overseas Highway (99020 Overseas Hwy., MM 99 Center), also in Key Largo. The newer location offers a similar menu, a full bar, and double the seating space. It's also kid-friendly. ⑤ *Average main: $15* ✉ *MM 99.4 BS, 99336 Overseas Hwy.*

☎ *305/451–3722, 305/451-6227* ⊕ *www.mrsmackitchen. com* ☉ *Closed Sun.*

$ ✕ **Snapper's.** *Seafood.* "You hook 'em, we cook 'em" is the motto here. Alas, "cleanin' 'em" is not part of the bargain. If you bring in your ready-for-the-grill fish, dinner here is $14 for a single, $15 per person family style with a mix of preparations. Otherwise, they'll catch and prepare you a plank-roasted yellowtail snapper, Thai-seared tuna, fish of the day baked with 36 herbs and spices, or a little something from the raw bar. The seviche of yellowtail, shrimp, and conch (merrily spiced) wins raves, too. The seafood burrito on the sandwich board is a keeper. All this is served up in a lively, mangrove-ringed waterfront setting with live music, an aquarium bar, Sunday brunch (including a build-your-own Bloody Mary bar), killer rum drinks, and seating alongside the fishing dock. Early bird dinners are available from 5 to 6 pm. ⑤ *Average main: $15* ⊠ *MM 94.5 OS, 139 Seaside Ave.* ☎ *305/852–5956* ⊕ *www.snapperskeylargo. com* ⌂ *Reservations not accepted.*

$$$ ✕ **Sundowners.** *American.* The name doesn't lie. If it's a clear night and you can snag a reservation, this restaurant will treat you to a sherbet-hued sunset over Florida Bay. If you're here in mild weather—anytime other than the dog days of summer or the rare winter cold snap—the best seats are on the patio. The food is excellent: try the key lime seafood, a happy combo of sautéed shrimp, lobster, and lump crabmeat swimming in a tangy sauce spiked with Tabasco served over penne or rice. Wednesday and Saturday are all about prime rib, and Friday draws the crowds with an all-you-can-eat fish fry. Vegetarian and gluten-free options are available. To beat the crowds, stop in for lunch, which offers the same great food, minus the hassle. ⑤ *Average main: $22* ⊠ *MM 104 BS, 103900 Overseas Hwy.* ☎ *305/451–4502* ⊕ *sundownerskeylargo.com* ⌂ *Reservations essential.*

WHERE TO STAY

$ ▦ **Amy Slate's Amoray Dive Resort.** *Resort.* You can read this hotel's name either as "a moray" (referring to the moray eels you'll encounter on the reef) or "amore" (Italian for love, which calls to mind the place's romantic atmosphere), and you'll understand the place's dual charms. **Pros:** top-notch dive operation; free use of kayaks and snorkel equipment. **Cons:** noise from highway; minimum stays during peak times. ⑤ *Rooms from: $179* ⊠ *MM 104.2 BS, 104250*

Overseas Hwy. ☎*305/451–3595, 800/426–6729* ⊕*www. amoray.com* ⇨*23 rooms, 8 apartments* ❘⊙❘*No meals.*

$$ ⊡ **Azul del Mar.** *B&B/Inn.* The dock points the way to many beautiful sunsets at this nonsmoking, adults-only boutique hotel, which Karol Marsden (an ad exec) and her husband Dominic (a travel photographer) have transformed from a run-down mom-and-pop place into a waterfront gem. **Pros:** great garden; good location; sophisticated design. **Cons:** small beach; high-priced; minimum stays during holidays. ⑤*Rooms from: $279* ⊠*MM 104.3 BS, 104300 Overseas Hwy.* ☎*305/451–0337, 888/253–2985* ⊕*www. azulkeylargo.com* ⇨*2 studios, 3 1-bedroom suites, 1 2-bedroom suite* ❘⊙❘*No meals.*

$ ⊡ **Coconut Bay Resort & Bay Harbor Lodge.** *Resort.* Some 200 feet of waterfront is the main attraction at these side-by-side sister properties that offer a choice between smaller rooms and larger separate cottages. **Pros:** bay front; neatly kept gardens; walking distance to restaurants; complimentary kayak and paddleboat use. **Cons:** a bit dated; small sea-walled sand beach. ⑤*Rooms from: $175* ⊠*MM 97.7 BS, 97702 Overseas Hwy.* ☎*305/852–1625, 800/385–0986* ⊕*www.coconutbaykeylargo.com* ⇨*7 rooms, 5 efficiencies, 2 suites, 1 2-bedroom villa, 6 1-bedroom cottages* ❘⊙❘*No meals.*

$$ ⊡ **Coconut Palm Inn.** *B&B/Inn.* You'd never find this waterfront haven unless someone told you it was there, as it's tucked into a residential neighborhood beneath towering palms and native gumbo-limbos. **Pros:** secluded; quiet; sophisticated feel. **Cons:** front desk closes early each evening; no access to ice machine when staff leaves; breakfast is ho-hum. ⑤*Rooms from: $279* ⊠*MM 92 BS, 198 Harborview Dr., via Jo-Jean Way off Overseas Hwy., Tavernier* ☎*305/852–3017* ⊕*www.coconutpalminn.com* ⇨*13 rooms, 7 suites* ❘⊙❘*Breakfast.*

$$ ⊡ **Dove Creek Lodge.** *B&B/Inn.* With its sherbet-hued rooms and plantation-style furnishings, these tropical-style units (19 in all) range in size from simple lodge rooms to luxury two-bedroom suites. **Pros:** luxurious rooms; walk to Snapper's restaurant; complimentary kayaks and Wi-Fi. **Cons:** no beach; some find the music from next door bothersome. ⑤*Rooms from: $229* ⊠*MM 94.5 OS, 147 Seaside Ave.* ☎*305/852–6200, 800/401–0057* ⊕*www.dovecreeklodge. com* ⇨*4 room, 10 suites* ❘⊙❘*Breakfast.*

★ Fodor'sChoice ⊡ **Hilton Key Largo Resort.** *Resort.* Nestled within
$$ a hardwood hammock (localese for uplands habitat where hardwood trees such as live oak grow) near the southern

border of Everglades National Park, this sprawling resort had a $12-million renovation in 2012 and offers a full slate of amenities in a woodsy setting. **Pros:** nice nature trail on bay side; pretty pools with waterfalls; awesome trees; bicycles available for rent. **Cons:** some rooms overlook the parking lot; pools near the highway; expensive per-night resort fee. ⑤ *Rooms from: $219* ✉ *MM 97 BS, 97000 Overseas Hwy.* ☎ *305/852–5553, 888/871–3437* ⊕ *www. keylargoresort.com* ⤴ *190 rooms, 10 suites* ⦿ *No meals.*

$$ ☒ **Island Bay Resort.** *Rental.* When Mike and Carol Shipley took over this off-the-beaten-path resort in 2000, they revamped the 10 bayside cottages, improved the landscaping, and added touches such as hammocks and Adirondack chairs that make you feel like this is your own personal tropical playground. **Pros:** on the water; sunset views. **Cons:** most units are small; no pool; lacks on-site amenities. ⑤ *Rooms from: $209* ✉ *92530 Overseas Hwy.* ☎ *305/852– 4087* ⊕ *www.islandbayresort.com* ⤴ *10 units* ⦿ *No meals.*

$$$$ ☒ **Jules' Undersea Lodge.** *Hotel.* You can truly sleep with the fishes at this underwater inn. **Pros:** one-of-a-kind experience; unbeatable views. **Cons:** must be a certified diver or take the special course to stay here; tight accommodations. ⑤ *Rooms from: $800* ✉ *MM 103.2 OS, 51 Shoreland Dr.* ☎ *305/451–2353* ⊕ *www.jul.com* ⤴ *2 rooms* ⦿ *Some meals.*

★ Fodor'sChoice ☒ **Kona Kai Resort, Gallery & Botanic Gardens.**
$$ *Resort.* Brilliantly colored bougainvillea, coconut palm, and guava trees—and a botanical garden of other rare species—make this 2-acre adult hideaway one of the prettiest places to stay in the Keys. **Pros:** free custom tours of botanical gardens for guests; free use of sports equipment; knowledgeable staff. **Cons:** expensive; some rooms are very close together. ⑤ *Rooms from: $289* ✉ *MM 97.8 BS, 97802 Overseas Hwy.* ☎ *305/852–7200, 800/365–7829* ⊕ *www.konakairesort.com* ⤴ *8 suites, 3 rooms* ⊙ *Closed Sept.* ⦿ *No meals.*

$ ☒ **Marriott's Key Largo Bay Beach Resort.** *Resort.* This 17-acre
FAMILY bayside resort has plenty of diversions, from diving to parasailing to a day spa. **Pros:** lots of activities; free, covered parking; dive shop on property; free Wi-Fi. **Cons:** rooms facing highway can be noisy; thin walls. ⑤ *Rooms from: $139* ✉ *MM 103.8 BS, 103800 Overseas Hwy.* ☎ *305/453– 0000, 866/849–3753* ⊕ *www.marriottkeylargo.com* ⤴ *132 rooms, 20 2-bedroom suites, 1 penthouse suite* ⦿ *No meals.*

$ ☒ **The Pelican.** *Hotel.* This 1950s throwback is reminiscent of the days when parents packed the kids into the station wagon and headed to no-frills seaside motels, complete with an old-timer fishing off the dock. **Pros:** free use of kayaks and a canoe; well-maintained dock; reasonable rates. **Cons:** some small rooms; basic accommodations and amenities. ⑤ *Rooms from: $110* ⊠ *MM 99.3, 99340 Overseas Hwy.* ☎ *305/451–3576, 877/451–3576* ⊕ *www. hungrypelican.com* ⟿ *13 rooms, 4 efficiencies, 4 suites, 2 trailers* ⎮◎⎮ *Breakfast.*

$ ▣ **Popp's Motel.** *Hotel.* Stylized metal herons mark the entrance to this 50-year-old family-run motel. **Pros:** beach; intimate feel; multiple night discounts. **Cons:** limited amenities; worn, outdated interiors. ⑤ *Rooms from: $149* ⊠ *MM 95.5 BS, 95500 Overseas Hwy.* ☎ *305/852–5201, 877/852–5201* ⊕ *www.popps.com* ⟿ *9 units* ⎮◎⎮ *No meals.*

$ ▣ **Seafarer Resort and Beach.** *Hotel.* It's very basic budget lodging, but the Seafarer Resort is not without its charms. **Pros:** sandy beach; complimentary kayak use; cheap rates. **Cons:** some rooms close to road noise; some complaints about cleanliness. ⑤ *Rooms from: $139* ⊠ *MM 97.6 BS, 97684 Overseas Hwy.* ☎ *305/852–5349* ⊕ *www. seafarerkeylargo.com* ⟿ *8 rooms, 3 studios, 3 1-bedroom cottages, 1 2-bedroom cottage, 2 apartments* ⎮◎⎮ *No meals.*

NIGHTLIFE

The semiweekly *Keynoter* (Wednesday and Saturday), weekly *Reporter* (Thursday), and Friday through Sunday editions of the *Miami Herald* are the best sources of information on entertainment and nightlife. Daiquiri bars, tiki huts, and seaside shacks pretty well summarize Key Largo's bar scene.

Breezers Tiki Bar & Grille. Mingle with locals over cocktails and sunsets at Marriott's Key Largo Bay Beach Resort. ⊠ *Marriott Key Largo Bay Beach Resort, 103800 Overseas Hwy.* ☎ *305/453–0000.*

Caribbean Club. Walls plastered with Bogart memorabilia remind customers that the classic 1948 Bogart–Bacall flick *Key Largo* has a connection with this worn watering hole. Although no food is served and the floors are bare concrete, this landmark draws boaters, curious visitors, and local barflies to its humble bar stools and pool tables. But the real magic is around back, where you can grab a seat on the deck and catch a postcard-perfect sunset. Live music draws revelers Thursday through Sunday. ⊠ *MM 104 BS, 10404 Overseas Hwy.* ☎ *305/451–4466.*

SHOPPING

For the most part, shopping is sporadic in Key Largo, with a couple of shopping centers and fewer galleries than you find on the other big islands. If you're looking to buy scuba or snorkel equipment, you'll have plenty of choices.

Bluewater Potters. Bluewater Potters creates functional and decorative ceramics ranging from signature vases and kitchenware to one-of-a-kind pieces where the owners' creative talent at the wheel blazes. In addition to their main gallery location in Key Largo, find them in the new Morada Way Arts and Culture District in Islamorada at MM 81.5. ⊠ *MM 102.9 OS, 102991 Overseas Hwy.* ☎ *305/453–1920* ⊕ *www.bluewaterpotters.com.*

Gallery at Kona Kai. Original works by major international artists—including sea captain–turned-painter Dirk Verdoorn, Italian artist Franco Passalaqua, and French sculptor Polles—are shown at this gallery in the Kona Kai Resort. ⊠ *MM 97.8 BS, 97802 Overseas Hwy.* ☎ *305/852–7200* ⊕ *www.g-k-k.com.*

★ **Fodor'sChoice Key Largo Chocolates.** Specializing in key lime truffles made with quality Belgian chocolate, this is the only chocolate factory in the entire Florida Keys. But you'll find much more than just the finest white, milk, and dark chocolate truffles; try their cupcakes, ice cream, and famous "chocodiles." Another fan favorite is the salted turtles, which are worth every calorie. Chocolate classes are also available for kids and adults, and a small gift area showcases local art, jewelry, hot sauces, and other goodies. Look for the bright green and pink building. ⊠ *MM100 BS, 100471 Overseas Hwy.* ☎ *305/453–6613* ⊕ *www.keylargochocolates.com.*

Key Lime Products. Go into olfactory overload—you'll find yourself sniffing every single bar of soap and scented candle inside this key lime treasure trove. Take home some key lime juice (supereasy pie-making directions are right on the bottle), marmalade, candies, sauces, even key lime shampoo. Outside, you'll find a huge selection of wood carvings, pottery, unique patio furniture, and artwork. They're even grilling up fresh fish sandwiches that alone are worth the stop. ⊠ *MM 95.2 BS, 95231 Overseas Hwy.* ☎ *305/853–0378, 800/870–1780* ⊕ *www.keylimeproducts.com.*

Randy's Florida Keys Gift Co. Since 1989, Randy's has been "the" place for unique gifts. Owner Randy and his wife

Lisa aren't only fantastic at stocking the store with a plethora of items, they're well respected in the community for their generosity and dedication. Stop in and say hello then browse the tight aisles and loaded shelves filled with key lime candles, books, wood carvings, jewelry, clothing, T-shirts, and eclectic, tropical decor items. This friendly shop prides itself on carrying wares from local craftsmen and there's something for every budget. ✉ *1102421 Overseas Hwy.* ✛ *Right on U.S. 1, next to the Sandal Factory Outlet* ☎ *305/453-9229* ⊕ *www.keysmermaid.com.*

Shell World. You can find lots of shops in the Keys that sell cheesy souvenirs—snow globes, alligator hats, and shell-encrusted anything. This is the granddaddy of them all. But this sprawling building in the median of Overseas Highway has much more than shell lamps and snow globes, you'll find high-end clothing, jewelry, housewares, artwork, and a wide selection of eclectic souvenirs from delightfully tacky to tasteful. ✉ *MM 97.5, 97600 Overseas Hwy.* ☎ *305/852–8245, 888/398–6233* ⊕ *www.shellworldflkeys.com.*

SPORTS AND THE OUTDOORS

BIKING

Not as big a pursuit as on other islands, biking can be a little dangerous along Key Largo's main drag. Parts of the still-developing Florida Keys Overseas Heritage Trail take you off Highway 1 along Old Highway.

Bubba's. Bubba's organizes one-week custom biking tours through the Keys along the heritage trail. A van accompanies tours to carry luggage and tired riders. Former police officer Bubba Barron also hosts an annual one-week ride down the length of the Keys every November. Riders can opt for tent camping ($695) or motel-room accommodations. Meals are included, but bike rentals are extra. ☎ *321/759–3433* ⊕ *www.bubbaspamperedpedalers.com* ▭ *From $695.*

BOATING

Everglades Eco-Tours. Captain Sterling operates Everglades and Florida Bay ecology tours and more expensive sunset cruises. You can see dolphins, manatees, and birds from the casual comfort of his pontoon boat, equipped with PVC chairs. Bring your own food and drinks. ✉ *MM 104 BS, Sundowners Restaurant, 103900 Overseas Hwy.* ☎ *305/853–5161, 888/224–6044* ⊕ *www.captainsterling. com* ▭ *From $50.*

M.V. *Key Largo Princess*. Two-hour glass-bottom-boat trips and sunset cruises on a luxury 70-foot motor yacht with a 280-square-foot glass viewing area depart from the Holiday Inn docks three times a day. ⊠ *Holiday Inn, MM 100 OS, 99701 Overseas Hwy.* ☎ *305/451–4655, 877/648–8129* ⊕ *www.keylargoprincess.com* ⊠ *$30.*

CANOEING AND KAYAKING

Sea kayaking continues to gain popularity in the Keys. You can paddle for a few hours or the whole day, on your own or with a guide. Some outfitters even offer overnight trips. The **Florida Keys Overseas Paddling Trail,** part of a statewide system, runs from Key Largo to Key West. You can paddle the entire distance, 110 miles on the Atlantic side, which takes 9 to 10 days. The trail also runs the chain's length on the bay side, which is a longer route.

Coral Reef Park Co. At John Pennekamp Coral Reef State Park, this operator has a fleet of canoes and kayaks for gliding around the 2½-mile mangrove trail or along the coast. Powerboat rentals are also available. ⊠ *MM 102.5 OS, 102601 Overseas Hwy.* ☎ *305/451–6300* ⊕ *www. pennekamppark.com* ⊠ *Rentals from $12 per hr.*

Florida Bay Outfitters. Rent canoes or sea kayaks from this company, which sets up self-guided trips on the Florida Keys Overseas Paddling Trail, helps with trip planning, and matches equipment to your skill level. It also runs myriad guided tours around Key Largo. Take a full-moon paddle or a one- to seven-day canoe or kayak tour to the Everglades, Lignumvitae Key, or Indian Key. ⊠ *MM 104 BS, 104050 Overseas Hwy.* ☎ *305/451–3018* ⊕ *www.kayakfloridakeys. com* ⊠ *From $25.*

FISHING

Private charters and big "head" boats (so named because they charge "by the head") are great for anglers who don't have their own vessel.

Sailors Choice. Fishing excursions depart twice daily (half-day trips are cash-only), but the company also does private charters. The 65-foot boat leaves from the Holiday Inn docks. Rods, bait, and license are included. ⊠ *Holiday Inn Resort & Marina, MM 100 OS, 99701 Overseas Hwy.* ☎ *305/451– 1802, 305/451–0041* ⊕ *www.sailorschoicefishingboat.com* ⊠ *From $40.*

SCUBA DIVING AND SNORKELING

Much of what makes the Upper Keys a singular dive destination is variety. Places like Molasses Reef, which begins 3 feet below the surface and descends to 55 feet, have something for everyone from novice snorkelers to experienced divers. The *Spiegel Grove*, a 510-foot vessel, lies in 130 feet of water, but its upper regions are only 60 feet below the surface. On rough days, Key Largo Undersea Park's Emerald Lagoon is a popular spot. Expect to pay about $80 to $85 for a two-tank, two-site dive trip with tanks and weights, or $35 to $40 for a two-site snorkel outing. Get big discounts by booking multiple trips.

Amy Slate's Amoray Dive Resort. This outfit makes diving easy. Stroll down to the full-service dive shop (NAUI, PADI, TDI, and BSAC certified), then onto a 45-foot catamaran. ✉ *MM 104.2 BS, 104250 Overseas Hwy.* ☎ *305/451–3595, 800/426–6729* ⊕ *www.amoray.com* ⬛ *From $85.*

Conch Republic Divers. Book diving instruction as well as scuba and snorkeling tours of all the wrecks and reefs of the Upper Keys. Two-location dives are the standard, and you'll pay an extra $20 for tank and weights. ✉ *MM 90.8 BS, 90800 Overseas Hwy.* ☎ *305/852–1655, 800/274–3483* ⊕ *www.conchrepublicdivers.com* ⬛ *From $65.*

Coral Reef Park Co. At John Pennekamp Coral Reef State Park, this company gives 3½-hour scuba and 2½-hour snorkeling tours of the park. In addition to the great location and the dependability, it's also suited for water adventurers of all levels. ✉ *MM 102.5 OS, 102601 Overseas Hwy.* ☎ *305/451–6300* ⊕ *www.pennekamppark.com* ⬛ *From $30.*

Horizon Divers. The company has customized diving and snorkeling trips that depart daily aboard a 45-foot catamaran. ✉ *100 Ocean Dr. #1* ☎ *305/453–3535, 800/984–3483* ⊕ *www.horizondivers.com* ⬛ *From $50 for snorkeling, from $80 for diving.*

Island Ventures. This operator provides daily excursions that take you snorkeling or scuba diving. Scuba trips, offered twice daily, include tanks and weights; snorkeling trips are also offered, and ride-alongs pay just $40. ✉ *Jules Undersea Lodge, 51 Shoreland Dr.* ☎ *305/451–4957* ⊕ *www. islandventure.com* ⬛ *Snorkel trips $50, diving $85.*

Keys Diver & Snorkel Center. This operator offers snorkel and dive trips that take you to Florida Keys National Marine Sanctuary. Two-tank dives include weights, tanks, and a restaurant lunch; snorkel excursions are also offered with two or three stops. A new offering is a night dive in a bioluminescent bay. ✉ *MM 100 BS, 99696 Overseas Hwy.* ☎ *305/451–1177* ⊕ *www.keysdiver.com* ⚑ *Snorkel trips from $29.95, dive trips from $85.*

Ocean Divers. The PADI five-star facility has been around since 1975 and offers day and night dives, a range of courses, and dive-lodging packages. Two-tank reef dives include tank and weight rental. There are also organized snorkeling trips with equipment. ✉ *MM 100 OS, 522 Caribbean Dr.* ☎ *305/451–1113, 800/451–1113* ⊕ *www.oceandivers.com* ⚑ *Snorkel trips from $35, diving from $85.*

★ Fodor'sChoice **Quiescence Diving Services.** This operator sets itself apart in two ways: it limits groups to six to ensure personal attention and offers both two-dive day and night dives, as well as twilight dives when sea creatures are most active. There are also organized snorkeling excursions. ✉ *MM 103.5 BS, 103680 Overseas Hwy.* ☎ *305/451–2440* ⊕ *www.quiescence.com* ⚑ *Snorkel trips $49, diving from $75.*

ISLAMORADA

Islamorada is between MM 90.5 and 70.

Early settlers named this key after their schooner, *Island Home,* but to make it sound more romantic they translated it into Spanish: *Isla Morada.* The Chamber of Commerce prefers to use its literal translation "Purple Island," which refers either to a purple-shelled snail that once inhabited these shores or to the brilliantly colored orchids and bougainvilleas.

Early maps show Islamorada as encompassing only Upper Matecumbe Key. But the incorporated "Village of Islands" is made up of a string of islands that the Overseas Highway crosses, including Plantation Key, Windley Key, Upper Matecumbe Key, Lower Matecumbe Key, Craig Key, and Fiesta Key. In addition, two state-park islands accessible only by boat—Indian Key and Lignumvitae Key—belong to the group.

Islamorada (locals pronounce it "*eye*-la-mor-*ah*-da") is one of the world's top fishing destinations. For nearly 100 years, seasoned anglers have fished these clear, warm waters teeming with trophy-worthy fish. There are numerous options for those in search of the big ones, including chartering a boat with its own crew or heading out on a vessel rented from one of the plethora of marinas along this 20-mile stretch of the Overseas Highway. More than 150 backcountry guides and 400 offshore captains are at your service.

Islamorada is one of the more affluent resort areas of the Keys. Sophisticated resorts and restaurants meet the needs of those in search of luxury, but there's also plenty for those looking for something more casual and affordable. Art galleries and boutiques make Islamorada's shopping scene the best in the Upper Keys, but if you need groceries, head to Marathon or Key Largo.

GETTING HERE AND AROUND

Most visitors arrive in Islamorada by car. If you're flying in to Miami International Airport or Key West International Airport, you can easily rent a car (reserve in advance) to make the drive.

VISITOR INFORMATION

Contact **Islamorada Chamber of Commerce & Visitors Center**
⊠ MM 87.1 BS, 87100 Overseas Hwy., Islamorada ☎ 305/664–4503, 800/322–5397 ⊕ www.islamoradachamber.com.

EXPLORING

TOP ATTRACTIONS

Florida Keys Memorial / Hurricane Monument. On Monday, September 2, 1935, more than 400 people perished when the most intense hurricane to make landfall in the United States swept through this area of the Keys. Two years later, the Florida Keys Memorial was dedicated in their honor. Native coral rock, known as keystone, covers the 18-foot obelisk monument that marks the remains of over 300 storm victims. A sculpted plaque of bending palms and waves graces the front (although many are bothered that the palms are bending in the wrong direction). In 1995, the memorial was placed on the National Register of Historic Places. ⊠ MM 81.5 OS, 81000 Overseas Hwy., Upper Matecumbe Key, Islamorada ☎ Free.

History of Diving Museum. Adding to the region's reputation for world-class diving, this museum plunges into the history of man's thirst for undersea exploration. Among its 13 galleries of interactive and other interesting displays are a submarine and helmet re-created from the film *20,000*

Islamorada

KEY
- **1** Restaurants
- **①** Hotels
- ◿ Dive Site
- ◿ Boat Launch
- ⚲ Beach

TO
TAVERNIER &
KEY LARGO

Plantation Key

❶

Islamorada
Founder's Park

①

Snake Creek

Windley Key

◿

Windley Key Fossil
Reef Geological
State Park

❷

②

Hens &
Chickens

◿

❸

Theater
of the Sea

*Whale Harbor
Bridge*

❹

Crocker
Reef

◿

❸ ❹

❺

History of Diving Museum

*Upper
Matecumbe
Key*

❺–❽

❻

Hammer
Head

◿

❼

Florida Keys Memorial/
Hurricane Monument

❽

❾

The Garden

◿

Beach Rd.

Cheeca
Rocks

◿

Parker Dr.

◿

Bayside

*Shell
Key*

Oceanside

The Eagle

◿

*Lignumvitae
Key*

Ligumvitae Key
Botanical State Park

◿

Alligator
Reef

◿

Robbie's Marina

Indian Key Historic
State Park

Indian Key

❿

①

Lasarra Ln.

Sea Ln.

Ocean Ln.

Sand Cove

*Lower
Matecumbe
Key*

*Costa
Bravo*

*Toll Gate
Blvd.*

Anne's Beach Park

TO
↙ MARATHON

Restaurants	Hotels
Chef Michael's, **9**	Casa Morada, **7**
Green Turtle Inn, **5**	Cheeca Lodge & Spa, **8**
Hungry Tarpon, **10**	Chesapeake Beach Resort, **4**
Islamorada Fish Company, **8**	Drop Anchor Resort and Marina, **3**
Island Grill, **2**	The Islander, A Guy Harvey Outpost Resort, **6**
Kaiyó Grill and Sushi, **4**	The Moorings Village, **9**
Lorelei Restaurant & Cabana Bar, **3**	Ocean House, **5**
Marker 88, **1**	Postcard Inn Beach Resort & Marina at Holiday Isle, **2**
Morada Bay Beach Café, **7**	Ragged Edge Resort, **1**
Pierre's, **6**	

Leagues Under the Sea. Vintage U.S. Navy equipment, diving helmets from around the world, and early scuba gear explore 4,000 years of diving history. For the grand finale, spend $3 for a mouthpiece and sing your favorite tune at the helium bar. There are extended hours (until 7 pm) on the third Wednesday of every month. ⊠ *MM 83 BS, 82990 Overseas Hwy., Upper Matecumbe Key, Islamorada* ☎ *305/664–9737* ⊕ *www.divingmuseum.org* 🖾 *$12* ⊙ *Daily 10–5.*

FAMILY **Robbie's Marina.** Huge, prehistoric-looking denizens of the not-so-deep, silver-sided tarpon congregate around the docks at this marina on Lower Matecumbe Key. Children—and lots of adults—pay $3 for a bucket of sardines to feed them and $1 each for dock admission. Spend some time hanging out at this authentic Keys community, where you can grab a bite to eat indoors or out, shop at a slew of artisans' booths, or charter a boat, kayak, or other watercraft. ⊠ *MM 77.5 BS, 77522 Overseas Hwy., Lower Matecumbe Key, Islamorada* ☎ *305/664–9814, 877/664–8498* ⊕ *www.robbies.com* 🖾 *Dock access $1* ⊙ *Daily sunrise–sunset.*

FAMILY **Theater of the Sea.** The second-oldest marine-mammal center in the world doesn't attempt to compete with more modern, more expensive parks. Even so, it's among the better attractions north of Key West, especially if you have kids in tow. In addition to marine life exhibits and shows, you can make reservations for up-close-and-personal encounters like a swim with a dolphin or sea lion, or stingray and turtle feedings (which include general admission; reservations required). These are popular, so reserve in advance. Ride a "bottomless" boat to see what's below the waves and take a guided tour of the marine-life exhibits. Nonstop animal shows highlight conservation issues. You can stop for lunch at the grill, shop in the extensive gift shop, or sunbathe and swim at their private beach. This easily could be an all-day attraction. ⊠ *MM 84.5 OS, 84721 Overseas Hwy., Windley Key, Islamorada* ☎ *305/664–2431* ⊕ *www.theaterofthesea. com* 🖾 *$31.95; interaction programs $35–$185* ⊙ *Daily 9:30–5 (last ticket sold at 3:30).*

WORTH NOTING

Anne's Beach Park. On Lower Matecumbe Key this popular village park is named for a local environmental activist. Its "beach" (really a typical Keys-style sand flat with a gentle slope) is best enjoyed at low tide. The nicest feature here is an elevated, wooden half-mile boardwalk that meanders through a natural wetland hammock. Covered picnic areas along the way give you places to linger and enjoy the view. Restrooms are at the north end. Weekends are packed with Miami day-trippers as it's the only public beach until you reach Marathon. **Amenities:** parking (no fee); toilets. **Best for:** partiers; snorkeling; swimming; windsurfing. ⊠ *MM 73.5 OS, Lower Matecumbe Key, Islamorada* ☎ *305/853–1685.*

Indian Key Historic State Park. Mystery surrounds 10-acre Indian Key, on the ocean side of the Matecumbe islands. Before it became one of the first European settlements outside of Key West, it was inhabited by Native Americans for several thousand years. The islet served as a base for 19th-century shipwreck salvagers until an Indian attack wiped out the settlement in 1840. Dr. Henry Perrine, a noted botanist, was killed in the raid. Today his plants grow in the town's ruins. Most people kayak or canoe here from Indian Key Fill or take a boat from Robbie's Marina to tour the nature trails and the town ruins or to snorkel. There are no restrooms or picnic facilities on Indian Key. ⊠ *Islamorada* ☎ *305/664–2540 park* ⊕ *www.floridastate-parks.org/indiankey* ⊒ *Free* ⊙ *Daily 8–5.*

Islamorada Founder's Park. This public park is the gem of Islamorada and boasts a palm-shaded beach, swimming pool, marina, skate park, tennis, and plenty of other facilities. If you want to rent a boat or learn to sail, businesses here can help you. If you're staying in Islamorada, admission is free. Those staying elsewhere pay $8 to enter the park. Either way, you pay an additional $3 to use the Olympic-size pool. A spiffy amphitheater hosts concerts, plays, and shows. The shallow water beach is ideal for swimming and families with little ones. Showers and bathrooms are beachside. ⊠ *MM 87 BS, 87000 Overseas Hwy., Plantation Key, Islamorada* ☎ *305/853–1685.*

Lignumvitae Key Botanical State Park. On the National Register of Historic Places, this 280-acre bayside island is the site of a virgin hardwood forest and the 1919 home of chemical magnate William Matheson. His caretaker's cottage serves as the park's visitor center. Access is by boat—your own, a rented vessel, or a tour operated from Robbie's Marina. The tour leaves at 8:30 am Friday through Sunday and takes in both Lignumvitae and Indian keys (reservations required). Paddling here from Indian Key Fill, at MM 78.5, is a popular pastime. The only way to do the trails is by a guided ranger walk, offered at 10 am and 2 pm Friday to Sunday. Wear long sleeves and pants, and bring mosquito repellent. On the first Saturday in December is the Lignumvitae Christmas Celebration, when the historic home is decorated 1930s-style. ✉ *Islamorada* ☎ *305/664–2540 park, 305/664–8070 boat tours* ⊕ *www.floridastateparks.org/lignumvitaekey* ▣ *$1 for ranger tours; $35 for boat tours* ⊙ *Park Thurs.–Mon. 8–5; house tours Fri.–Sun at 10 and 2.*

Upper Matecumbe Key. This was one of the first of the Upper Keys to be permanently settled. Early homesteaders were so successful at growing pineapples in the rocky soil that at one time the island yielded the country's largest annual crop; however, foreign competition and the hurricane of 1935 killed the industry. Today, life centers on fishing and tourism, and the island is filled with everything from bait shops and charter boats to eclectic galleries and fusion restaurants. ✉ *MM 84–79, Islamorada.*

Windley Key. This is the highest point in the Keys, though at 16 feet above sea level it's not likely to give anyone altitude sickness. Originally two islets, this area was first inhabited by Native Americans, who left behind a few traces of their dwellings, and then by farmers and fishermen who built their homes here in the mid-1800s. Henry Flagler bought the land from homesteaders in 1908 for his Florida East Coast Railway, filling in the inlet between what were then called the Umbrella Keys. His workers quarried coral rock for the rail bed and bridge approaches—the same rock used in many historic South Florida structures, including Miami's Vizcaya and the Hurricane Monument on Upper Matecumbe. Although the Quarry Station was destroyed by the 1935 hurricane, quarrying continued until the 1960s. Today, this is where you'll find Theater of the Sea, the famous Holiday Isle (now Postcard Inn), and Windley Key Fossil Reef Geological State Park. ✉ *MM 86–84, Islamorada.*

Windley Key Fossil Reef Geological State Park. The fossilized-coral reef, dating back about 125,000 years, demonstrates that the Florida Keys were once beneath the ocean. Excavation of Windley Key's limestone bed by the Florida East Coast Railway exposed the petrified reef, full of beautifully fossilized brain coral and sea ferns. Visitors can see the fossils along a 300-foot quarry wall when hiking the park's three trails. There are guided (Friday, Saturday, and Sunday only) and self-guided tours along the trails, which lead to the railway's old quarrying equipment and cutting pits, where you can make rubbings of the quarry walls. The **Alison Fahrer Environmental Education Center** holds historic, biological, and geological displays about the area, including videos. The first Saturday in March is Windley Key Day, when the park sells native plants and hosts environmental exhibits. ⊠ *MM 84.9 BS, Windley Key, Islamorada* ☎ *305/664–2540* ⊕ *www.floridastateparks.org/windleykey* ⊠ *$2.50; additional $2 for guided tours (self-guided is free)* ☉ *Education center Fri.–Sun. 9–5 (tours at 10 and 2).*

WHERE TO EAT

★ Fodor's Choice × **Chef Michael's.** *Seafood.* Peace. Love. Hogfish.
$$$ That's the motto of this local favorite that's been making big waves since its opening in 2011 with Chef Michael Ledwith at the helm. Sit outdoors on the covered wood deck and tap your toes to the live music, or dine inside amid dark wood floors and white linens. Seafood is selected fresh daily, then elegantly prepared with a splash of tropical flair. Try hogfish with mango sauce, or the catch "Juliette" with shrimp, scallops, Chardonnay butter, and toasted almonds. Carnivores can feast on prime-grade beef, carved in-house—that kind of marbling just melts in your mouth. Chef Michael even grows his own herbs, right out the kitchen door. How about a watermelon mint sangria? Just say yes. Gluten-free and vegetarian dishes are available. ⑤ *Average main: $29* ⊠ *MM81.7, 81671 Overseas Hwy., Upper Matecumbe Key, Islamorada* ☎ *305/664–0640* ⊕ *www.foodtotalkabout.com* ⌂ *Reservations essential* ☉ *No lunch Mon.–Sat.*

$$$ × **Green Turtle Inn.** *Seafood.* This circa-1947 landmark inn and its vintage neon sign is a slice of Florida Keys history. Period photographs decorate the wood-paneled walls. Breakfast options include surprises like French toast made with challah bread and Captain Morgan batter, and Keys Benedict with a blue crab cake. For lunch, skip the fish dip, and opt for lobster mac and cheese. Turtle chowder (don't gasp; it's made from farm-raised, freshwater turtles) is a staple. For dessert, the seventh-generation pound cake gets a standing ovation. ⑤ *Average main: $24* ⊠ *MM 81.2 OS, 81219 Overseas Hwy., Upper Matecumbe Key, Islamorada* ☎ *305/664–2006* ⊕ *www.greenturtlekeys.com* ⌂ *Reservations essential* ☉ *Closed Mon.*

$$ × **Hungry Tarpon.** *Seafood.* As part of the colorful, bustling Old Florida scene at Robbie's Marina, you know that the seafood here is fresh and top quality. The extensive menu seems as if it's bigger than the dining space, which consists of a few tables and counter-seating indoors, plus tables out back under the mangrove trees, close to where tourists pay to feed the tarpon in the marina. While tarpon are snacking on sardines, diners enjoy quite the impressive smattering of dishes for breakfast, lunch, and dinner. Specialties include biscuits and gravy, grilled ahi tuna nachos, a Matecumbe fish sandwich with provolone and bacon on grilled sourdough, and a shrimp burrito. Ⓢ *Average main: $19* ✉ *MM 77.5 BS, 77522 Overseas Hwy., Lower Matecumbe Key, Islamorada* ☎ *305/664–0535* ⊕ *www.hungrytarpon.com* ⌧ *Reservations not accepted.*

$ ✕ **Islamorada Fish Company.** *Seafood.* When a restaurant is
FAMILY   owned by Bass Pro Shops, you know the seafood should be as fresh as you can get it. The fun begins in the parking lot with painted white fish marking the parking spaces. The restaurant is housed in an open-air, oversized tiki hut right on Florida Bay, making this the quintessential Keys experience. There's a small, low-key tiki bar area if you prefer a stool to a table. Menu highlights include cracked conch beaten till tender and fried crispy, and Grouper Portofino, which will keep you coming back for more. Each afternoon, the staff feed the fish in the bay. Jump out of your seat and walk over for a close-up view of snapper, large tarpon, and even sharks. Ⓢ *Average main: $15* ✉ *MM 81.5 BS, 81532 Overseas Hwy., Windley Key, Islamorada* ☎ *305/664–9271* ⊕ *restaurants.basspro.com/fishcompany/ Islamorada/* ⊘ *Daily 11–10.*

$ ✕ **Island Grill.** *Seafood.* Don't be fooled by appearances; this shack on the waterfront takes island breakfast, lunch, and dinner up a notch. The eclectic menu tempts you with such dishes as its famed "original tuna nachos," lobster rolls, and a nice selection of seafood and sandwiches. Southern-style shrimp and andouille sausage with grits join island-style specialties such as grilled ribs with guava barbecue sauce on the list of entrées. There's an air-conditioned dining room and bar as well as open seating under a vaulted porch ceiling. The outdoor bar hosts live entertainment Wednesday to Sunday. Don't be in a hurry; service is usually slow. Ⓢ *Average main: $12* ✉ *MM 85.5 OS, 85501 Overseas Hwy., Windley Key, Islamorada* ☎ *305/664–8400* ⊕ *www. keysislandgrill.com* ⌧ *Reservations not accepted.*

$$$ ✕ **Kaiyo Grill & Sushi.** *Japanese.* The decor—an inviting setting that includes colorful abstract mosaics, polished wood floors, and upholstered banquettes—almost steals the show

at Kaiyo, but the food is equally interesting. The menu, a fusion of East and West, offers sushi rolls that combine local ingredients with traditional Japanese tastes. A wood grill is used to prepare such dishes as grilled catch of the day and hardwood-grilled rack of lamb. Drunken scallops are a must. Wine and sake choices are abundant, and the manager is a sommelier, so take advantage of his expertise and try pairings customized to your liking. [$] *Average main:* $28 ⊠ MM 81.5 OS, 81701 *Overseas Hwy., Upper Matecumbe Key, Islamorada* ☎ 305/664-5556 ⊕ *www.kaiyogrill. com* ⚑ *Reservations essential* ☺ *No lunch.*

$ ✕ **Lorelei Restaurant & Cabana Bar.** *American.* Local anglers gather here for breakfast. Lunch and dinner bring a mix of islanders and visitors for straightforward food and front row seats to the sunset. Live music seven nights a week ensures a lively nighttime scene, and the menu staves off inebriation with burgers, barbecued baby back ribs, and Parmesan-crusted snapper. Key lime pie comes frozen with mango sauce. Service can be less than stellar and the gathering at sunset is always crowded. [$] *Average main:* $15 ⊠ MM 82 BS, 81924 *Overseas Hwy., Upper Matecumbe Key, Islamorada* ☎ 305/664-2692 ⊕ *www.loreleicabanabar. com* ⚑ *Reservations not accepted.*

$$$ ✕ **Marker 88.** *Seafood.* A few yards from Florida Bay, this seafood restaurant has been popular since the late '60s. Large picture windows offer great sunset views, but the bay is lovely no matter what time of day you visit. Outdoor dining is popular, too. Chef Bobby Stoky serves such irresistible entrées as onion-crusted mahimahi, crispy yellowtail snapper, and mangrove-honey-and-chipotle–glazed rib eye. In addition, there are a half-dozen burgers and sandwiches, and you can't miss the restaurant's famous key lime baked Alaska dessert. The extensive wine list is an oenophile's delight. [$] *Average main:* $28 ⊠ MM 88 BS, 88000 *Overseas Hwy., Plantation Key, Islamorada* ☎ 305/852-9315 ⊕ *www. market88.info* ⚑ *Reservations essential.*

$$$ ✕ **Morada Bay Beach Café.** *Eclectic.* This bay-front restaurant **FAMILY** wins high marks for its surprisingly stellar cuisine, tables planted in the sand, and tiki torches that bathe the evening in romance. Entrées feature alluring combinations like fresh fish of the day sautéed with Meyer lemon butter and whole fried snapper with coconut rice. Seafood takes center stage, but you can always get roasted organic chicken or prime rib. Tapas and raw bar menus cater to smaller appetites or those who can't decide with offerings like fried calamari, conch fritters, and Wagyu beef sliders. Lunch adds interest-

ing sandwiches to the mix. Sit in a dining room outfitted with surfboards or outdoors on a beach where the sunset puts on a mighty show and kids (and your feet) play in the sand. $ *Average main: $27* ⊠ MM 81 BS, 81600 Overseas Hwy., Upper Matecumbe Key, Islamorada ☎ 305/664-0604 ⊕ *www.moradabay-restaurant.com.*

$$$$ ★ Fodor'sChoice ✕ **Pierre's.** *French.* One of the Keys' most elegant restaurants, Pierre's marries colonial style with modern food trends. Full of interesting architectural artifacts, the place oozes style, especially the wicker chair–strewn veranda overlooking the bay. Save your best "tropical chic" duds for dinner here, so you don't stand out from your surroundings. The food, drawn from French and Floridian influences, is multilayered and beautifully presented. Among the season-ally changing appetizer choices, you might find smoked hogfish chowder and foie gras sliders with a butternut squash milk shake. A changing list of entrées might include hogfish meunière and scallops with pork belly tortellini. The downstairs bar is a perfect spot for catching sunsets, sip-ping martinis, and enjoying light eats. $ *Average main: $35* ⊠ MM 81.5 BS, 81600 Overseas Hwy., Upper Matecumbe Key, Islamorada ☎ 305/664-3225 ⊕ *www.moradabay.com* ⊘ *No lunch.* ⚘ *Reservations essential.*

WHERE TO STAY

$$ ★ Fodor'sChoice ☑ **Casa Morada.** *B&B/Inn.* This relic from the 1950s has been restyled into a suave, design-forward, all-suites property with outdoor showers and Jacuzzis in some of the suites. **Pros:** cool design; complimentary snacks and bottled water; complimentary use of bikes, kayaks, and snorkel gear. **Cons:** trailer park across the street; beach is small and inconsequential. *Rooms from: $299* ⊠ MM 82 BS, 136 Madeira Rd., Upper Matecumbe Key, Islamorada ☎ 305/664-0044, 888/881-3030 ⊕ *www.casamorada.com* ⚘ *16 suites* ⊘ *Breakfast.*

$$ ★ Fodor'sChoice ☑ **Cheeca Lodge & Spa.** *Resort.* At 27 acres, this may be the largest resort in the Keys, and it's also big on included amenities. **Pros:** beautifully landscaped grounds; new designer rooms; water-sports center on property. **Cons:** expensive rates; expensive resort fee; very busy. *Rooms from: $299* ⊠ MM 82 OS, Upper Matecumbe Key, Islamo-rada ☎ 305/664-4651, 800/327-2888 ⊕ *www.cheeca.com* ⚘ *60 1-bedroom suites, 64 junior suites* ⊘ *No meals.*

$ ☑ **Chesapeake Beach Resort.** *Resort.* This boutique hotel on the beach mixes modern conveniences with a retro look.

Pros: oceanfront location; free use of water-sports equipment and Wi-Fi (included in resort fee). **Cons:** dated exterior; mandatory resort fee (per room per night). $ Rooms from: $179 ⊠ MM 83.5, 83409 Overseas Hwy., Upper Matecumbe Key, Islamorada ☎ 305/664–4662, 800/338–3395 ⊕ www.chesapeake-resort.com ⤴ 44 rooms, 8 suites, 13 villas ⊙ Breakfast.

$ ⚅ **Drop Anchor Resort and Marina.** *Hotel.* Immaculately maintained, this place has the feel of an old friend's beach house. **Pros:** bright and colorful; attention to detail; laid-back charm. **Cons:** noise from the highway; beach is better for fishing than swimming. $ Rooms from: $149 ⊠ MM 85 OS, 84959 Overseas Hwy., Windley Key, Islamorada ☎ 305/664–4863, 888/664–4863 ⊕ www.dropanchorresort.com ⤴ 18 suites ⊙ No meals.

$$ ⚅ **The Islander, A Guy Harvey Outpost Resort.** *Resort.* Guests here get to choose between a self-sufficient town home on the bay with room for a boat, or an oceanfront resort with on-site restaurants and oodles of amenities. **Pros:** spacious rooms; nice kitchens; eye-popping views. **Cons:** pricey for what you get; beach has rough sand. $ Rooms from: $249 ⊠ MM 82.1 OS, 82200 Overseas Hwy., Upper Matecumbe Key, Islamorada ☎ 305/664–2031, 800/753–6002 ⊕ www.guyharveyoutpostislamorada.com ⤴ 114 rooms, 12 suites, 25 townhomes ⊙ Breakfast.

★ Fodor'sChoice ⚅ **The Moorings Village.** *Hotel.* This tropical
$$$ retreat is everything you imagine when you think of the Keys—from hammocks swaying between towering trees to sugar-white sand (arguably the Keys' best resort beach) lapped by aqua-green waves. **Pros:** romantic setting; good dining options with room-charging privileges; beautiful beach. **Cons:** no room service; extra fee for housekeeping; daily resort fee for activities. $ Rooms from: $375 ⊠ MM 81.6 OS, 123 Beach Rd., Upper Matecumbe Key, Islamorada ☎ 305/664–4708 ⊕ www.themooringsvillage.com ⤴ 6 cottages, 12 houses ⊙ No meals.

★ Fodor'sChoice ⚅ **Ocean House.** *Hotel.* Islamorada's newest adult
$$ boutique hotel is situated right on the Atlantic, yet it's hidden from passersby amidst lush gardens. **Pros:** complimentary use of kayaks, snorkel equipment, and bicycles; luxurious facilities and amenities. **Cons:** limited number of units means they're often booked solid; luxury comes at a price. $ Rooms from: $299 ⊠ MM 82 OS, 82885 Old Hwy., Windley Key, Islamorada ☎ 866/540–5520 ⊕ www.oceanhousefloridakeys.com ⤴ 8 suites ⊙ Some meals.

$$ ⊞ **Postcard Inn Beach Resort & Marina at Holiday Isle.** *Resort.* After an $11-million renovation that encompassed updating everything from the rooms to the public spaces, this iconic property (formerly known as the Holiday Isle Beach Resort) has found new life. **Pros:** large private beach; heated pools; on-site restaurants including Shula's 2. **Cons:** rooms near Tiki bar are noisy; minimum stay required during peak times; bathrooms need updating. ⑤*Rooms from: $215* ⊠ *MM 84 OS, 84001 Overseas Hwy., Plantation Key, Islamorada* ☎ *305/664–2321* ⊕ *www.holidayisle.com/ Islamorada-beachclub* ⌑ *143 rooms* ⦿*No meals.*

$ ⊞ **Ragged Edge Resort.** *Hotel.* Nicely tucked away in a residential area at the ocean's edge, this family-owned hotel draws returning guests who'd rather fish off the dock and grill up dinner than loll around in Egyptian cotton sheets. **Pros:** oceanfront; boat docks and ramp; cheap rates. **Cons:** dated decor; off the beaten path. ⑤*Rooms from: $110* ⊠ *MM 86.5 OS, 243 Treasure Harbor Rd., Plantation Key, Islamorada* ☎ *305/852–5389, 800/436–2023* ⊕ *www. ragged-edge.com* ⌑ *6 studios, 1 efficiency, 3 2-bedroom suites* ⦿*No meals.*

FAMILY

NIGHTLIFE

Islamorada is not known for its raging nightlife, but for local fun. Lorelei's is legendary, as is the Postcard Inn at Holiday Isle. Others cater to the town's sophisticated clientele and fishing fervor.

Hog Heaven. Come by boat or car to this oceanfront restaurant and sports bar where you can soak in the views dockside or relax in the air-conditioning. Munch on fresh fish sandwiches or barbecue dishes while you shoot pool, catch the big game on large flat screens, or dance to a live band or DJ. Late night can get a bit wild and loud. ⊠ *MM 85.3 OS, 85361 Overseas Hwy., Islamorada* ☎ *305/664–9669* ⊕ *www.hogheavensportsbar.com.*

Lorelei Restaurant & Cabana Bar. Behind a larger-than-life mermaid, this is the kind of place you fantasize about during those long cold winters up north. It's all about good drinks, tasty pub grub, and beautiful sunsets set to live bands playing island tunes and light rock nightly. Dining is all outdoors, on a deck or under the trees. Service is slow, sometime even nonexistent. ⊠ *MM 82 BS, 81924 Overseas Hwy., Upper Matecumbe Key, Islamorada* ☎ *305/664–2692* ⊕ *www.loreleicabanabar.com.*

Safari Lounge. Locals often refer to Safari Lounge as the Dead Animal Bar, or simply DAB, because of the mounted big-game trophies lining the walls and ceiling. Within eyeshot of the sea, it's a good spot to hoist a few with the island drinking crowd. Happy hour is daily 5–7. ⊠ *MM 73.5 OS, 73814 Overseas Hwy., Islamorada* ☎ *305/664–8142.*

Zane Grey Long Key Lounge. Above the World Wide Sportsman, Zane Grey Long Key Lounge was created to honor writer Zane Grey, one of the most famous members of the Long Key Fishing Club. The lounge displays the author's photographs, books, and memorabilia. Listen to live blues, jazz, and Motown on a wide veranda that invites sunset watching. Full menu is available. ⊠ *MM 81.5, BS, 81576 Overseas Hwy., Upper Matecumbe Key, Islamorada* ☎ *305/664–4615* ⊕ *restaurants.basspro.com/ ZaneGreyLounge.*

Ziggie & Mad Dog's. The area's glam celebrity hangout, Ziggie & Mad Dog's serves appetizers with its happy-hour drink specials. Its wine list and outrageous steaks have become legendary. ⊠ *MM 83 BS, 83000 Overseas Hwy., Upper Matecumbe Key, Islamorada* ☎ *305/664–3391* ⊕ *www. ziggieandmaddogs.com.*

SHOPPING

Art galleries, upscale gift shops, and the mammoth World Wide Sportsman (if you want to look the part of a local fisherman, you must wear a shirt from here) make up the variety and superior style of Islamorada shopping.

BOOKS

Hooked on Books. Among the best buys in town are the used best sellers at this bookstore, which also sells new titles, audiobooks, and CDs. ⊠ *MM 81.9 OS, 81909 Overseas Hwy., Upper Matecumbe Key, Islamorada* ☎ *305/517–2602* ⊕ *www.hookedonbooksfloridakeys.com.*

GALLERIES

Gallery Morada. This gallery is a go-to destination for one-of-a-kind gifts, beautifully displayed blown glass, original sculptures, paintings, lithographs, and jewelry by 200 artists. Its location, front and center, makes it the gateway to the Morada Way Arts & Cultural District, an area with artist galleries, shops, potters, gardens, and culinary classes. ⊠ *MM 81.6 OS, 81611 Old Hwy., Upper Matecumbe Key, Islamorada* ☎ *305/664–3650* ⊕ *www.gallerymorada.com.*

Rain Barrel Artisan Village. This is a natural and unhurried shopping showplace. Set in a tropical garden of shady trees, native shrubs, and orchids, the crafts village has shops selling the work of local and national artists as well as resident artists who sell work from their own studios. Have your photo taken with "Betsy," the giant Florida lobster, roadside. ⊠ *MM 86.7 BS, 86700 Overseas Hwy., Plantation Key, Islamorada* ☎ *305/852–3084* ⊕ *www.seefloridaonline.com/rainbarrel/index.html.*

Redbone Gallery. One of the largest sportfishing–art galleries in Florida stocks hand-stitched clothing and giftware, in addition to work by wood and bronze sculptors such as Kendall van Sant; watercolorist C.D. Clarke; and painters Daniel Caldwell, David Hall, Steven Left, and Stacie Krupa. Proceeds benefit cystic fibrosis research. Find them in the Morada Way Arts & Cultural District. ⊠ *MM 81.5 OS, 200 Morada Way, Upper Matecumbe Key, Islamorada* ☎ *305/664–2002* ⊕ *www.redbone.org.*

GIFTS

Banyan Tree. A sharp-eyed husband-and-wife team successfully combines antiques and contemporary gifts for the home and garden with plants, pots, and trellises in a stylishly sophisticated indoor-outdoor setting. ⊠ *MM 81.2 OS, 81197 Overseas Hwy., Upper Matecumbe Key, Islamorada* ☎ *305/664–3433* ⊕ *www.banyantreegarden.com.*

Island Silver & Spice. This upscale shop is the place to go for women's and men's resort wear, fine tropical jewelry, and high-end watches. Island-themed glassware and elegant kitchen items make excellent gifts. Upstairs is unique tropical home decor, as well as the clearance section. ⊠ *MM 82 OS, 81981 Overseas Hwy., Upper Matecumbe Key, Islamorada* ☎ *305/664–2714.*

SHOPPING CENTERS

Casa Mar Village. Change is good, and in this case, it's fantastic. What was once a row of worn-down buildings is now a merry blend of gift shops and galleries with the added bonus of a place selling fresh-roasted coffee. By day, these colorful shops glisten at their canal-front location; by nightfall, they're lit up like a lovely Christmas town. The offerings include the Jolly Pelican, Jewels by Vivi, the Little White Gallery, Olive Morada (upscale oils and vinegars), and the Fresh Press Cafe. ⊠ *MM90 OS, 90775 Old Hwy., Upper Matecumbe Key, Islamorada* ☎ *305/522-0330.*

SPORTING GOODS

World Wide Sportsman. This two-level retail center sells upscale and everyday fishing equipment, resort clothing, sportfishing art, and other gifts. When you're tired of shopping, relax at the Zane Grey Long Key Lounge, located above the store—but not before you step up and into *Pilar*, a replica of Hemingway's boat. ⊠ *MM 81.5 BS, 81576 Overseas Hwy., Upper Matecumbe Key, Islamorada* ☎ *305/664–4615, 800/327–2880.*

2

SPORTS AND THE OUTDOORS

BOATING

Bump & Jump. You can rent both fishing and deck boats here (from 15 to 29 feet) by the day or the week. There's free local delivery for those without trailers. ⊠ *MM 81.2 OS, 81197 Overseas Hwy., Upper Matecumbe Key, Islamorada* ☎ *305/664–9404, 877/453–9463* ⊕ *www.keysboatrental. com* ⊠ *Rentals from $145 per day.*

Houseboat Vacations of the Florida Keys. See the islands from the comfort of your own boat (captain's cap optional). The company maintains a fleet of 44- to 55-foot boats that accommodate up to 10 people and come outfitted with everything you need besides food. (You may provision yourself at a nearby grocery store.) There's a three-day minimum; weekly rates are available. Kayaks and paddleboards suitable for bayside use are also available. ⊠ *MM 85.9 BS, 85944 Overseas Hwy., Islamorada* ☎ *305/664–4009* ⊕ *www.baysidetikiboats.com* ⊠ *From $1,150.*

Nauti-Limo. Captain Joe Fox has converted the design of a 1983 pink Caddy stretch limo into a less-than-luxurious but certainly curious watercraft. The seaworthy hybrid—complete with wheels—can sail with the top down if you're in the mood. Only in the Keys! One-hour and longer tours are available. ⊠ *Lorelei Restaurant & Yacht Club, MM 82 BS, 96 Madeira Rd., Upper Matecumbe Key, Islamorada* ☎ *305/942–3793* ⊕ *www.nautilimo.com* ⊠ *From $60.*

Robbie's Boat Rentals & Charters. This full-service company will even give you a crash course on how not to crash your boat. The rental fleet includes an 18-foot skiff with a 90-horsepower outboard to a 21-foot deck boat with a 130-horsepower engine. Robbie's also rents snorkeling gear (there's good snorkeling nearby) and sells bait, drinks and snacks. Want to hire a guide who knows the local waters and where the fish lurk? Robbie's offers offshore-fishing trips, patch-reef trips, and party-boat fishing. Backcountry flats trips are a specialty. ⊠ *MM 77.5 BS, 77522 Overseas Hwy., Lower Matecumbe Key, Islamorada* ☎ *305/664–9814, 877/664–8498* ⊕ *www.robbies.com* ⊠ *From $185 per day.*

Treasure Harbor Marine. The Anderson family will provide everything you need for a bareboat sailing vacation at sea. They also give excellent advice on where to find the best anchorages, snorkeling spots, or lobstering sites. Vessels range from a 23.5-foot Hunter to a 41-foot Morgan Out Island. Boats can be rented by the day or week. Marina facilities include water, electric, ice machine, laundry, picnic tables, and restrooms with showers. Transient and long-term dockages are available. A store sells snacks, beverages, and sundries. ⊠ *MM 86.5 OS, 200 Treasure Harbor Dr., Plantation Key, Islamorada* ☎ *305/852–2458, 800/352–2628* ⊕ *www.treasureharbor.com* ⊠ *From $160 per day.*

FISHING

Here in the self-proclaimed "Sportfishing Capital of the World," sailfish is the prime catch in the winter and mahimahi in the summer. Buchanan Bank just south of Islamorada is a good spot to try for tarpon in the spring. Blackfin tuna and amberjack are generally plentiful in the area, too. ■TIP→ **The Hump at Islamorada ranks highest among anglers' favorite fishing spots in Florida (declared Florida Monthly magazine's best for seven years in a row) due to the incredible offshore marine life.**

Captain Ted Wilson. Go into the backcountry for bonefish, tarpon, redfish, snook, and shark aboard a 17-foot boat that accommodates up to three anglers. Two people can choose half- or full-day trips, two-hour sunset bonefishing excursions, or evening fishing excursions. There's an extra $100 charge for each additional person. ⊠ *MM 79.9 OS, 79851 Overseas Hwy., Upper Matecumbe Key, Islamorada* ☎ *305/942–5224, 305/664–9463* ⊕ *www.captaintedwilson. com* ⊠ *Bonefishing from $250, half-day trips from $400.*

Florida Keys Fly Fish. Like other top fly-fishing and light-tackle guides, Captain Geoff Colmes helps his clients land trophy fish in the waters around the Keys. ⊠ *105 Palm La., Upper Matecumbe Key, Islamorada* ☎ *305/853–0741* ⊕ *www.floridakeysflyfish.com* ⊠ *From $400.*

Florida Keys Outfitters. Long before fly-fishing became popular, Sandy Moret was fishing the Keys for bonefish, tarpon, and redfish. Now he attracts anglers from around the world on a quest for the big catch. His weekend fly-fishing classes include classroom instruction, equipment, and daily lunch. Guided fishing trips can be done for a half-day or full day. Packages combining fishing and accommodations at Islander Resort are available. ✉ *MM 81.2, Green Turtle, 81219 Overseas Hwy., Upper Matecumbe Key, Islamorada* ☎ *305/664–5423* ⊕ *www.floridakeysoutfitters.com* 🖅 *Half-day trips from $496.*

Hubba Hubba Charters. Captain Ken Knudsen has fished the Keys waters since the 1970s. A licensed backcountry guide, he's ranked among Florida's top 10 by national fishing magazines. He offers four-hour sunset trips for tarpon and two-hour sunset trips for bonefish, as well as half- and full-day outings. Prices are for one or two anglers, and tackle and bait are included. ✉ *MM 79.8 OS, Upper Matecumbe Key, Islamorada* ☎ *305/664–9281* 🖅 *From $200.*

Miss Islamorada. This 65-foot party boat offers full-day trips. Bring your lunch or buy one from the dockside deli. ✉ *Bud n' Mary's Marina, MM 79.8 OS, 79851 Overseas Hwy., Upper Matecumbe Key, Islamorada* ☎ *305/664–2461, 800/742–7945* ⊕ *www.budnmarys.com* 🖅 *From $65.*

SCUBA DIVING AND SNORKELING

About 1 ¼ nautical miles south of Indian Key is the San Pedro Underwater Archaeological Preserve State Park, which includes the wreck of a Spanish treasure-fleet ship that sank in 1733. The state of Florida protects the site for divers; no spearfishing or souvenir collecting is allowed. Resting in only 18 feet of water, its ruins are visible to snorkelers as well as divers and attract a colorful array of fish.

Florida Keys Dive Center. Dive from John Pennekamp Coral Reef State Park to Alligator Light with this outfitter. The center has two 46-foot Coast Guard–approved dive boats, offers scuba training, and is one of the few Keys dive centers to offer Nitrox and Trimix (mixed gas) diving. ✉ *MM 90.5 OS, 90451 Overseas Hwy., Plantation Key, Islamorada* ☎ *305/852–4599, 800/433–8946* ⊕ *www.floridakeysdivectr.com* 🖅 *Snorkeling from $38, diving from $65.*

Islamorada Dive Center. This one-stop dive shop has a resort, pool, restaurant, lessons, and twice-daily dive and snorkel trips. You can take a day-trip with a two-tank dive or a one-tank night trip without equipment. Snorkel trips are also available. ✉ *MM 84 OS, 84001 Overseas Hwy., Windley*

Key, Islamorada ☎*305/664–3483, 800/327–7070* ⊕*www. islamoradadivecenter.com* ⊠*Snorkel trips from $45, diving from $80.*

San Pedro Underwater Archaeological Preserve State Park. About 1¼ nautical mile south of Indian Key is the San Pedro Underwater Archaeological Preserve State Park, which includes the remains of a Spanish treasure-fleet ship that sank in 1733. The state of Florida protects the site for divers; no spearfishing or souvenir collecting is allowed. Seven replica cannons and a plaque enhance what basically amounts to a 90-foot-long pile of ballast stones. Resting in only 18 feet of water, its ruins are visible to snorkelers as well as divers and attract a colorful array of fish. ⊠*MM 85.5 OS, Islamorada* ☎*305/664–2540* ⊕*www. floridastateparks.org/sanpedro.*

WATER SPORTS

The Kayak Shack. You can rent kayaks for trips to Indian (about 20 minutes one way) and Lignumvitae (about 45 minutes one way) keys, two favorite destinations for paddlers. Kayaks can be rented for a half day (and you'll need plenty of time to explore those mangrove canopies). Pedal kayaks are also available and are a bit more expensive. The company also offers guided three-hour tours, including a snorkel trip to Indian Key. It also rents stand-up paddleboards, including instruction, and canoes. ⊠*MM 77.5 BS, Robbie's Marina, 77522 Overseas Hwy., Lower Matecumbe Key, Islamorada* ☎*305/664–4878* ⊕*www. kayakthefloridakeys.com* ⊠*From $40 for single, $55 for double, guided trips from $45.*

LONG KEY

MM 70–65.5.

Long Key isn't a tourist hot spot, making it a favorite destination for those looking to avoid the masses and enjoy some natural history.

EXPLORING

Layton Nature Trail. Across the road from Long Key State Park, beginning at a close-to-the-ground marker, is a free trail that leads through a tropical-hardwood forest to a rocky Florida Bay shoreline overlooking shallow grass flats. It takes about 20 minutes to walk the trail. ⊠*MM 67.7 BS.*

Long Key State Park. Come here for solitude, hiking, fishing, and camping. On the ocean side, the Golden Orb Trail leads to a boardwalk that cuts through the mangroves (may require some wading) and alongside a lagoon where waterfowl congregate (as do mosquitoes, so be prepared). A 1¼-mile canoe trail leads through a tidal lagoon, and a broad expanse of shallow grass flats is perfect for bonefishing. Bring a mask and snorkel to observe the marine life in the shallow water. The park is particularly popular with campers who long to stake their tent at the campground on a beach. In summer, no-see-ums (biting sand flies) also love the beach, so again—be prepared. The picnic area is on the water, too, but lacks a beach. Canoes rent for $10 per day, and kayak rentals start at $17 for a single for two hours, $21.50 for a double. Rangers lead tours every Wednesday and Thursday at 10 on birding, boating, or beachcombing. ⊠ *MM 67.5 OS, 67400 Overseas Hwy.* ☎ *305/664–4815* ⊕ *www.floridastateparks.org/longkey* ⌨ *$4.50 for 1 person, $5.50 for 2 people, and 50¢ for each additional person in the group* ☉ *Daily 8–sunset.*

Long Key Viaduct. As you cross Long Key Channel, look beside you at the old viaduct. The second-longest bridge on the former rail line, this 2-mile-long structure has 222 reinforced-concrete arches. The old bridge is popular with cyclists and anglers, who fish off the sides day and night.

BEACHES

Long Key State Park Beach. Camping, snorkeling, and bonefishing are the favored activities along this narrow strip of natural, rocky shoreline and its shallow, seagrass-bottom waters. It lines the park's campground, which is open only to registered campers. While the campground is open only to registered campers, the "day" area offers a nice respite, although those expecting a wide, sandy beach will be thoroughly disappointed. If you're seeking a spot by the shoreline, this could be your place in the sun. **Amenities:** showers; toilets. **Best for:** snorkeling; swimming; walking. ⊠ *MM 67.5 OS, 67400 Overseas Hwy.* ☎ *305/664–4815* ⊕ *www.floridastateparks.org/longkey* ⌨ *$4.50 for 1 person, $5.50 for 2 people, and 50¢ for each additional person in the group* ☉ *Daily 8–sunset.*

WHERE TO STAY

$ ⬚ **Lime Tree Bay Resort.** *Resort.* Easy on the eye and the wallet, this 2½-acre resort on Florida Bay offers simple accommodations that are far from the hustle and bustle of the larger islands. **Pros:** great views; friendly staff; close to Long Key State Park. **Cons:** no restaurants nearby; shared balconies; gravel beach. ⑤ *Rooms from: $199* ✉ *MM 68.5 BS, 68500 Overseas Hwy., Layton* ☎ *305/664–4740, 800/723–4519* ⊕ *www.limetreebayresort.com* ⇨ *10 rooms, 10 studios, 4 two-bedroom suites, 20 mini suites, 4 efficiencies* ⦿ *Breakfast.*

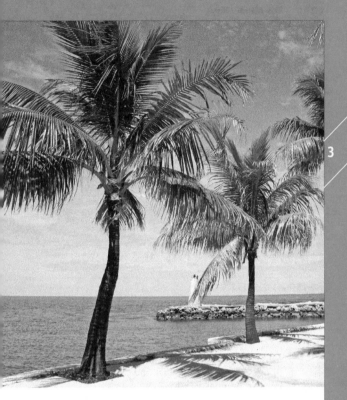

3

THE MIDDLE KEYS

Updated
by Jill
Martin **MOST OF THE ACTIVITY IN THE MIDDLE KEYS** revolves around the town of Marathon, the region's third-largest metropolitan area. On either end of it, smaller keys hold resorts, wildlife research and rehab facilities, a historic village, and a state park. The Middle Keys make a fitting transition from the Upper Keys to the Lower Keys not only geographically but also mentally. Crossing Seven Mile Bridge prepares you for the slow pace and don't-give-a-damn attitude you'll find a little farther down the highway. Fishing is one of the main attractions—in fact, the region's commercial fishing industry was founded here in the early 1800s. Diving is another popular pastime. There are also beaches and natural areas to enjoy in the Middle Keys, where mainland stress becomes an ever more distant memory.

ORIENTATION AND PLANNING

GETTING ORIENTED

If you get bridge fever—the heebie-jeebies when driving over long stretches of water—you may need a pair of blinders (or a couple of tranquilizers) before tackling the Middle Keys. Stretching from Conch Key to the far side of the Seven Mile Bridge, this zone is home to the region's two longest bridges: Long Key Viaduct and Seven Mile Bridge, both historic landmarks.

PLANNING

GETTING HERE AND AROUND

To get to the Middle Keys you can fly into either Miami International Airport or Key West International Airport. Key West is closer, but there are far fewer flights coming in and going out. Rental cars are available at both airports. In addition, there is bus service from the Key West airport, $4 one-way with Key West Transit. SuperShuttle charges $250 for up to 11 passengers from Miami International Airport (MIA) to Big Pine Key. Keys Shuttle charges $80 per passenger from MIA to Marathon.

U.S. 1 takes you from one end of the region to the other in a direct line that takes in most of the sights, but you'll find some interesting resorts and restaurants off the main drag. *See Ground Transportation and Bus Travel in Travel Smart.*

TOP REASONS TO GO

■ **Crane Point.** Visit 63-acre Crane Point Museum, Nature Center & Historic Site in Marathon for a primer on local natural and social history.

■ **A Beach for the Whole Family.** Sun, swim, and play with abandon at Marathon's family-oriented Sombrero Beach.

■ **Pigeon Key.** Step into the era of railroad building with a ferry ride to Pigeon Key's historic village, which was once a residential camp for workers on Henry M. Flagler's Overseas Railroad.

■ **Dolphins.** Kiss a dolphin, and maybe even watch one paint, at Dolphin Research Center, which was begun by the maker of the movie *Flipper*.

■ **Fishing.** Anglers will be happy to hear that the deep-water fishing off Marathon is superb in both the bay and the ocean.

HOTELS

From quaint old cottages to newly built town-house communities, the Middle Keys have it all, often with prices that are more affordable than at the chain's extremes. Hawks Cay has the region's best selection of lodgings.

Hotel reviews have been shortened. For full information, visit Fodors.com.

RESTAURANTS

Hope you're not tired of seafood, because the run of fish houses continues in the Middle Keys. In fact, Marathon boasts some of the best. Several are not so easy to find, but worth the search because of their local color and water views. Expect casual and friendly service with a side of sass. Restaurants may close for two to four weeks during the slow season between September and mid-November, so call ahead if you have a particular place in mind.

CONCH KEY

MM 63–60.

This stretch of islands ranges from rustic fishing village to boating elite. Fishing dominates the economy, and many residents are descendants of immigrants from the mainland South. Across a causeway from the tiny fishing village of Conch Key is Duck Key, home to a more upscale community. There are a few lodging options here for those

The Middle Keys

0   10 miles

0   10 km

Florida Bay

Seven Mile Bridge

Marathon   see detail map

Marathon Airport

Grassy Key

Gulf View Waterfront Resort

Conch Key

Duck Key

Conch Key Cottages

Hawks Cay Resort

Pigeon Key

Vaca Key

Curry Hammock State Park

ATLANTIC OCEAN

exploring Marathon or taking advantage of the water sports on Duck Key.

WHERE TO STAY

$$$ **Conch Key Cottages.** *Hotel.* Brightly colored American-Caribbean style cottages, each named for a shell or sea creature, are furnished Bali-style in a secluded island setting on a mangrove-framed beach between Marathon and Islamorada. **Pros:** far from the traffic noise; sandy beach; lots of sunny decks. **Cons:** far from restaurants. ⓢ *Rooms from: $300* ⊠ *MM 62.3 OS, 62250 Overseas Hwy., Conch Key* ☎ *800/330–1577* ⊕ *www.conchkeycottages.com* ↝ *9 cottages, 2 apartments, 2 seaside villas, 2 rooms* ⍟ *Breakfast.*

DUCK KEY

MM 61.

Duck Key holds one of the region's nicest marina resorts, Hawks Cay, plus a boating-oriented residential community.

WHERE TO EAT

$$$ ✕**Alma.** *Latin American.* A refreshing escape from the Middle Keys' same-old menus, Alma serves expertly prepared Florida and Latin-Caribbean dishes in an elegant setting. Nightly changing menus might include a trio of ceviche, ahi tuna with a wonderful garbanzo bean tomato sauce, gnocchi and exotic mushroom ragout, or pan-seared Wagyu steak. Finish your meal with the silky, smooth, passion fruit crème brûlée, which has just the right amount of tartness to balance the delicate caramelized crust. ⑤ *Average main: $28 ⊠Hawks Cay Resort, 61 Hawks Cay Blvd., Duck Key ☎305/743–7000, 888/432–2242 ⊕www.hawkscay. com ⊘No lunch.*

WHAT IT COSTS				
	$	**$$**	**$$$**	**$$$$**
Restaurants	Under $15	$16–$20	$21–$30	Over $30
Hotels	Under $200	$201–$300	$301–$400	Over $400

Prices in the restaurant reviews are the average cost of a main course at dinner or, if dinner isn't served, at lunch. Prices in the hotel reviews are the lowest cost of a standard double room in high season. Prices don't include taxes (6%, more in some counties, and 1%–5% tourist tax for hotel rooms).

WHERE TO STAY

★ **Fodor's**Choice ☷**Hawks Cay Resort.** *Resort.* The 60-acre,
$$ Caribbean-style retreat with a full-service spa and res-
FAMILY taurants has plenty to keep the kids occupied (and adults happy). **Pros:** huge rooms; restful spa; full-service marina and dive shop. **Cons:** no real beach; far from Marathon's attractions. ⑤ *Rooms from: $240 ⊠MM 61 OS, 61 Hawks Cay Blvd., Duck Key ☎305/743–7000, 888/432–2242 ⊕www.hawkscay.com ⇋161 rooms, 16 suites, 225 2- and 3-bedroom villas ⑩No meals.*

SPORTS AND THE OUTDOORS

DOLPHIN INTERACTION

Dolphin Connection. Hawk's Cay Resort's Dolphin Connection offers three programs, including Dockside Dolphins, a 30-minute encounter from the dry training docks; Dolphin Discovery, an in-water program that lasts about 45 minutes and lets you kiss, touch, and feed the dolphins; and Trainer for a Day, a three-hour session with the animal training team. ✉ *Hawk's Cay Resort, MM 61 OS, 61 Hawks Cay Blvd., Duck Key* ☎ *305/743–7000* ⊕ *www. dolphinconnection.com* ✎ *From $60.*

SCUBA DIVING AND SNORKELING

Dive Duck Key. Dive Duck Key is a full-service dive shop offering rentals, charters, lessons, and certification courses. Scuba trips are offered with and without gear. Basic open-water certification courses are also available, but these require four days of your time; a shorter resort course can be finished in a day. There's also snuba, a snorkel-scuba hybrid where your tanks float on the surface rather than being attached to your back. ✉ *Hawks Cay Resort, MM 61 OS, 61 Hawks Cay Blvd., Duck Key* ☎ *305/289–4931, 877/386–3483* ⊕ *www.diveduckkey.com* ✎ *Diving from $65, excursions from $115.*

WATER SPORTS

Sundance Watersports. Go on a one-hour guided Jet Ski tour, soar on a parasail flight, go reef snorkeling (including equipment rentals), or enjoy a sunset cruise. ✉ *Hawks Cay Resort, MM 61 OS, 61 Hawks Cay Blvd., Duck Key* ☎ *305/743–0145* ⊕ *www.sundancewatersports.net* ✎ *From $42.*

GRASSY KEY

MM 60–57.

Local lore has it that this sleepy little key was named not for its vegetation—mostly native trees and shrubs—but for an early settler by the name of Grassy. A few families operating small fishing camps and roadside motels primarily inhabit the key. There's no marked definition between it and Marathon, so it feels sort of like a suburb of its much larger neighbor to the south. Grassy Key's sights tend toward the natural, including a worthwhile dolphin attraction and a small state park.

GETTING HERE AND AROUND

Most visitors arriving by air drive to this destination either from Miami International Airport or Key West International Airport. Rental cars are readily available at both, and in the long run, are the most convenient means of transportation for getting here and touring around the Keys.

EXPLORING

Curry Hammock State Park. Looking for a slice of the Keys that's far removed from tiki bars? On the ocean and bay sides of Overseas Highway are 260 acres of upland hammock, wetlands, and mangroves. On the bay side, there's a trail through thick hardwoods to a rocky shoreline. The ocean side is more developed, with a sandy beach, a clean bathhouse, picnic tables, a playground, grills, and a 28-site campground. Locals consider the paddling trails under canopies of arching mangroves one of the best kayaking spots in the Keys. Manatees frequent the area, and it's a great spot for bird-watching. Herons, egrets, ibis, plovers, and sanderlings are commonly spotted. Raptors are often seen in the park, especially during migration periods. ⊠ *MM 57 OS, 56200 Overseas Hwy., Little Crawl Key* ☎ *305/289–2690* ⊕ *www.floridastateparks.org/curryhammock* ☜ *$4.50 for 1 person, $6 for 2, 50¢ per additional person* ☉ *Daily 8–sunset.*

FAMILY **Dolphin Research Center.** The 1963 movie *Flipper* popularized the notion of humans interacting with dolphins, and Milton Santini, the film's creator, also opened this center, which is home to a colony of dolphins and sea lions. The nonprofit center has educational sessions and programs that allow you to greet the dolphins from dry land or play with them in their watery habitat. You can even paint a T-shirt with a dolphin—you pick the paint, the dolphin "designs" your shirt. The center also offers five-day programs for children and adults with disabilities. ⊠ *MM 59 BS, 58901 Overseas Hwy.* ☎ *305/289–1121 information, 305/289–0002 reservations* ⊕ *www.dolphins.org* ☜ *$20* ☉ *Daily 9–4:30.*

WHERE TO EAT

$$$ ✕ **Hideaway Café.** *American.* The name says it all. Tucked between Grassy Key and Marathon, it's easy to miss if you're barnstorming through the middle islands. When you find it (upstairs at Rainbow Bend Resort), you'll discover a favorite of locals who appreciate a well-planned menu, lovely ocean view, and quiet evening away from the crowds—fancy with white tablecloths, but homey with worn carpeting. For starters, dig into escargots à la Edison (sautéed with vegetables, pepper, cognac, and cream). Then feast on several specialties, such as a rarely found chateaubriand for one, a whole roasted duck, or the seafood medley combining the catch of the day with scallops and shrimp in a savory sauce. ⑤ *Average main: $30* ✉ *Rainbow Bend Resort, 57784 Overseas Hwy., MM 58 OS* ☎ *305/289–1554* ⊕ *www.hideawaycafe.com* ⊘ *No lunch.*

WHERE TO STAY

$ ⬚ **Gulf View Waterfront Resort.** *Resort.* With a flock of 15 caged birds, a tortoise, and an iguana on the property, this homey duplex is part resort, part menagerie. **Pros:** park-like setting; sandy beach area with hammocks; close to restaurants. **Cons:** no elevator to office and second-story accommodations; some traffic noise. ⑤ *Rooms from: $123* ✉ *MM 58.7 BS, 58743 Overseas Hwy.* ☎ *305/289–1414, 877/289–0111* ⊕ *www.gulfviewwaterfrontresort.com* ⊅ *2 rooms, 3 efficiencies, 3 1-bedroom apartments, 3 2-bedroom apartments* ⊘ *No meals.*

MARATHON

MM 53–47.5.

New Englanders founded this former fishing village in the early 1800s. The community on Vaca Key subsequently served as a base for pirates, salvagers (also known as "wreckers"), spongers, and, later, Bahamian farmers who eked out a living growing cotton and other crops. More Bahamians arrived in the hope of finding work building the railroad. According to local lore, Marathon was renamed when a worker commented that it was a marathon task to position the tracks across the six-mile-long island.

During the building on the railroad, Marathon developed a reputation for lawlessness that rivaled that of the Old West. It is said that to keep the rowdy workers from descending on Key West for their off-hours endeavors, residents would send boatloads of liquor up to Marathon. Needless to say, things have quieted down considerably since then.

Still, Marathon is a bustling town, at least compared to other communities in the Keys. As it leaves something to be desired in the charm department, Marathon may not be your first choice of places to stay, but water-sports types will find plenty to enjoy, and its historic and natural attractions merit a visit. Surprisingly good dining options abound, so you'll definitely want to stop for a bite even if you're just passing through on the way to Key West.

Throughout the year, Marathon hosts fishing tournaments (practically monthly), a huge seafood festival in March, and lighted boat parades around the holidays.

GETTING HERE AND AROUND

SuperShuttle charges $102 per passenger for trips from Miami International Airport to the Upper Keys. To go farther into the Keys, you must book an entire 11-person van, which costs about $250 to Marathon. For a trip to the airport, place your request 24 hours in advance.

Miami-Dade Transit provides daily bus service from MM 50 in Marathon to the Florida City Wal-Mart Supercenter on the mainland. The bus stops at major shopping centers as well as on-demand anywhere along the route during daily round trips on the hour from 6 am to 10 pm. The cost is $2 one-way, exact change required. The Kew West Transit bus runs from Marathon to Key West ($4 one-way), with scheduled stops along the way. *For details, see Ground Transportation and Bus Travel in Travel Smart.*

VISITOR INFORMATION

Contact **Greater Marathon Chamber of Commerce and Visitor Center** ⊠ *MM 53.5 BS, 12222 Overseas Hwy.* ☎ *305/743–5417, 800/262–7284* ⊕ *www.floridakeysmarathon.com.*

EXPLORING

Grassy Key segues into Marathon with little more than a slight increase in traffic and higher concentration of commercial establishments. Marathon's roots are anchored in fishing and boating, so look for marinas to find local color, fishing charters, and good restaurants. At its north end, Key Colony Beach is an old-fashioned island neighborhood worth a visit for its shops and restaurants. Nature lovers shouldn't miss the attractions on Crane Point. Other good places to leave the main road are at Sombrero Beach Road (MM 50), which leads to the beach, and 35th Street (MM 49), which takes you to a funky little marina and restaurant. U.S. 1 hightails through Hog Key and Knight Key before the big leap over Florida Bay and Hawk's Channel via the Seven Mile Bridge.

FAMILY **Crane Point Museum, Nature Center, and Historic Site.** Tucked away from the highway behind a stand of trees, Crane Point—part of a 63-acre tract that contains the last-known undisturbed thatch-palm hammock—is delightfully undeveloped. This multiuse facility includes the **Museum of**

Marathon

KEY

- ● Restaurants
- ① Hotels
- ◿ Dive Site
- ◿ Boat Launch

Conch Key
Conch Cotta

TO ISLAMORADA

Duck Key
Hawk Reso Alma

Dolphin Research Center

Grassy Key

Gulf View Waterfront Resor
Bonefish Resort
Hideaway Café

Bamboo Key

Crawl Key

Curry Hammock State Park

Thunderbolt

Greater Marathon Chamber of Commerce

125 St. Key Colony Bch.
Coco Plum Dr.
117 St.
107 St.
110 St.
100 St.

● ①
Golf Course
Key Colony Beach
②

Marathon

Dolphin Dr.
Marathon Airport

83 St.
72 St.
64 St.

Crane Point Museum, Nature Center, and Historic Site
The Turtle Hospital

❸
62 St.
49 St.
❹
47 St.

Vaca Key

Gull Terr. Ave
②
126 St.

Sombrero Beach

❺
111 St.

The American

❻
Boot Key Bridge

Boot Key

Old Seven Mile Bridge
Pigeon Key
Seven Mile Bridge

Sombrero Reef

↙ TO LOWER KEYS

Restaurants	Lazy Days South, **5**	**Hotels**
Fish Tales Market and Eatery, **1**	The Stuffed Pig, **4**	Glunz Ocean Beach Hotel & Resort, **1**
Key Colony Inn, **2**	Sunset Grille & Raw Bar, **6**	Tranquility Bay, **2**
Keys Fisheries Market & Marina, **3**		

Natural History of the Florida Keys, which has displays about local wildlife, a seashell exhibit, and a marine-life display that makes you feel you're at the bottom of the sea. Kids love the replica 17th-century galleon and pirate dress-up room where they can play, and the re-created **Cracker House** filled with insects, sea-turtle exhibits, and children's activities. On the 1-mile indigenous loop trail, visit the **Laura Quinn Wild Bird Center** and the remnants of a Bahamian village, site of the restored **George Adderly House.** It is the oldest surviving example of Bahamian tabby (a concrete-like material created from sand and sea-shells) construction outside Key West. A boardwalk crosses wetlands, rivers, and mangroves before ending at Adderly Village. From November to Easter, docent-led tours are available; bring good walking shoes and bug repellent during warm weather. ⊠ *MM 50.5 BS, 5550 Overseas Hwy.* ☎ *305/743–9100* ⊕ *www.cranepoint.net* ⊠ *$12.50* ⊗ *Mon.–Sat. 9–5, Sun. noon–5; call to arrange trail tours.*

Pigeon Key. There's much to like about this 5-acre island under the Old Seven Mile Bridge. You might even recognize it from one season finale of the TV show *The Amazing Race.* You can reach it via a ferry that departs from behind the visitor center (look for the old red railroad car on Knight's Key, MM 47 OS). Once there, tour the island on your own or join a guided tour to explore the buildings that formed the early-20th-century work camp for the Overseas Railroad that linked the mainland to Key West in 1912. Later the island became a fish camp, a state park, and then government-administration headquarters. Exhibits in a small museum recall the history of the Keys, the railroad, and railroad baron Henry M. Flagler. The ferry ride with tour lasts two hours; visitors can self-tour and catch the ferry back in a half hour. ⊠ *MM 45 OS, 1 Knights Key Blvd., Pigeon Key* ☎ *305/743–5999* ⊕ *pigeonkey.net* ⊠ *$12* ⊗ *Daily 9:30–2:30; ferry departures at 10, 12 and 2 pm.*

Seven Mile Bridge. This is one of the most photographed images in the Keys. Actually measuring slightly less than 7 miles, it connects the Middle and Lower Keys and is believed to be the world's longest segmental bridge. It has 39 expansion joints separating its various concrete sections. Each April runners gather in Marathon for the annual Seven Mile Bridge Run. The expanse running parallel to Seven Mile Bridge is what remains of the **Old Seven Mile Bridge,** an engineering and architectural marvel in its day that's now on the National Register of Historic Places. Once proclaimed the Eighth Wonder of the World, it rested on a record 546 concrete piers. No cars are allowed on the old bridge today.

FAMILY **Sombrero Beach.** No doubt one of the best beaches in the Keys, here you'll find pleasant, shaded picnic areas that overlook a coconut palm–lined grassy stretch and the Atlantic Ocean. Roped-off areas allow swimmers, boaters, and windsurfers to share the narrow cove. Facilities include barbecue grills, a large playground, a pier, a volleyball court, and a paved, lighted bike path off Overseas Highway. Sunday afternoons draw lots of local families toting coolers. The park is accessible for those with disabilities and allows leashed pets. Turn east at the traffic light in Marathon and follow signs to the end. **Amenities:** showers; toilets. **Best for:** families; swimming; windsurfing. ⊠ *MM 50 OS, Sombrero Beach Rd.* ☎ *305/743–0033* ⊠ *Free* ⊙ *Daily 8–sunset.*

FAMILY **The Turtle Hospital.** More than 100 injured sea turtles check in here every year. The 90-minute guided tours take you into recovery and surgical areas at the world's only state-certified veterinary hospital for sea turtles. In the "hospital bed" tanks, you can see recovering patients and others that are permanent residents due to their injuries. After the tour, you can feed some of the "residents." Call ahead—space is limited and tours are sometimes cancelled due to medical emergencies. The turtle ambulance out front makes for a memorable souvenir photo. ⊠ *MM 48.5 BS, 2396 Overseas Hwy.* ☎ *305/743–2552* ⊕ *www.turtlehospital.org* ⊠ *$18* ⊙ *Daily 9–5.*

WHERE TO EAT

$ ✕ **Fish Tales Market and Eatery.** *Seafood.* This roadside eatery with its own seafood market serves signature dishes such as snapper on grilled rye with coleslaw and melted Muenster cheese and a fried fish burrito. You also can slurp luscious lobster bisque or tomato-based conch chowder. There are burgers, chicken, and dogs for those who don't do seafood. Plan to dine early; it's only open until 6:30 pm (4 pm on Saturdays). This is a no-frills kind of place with a loyal local following, unfussy ambience, a couple of outside picnic tables, and friendly service. ⑤ *Average main: $9* ⊠ *MM 52.5 OS, 11711 Overseas Hwy.* ☎ *305/743–9196, 888/662–4822* ⊕ *www.floridalobster.com* ⚑ *Reservations not accepted* ⊙ *Closed Sun. No dinner Sat.*

TURTLE TIME

Five species of threatened and endangered sea turtles frequent the waters of the Florida Keys. The **loggerhead**, the most common, is named for the shape of its noggin. It grows to a heft of 300 pounds. It is the only one of the local turtles listed as threatened rather than endangered.

The vegetarian **green turtle** was once hunted for its meat, which has brought populations to their endangered stage. It can reach an impressive 500 pounds.

Named for the shape of its mouth, the **hawksbill turtle** is a relative lightweight at 150 pounds. It prefers rocks and reefs for habitat. The Keys are the only U.S. breeding site for the endangered critter.

The largest reptile alive, the **leatherback turtle** can weigh in at up to 2,000 pounds, attained from a diet of mainly jellyfish.

The rarest of local sea turtles, the **Kemps Ridley** is named after a Key West fisherman. A carnivore, it grows to 100 pounds.

The biggest threats to sea turtle survival include fibropapilloma tumors, monofilament fishing lines (which can sever their flippers), entanglement in ropes and nets, boat propeller run-ins, swallowing plastic bags (which appear to them as jellyfish), oil spills, and other human and natural impact.

$$ ✕ **Key Colony Inn.** *Italian.* The inviting aroma of an Italian kitchen pervades this family-owned favorite with a supperclub atmosphere. As you'd expect, the service is friendly and attentive. For lunch there are fish and steak entrées served with fries, salad, and bread in addition to Italian specialties. At dinner you can't miss with traditional dishes like veal Oscar and New York strip, or such specialties as seafood *Italiano*, a dish of scallops and shrimp sautéed in garlic butter and served with marinara sauce over a bed of linguine. The place is renowned for its Sunday brunch, served from November to April. ⑤ *Average main: $19* ⊠ *MM 54 OS, 700 W. Ocean Dr., Key Colony Beach* ☎ *305/743–0100* ⊕ *www.kcinn.com.*

$$ ✕ **Keys Fisheries Market & Marina.** *Seafood.* From the parking
FAMILY lot, you can't miss the enormous tiki bar on stilts, but the walk-up window on the ground floor is the heart of this warehouse-turned-restaurant. Order at the window, pick up your food, then dine at one of the waterfront tables outfitted with rolls of paper towels. The menu is comprised of fresh

seafood and a token hamburger and chicken sandwich. A huge lobster Reuben ($14.95) served on thick slices of toasted bread is the signature dish. Other delights include the shrimp burger, very rich whiskey-peppercorn snapper, and the Keys Kombo (grilled lobster, shrimp, scallops, and mahimahi for $29). The adults-only upstairs tiki bar offers a sushi and raw bar for eat-in only. Bring quarters for fish food—you can feed the tarpon while you wait for your food. ⑤ *Average main: $16* ⊠ *MM 49 BS, 3390 Gulfview Ave., at the end of 35th St.* ⊹ *Turn right on 35th St. off Gulfview Ave.* ☎ *305/743–4353, 866/743–4353* ⊕ *www. keysfisheries.com* ⊲ *Reservations not accepted.*

★ **Fodor$Choice** × **Lazy Days South.** *Seafood.* Tucked into Mara-
$$$ thon Marina a half mile north of the Seven Mile Bridge, this restaurant offers views just as spectacular as its highly lauded food. A spin-off of an Islamorada favorite, here you'll find a wide range of daily offerings from fried or sautéed conch and a coconut-fried fish du jour sandwich to seafood pastas and beef tips over rice. Choose a table on the outdoor deck or inside underneath paddle fans and surrounded by local art. ⑤ *Average main: $22* ⊠ *MM 47.3 OS, 725 11th St.* ☎ *305/289–0839* ⊕ *www.keysdining.com/ lazydays.*

$ × **The Stuffed Pig.** *Diner.* With only nine tables and a coun-
ter inside, this breakfast-and-lunch place is always hopping. When the weather's right, grab a table out back. The kitchen whips up daily lunch specials like burgers, seafood platters, or pulled pork with hand-cut fries, but a quick glance around the room reveals that the all-day breakfast is the main draw. You can get the usual breakfast plates, but most newcomers opt for oddities like the lobster omelet, alligator tail and eggs, or "grits and grunts" (that's fish, to the rest of us). ⑤ *Average main: $9* ⊠ *MM 49 BS, 3520 Overseas Hwy.* ☎ *305/743–4059* ⊕ *www.thestuffedpig.com* ⊲ *Reservations not accepted* ▬ *No credit cards* ☉ *No dinner.*

$$$ × **Sunset Grille & Raw Bar.** *Seafood.* After a walk or bike ride along the Old Seven Mile Bridge, treat yourself to a seafood lunch or dinner at this vaulted tiki hut by the bridge. For lunch, start with the conch chowder or frit-ters, and then move on to the Voodoo grouper sandwich topped with mango-guava mayo, and finish with a tasty key lime pie. Wear your swimsuit if you want to take a dip in the pool for a post-lunch swim. Dinner specialties add a creative twist, like the Brie-stuffed filet mignon, coconut curry lobster, and Thai peanut shrimp. This is a popular place to catch the sunset, hence the name. Pool

parties/barbecues are the weekend norm. ⑤ *Average main: $22* ✉ *MM 47 OS, 7 Knights Key Blvd.* ☎ *305/396–7235* ⊕ *www.sunsetgrille7milebridge.com.*

WHERE TO STAY

$$ 🏨 **Glunz Ocean Beach Hotel & Resort.** *Rental.* The Glunz family got it right when they purchased this former timeshare property and put a whole lot of love into renovating it to its full oceanfront potential. **Pros:** oceanfront; convenient amenities; excellent free Wi-Fi. **Cons:** neighbor noise; small elevator; no interior corridors; not cheap. ⑤ *Rooms from: $260* ✉ *MM 53.5 OS, 351 East Ocean Dr, Key Colony Beach* ☎ *305/289–0525* ⊕ *www.GlunzOceanBeachHotel. com* ⌇ *22 rooms, 16 suites* �🍽 *No meals.*

★ **Fodor's**Choice 🏨 **Tranquility Bay.** *Resort.* Ralph Lauren could
$$$ have designed the rooms at this stylish, luxurious resort on
FAMILY a nice beach. **Pros:** secluded setting; gorgeous design; lovely crescent beach. **Cons:** a bit sterile; no real Keys atmosphere; cramped building layout. ⑤ *Rooms from: $399* ✉ *MM 48.5 BS, 2600 Overseas Hwy.* ☎ *305/289–0888, 866/643–5397* ⊕ *www.tranquilitybay.com* ⌇ *16 guestrooms, 45 2-bedroom suites, 41 3-bedroom suites* �🍽 *No meals.*

SPORTS AND THE OUTDOORS

BIKING

Tooling around on two wheels is a good way to see Marathon. There's easy cycling on a one-mile off-road path that connects to the two miles of the Old Seven Mile Bridge leading to Pigeon Key.

Bike Marathon Bike Rentals. "Have bikes, will deliver" could be the motto of this company, which gets beach cruisers to your hotel door, including a helmet and basket. They also rent kayaks. Note that there's no physical location, but services are available Monday through Saturday 9–4 and Sunday 9–2. ☎ *305/743–3204* ⊕ *www. bikemarathonbikerentals.com* ⌸ *$35 per week.*

Overseas Outfitters. Aluminum cruisers and hybrid bikes are available for rent at this outfitter. It's open weekdays 9–5:30 and Saturday 9–3. All rentals include a helmet and lock. ✉ *MM 48 BS, 1700 Overseas Hwy.* ☎ *305/289–1670* ⊕ *www.overseasoutfitters.com* ⌸ *Rentals from $15 per day.*

BOATING

Sail, motor, or paddle: Whatever your choice of modes, boating is what the Keys is all about. Brave the Atlantic waves and reefs or explore the backcountry islands on the gulf side. If you don't have a lot of boating and chart-reading experience, it's a good idea to tap into local knowledge on a charter.

Captain Pip's. This operator rents 20- to 24-foot outboards as well as tackle and snorkeling gear. Fishing charters are also available with a captain and a mate (full-day charters are also available). Ask about multiday deals, or try one of their accommodation packages and walk right from your bay-front room to your boat. ✉ *MM 47.5 BS, 1410 Overseas Hwy.* ☎ *305/743–4403, 800/707–1692* ⊕ *www.captainpips.com* ⊠ *Rentals from $195 per day; half-day charters from $650.*

Fish 'n Fun. Get out on the water on 19- to 26-foot powerboats. Rentals can be for a half or full day. The company also offers free delivery in the Middle Keys. ✉ *MM 49.5 OS, 4590 Overseas Hwy., at Banana Bay Resort & Marina* ☎ *305/743–2275, 800/471–3440* ⊕ *www.fishnfunrentals.com* ⊠ *From $175.*

FISHING

For recreational anglers, the deepwater fishing is superb in both bay and ocean. Marathon West Hump, one good spot, has depths ranging from 500 to more than 1,000 feet. Locals fish from a half-dozen bridges, including Long Key Bridge, the Old Seven Mile Bridge, and both ends of Tom's Harbor. Barracuda, bonefish, and tarpon all frequent local waters. Party boats and private charters are available.

Marathon Lady. Morning, afternoon, and night, fish for mahimahi, grouper, and other tasty catch aboard this 73-footer, which departs on half-day excursions from the Vaca Cut Bridge (MM53), north of Marathon. Join the crew for night fishing ($55) from 6:30 to midnight from Memorial Day to Labor Day; it's especially beautiful on a full-moon night. ✉ *MM 53 OS, at 117th St., 11711 Overseas Hwy.* ☎ *305/743–5580* ⊕ *www.marathonlady.net* ⊠ *From $50.*

Sea Dog Charters. Captain Jim Purcell, a deep-sea specialist for ESPN's *The American Outdoorsman,* provides one of the best values in Keys fishing. Next to the Seven Mile Grill, his company offers half- and full-day offshore, reef and wreck, and backcountry fishing trips, as well as fishing and snorkeling trips aboard 30- to 37-foot boats. The per-person for a half-day trip is the same regardless of whether your group fills the boat, and includes bait, light tackle, ice, coolers, and fishing licenses. If you prefer an all-day private charter on a 37-foot boat, he offers those, too, for up to six people. A fuel surcharge may apply. ⊠ *MM 47.5 BS, 1248 Overseas Hwy.* ☎ *305/743–8255* ⊕ *www.seadogcharters. net* ⊠ *From $60.*

GOLF

Key Colony Beach Golf & Tennis. Designed by Wayne Spano and opened in 1973, this 9-holer near Marathon has no reserved tee times, and there's never a rush to hurry up and play through. In fact, you can finish in about 45 minutes even with slow greens, as it's an easy, flat course to walk. Just show up anytime from 7:30 am to dusk. Regulars say you only need three clubs to play the entire course, making it perfect for beginners or those that can't hit far. A little pro shop meets basic golf needs. Club rentals are only $3 per person, but the choices are a bit worn; pull carts are $2. You'll also have free use of the club's tennis courts. ⊠ *MM 53.5 OS, 460 8th St., Key Colony Beach* ⊕ *www. keycolonybeach.net/recreation.html* ⊠ *9 holes for $13; $8 for each additional 9 holes* ⅃ *9 holes. 972 yards. Par 3.*

SCUBA DIVING AND SNORKELING

Local dive operations take you to Sombrero Reef and Lighthouse, the most popular down-under destination in these parts. For a shallow dive and some lobster nabbing, Coffins Patch, off Key Colony Beach, is a good choice. A number of wrecks such as *Thunderbolt* serve as artificial reefs. Many operations out of this area will also take you to Looe Key Reef.

Hall's Diving Center & Career Institute. The institute has been training divers for more than 40 years. Along with con-ventional twice-a-day snorkel and two-tank dive trips to the reefs at Sombrero Lighthouse and wrecks like the *Thunderbolt,* the company has more unusual offerings like rebreather, photography, and Nitrox courses. ⊠ *MM 48.5 BS, 1994 Overseas Hwy.* ☎ *305/743–5929, 800/331–4255* ⊕ *www.hallsdiving.com* ⊠ *From $40.*

Spirit Snorkeling. Join regularly scheduled snorkeling excur-sions to Sombrero Reef and Lighthouse Reef on this compa-ny's comfortable catamaran. They also offer sunset cruises, private charters, and New Age yoga cruises. ⊠ *MM 47.5 BS,*

1410 Overseas Hwy., Slip No. 1 ☎ *305/289–0614* ⊕ *www. spiritsnorkeling.net* ✉ *From $30.*

Tildens Scuba Center. Since the mid-1980s, Tildens Scuba Center has been providing lessons, tours, gear rental, and daily snorkel, scuba, and snuba adventures. Look for the huge, colorful angelfish sculpture outside the building. ✉ *MM 49.5 BS, 4650 Overseas Hwy.* ☎ *305/743–7255, 888/728–2235* ✉ *From $40 for snorkel trips from $65 for dive trips.*

WATER SPORTS

Jerry's Charter Service & Watersport Rentals. For all your watersports-rental needs, head to this one-stop shop. It rents kayaks, Jet Skis, deckboats, snorkel equipment, fishing rods, and power- and pontoon boats. Two-hour guided Jet Ski tours (two Jet Ski minimum) are offered. ✉ *Banana Bay Resort & Marina, MM 49.5 BS, 4590 Overseas Hwy.* ☎ *305/743–7298, 800/775–2646* ⊕ *www.jerryscharters.com* ✉ *Jet Ski tours from $190.*

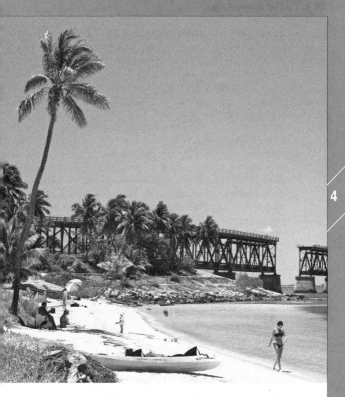

4

THE LOWER KEYS

Updated by Jill Martin

BEGINNING AT BAHIA HONDA KEY, the islands of the Florida Keys become smaller, more clustered, and more numerous, a result of ancient tidal water flowing between the Florida Straits and the gulf. Here you're likely to see more birds and mangroves than other tourists, and more refuges, beaches, and campgrounds than museums, restaurants, and hotels. The islands are made up of two types of limestone, both denser than the highly permeable Key Largo limestone of the Upper Keys. As a result, freshwater forms in pools rather than percolating through the rock, creating watering holes that support alligators, snakes, deer, rabbits, raccoons, and migratory ducks. (Many of these animals can be seen in the National Key Deer Refuge on Big Pine Key.) Nature was generous with her beauty in the Lower Keys, which have both Looe Key Reef, arguably the Keys' most beautiful tract of coral, and Bahia Honda State Park, considered one of the best beaches in the world for its fine sand dunes, clear warm waters, and panoramic vista of bridges, hammocks, and azure sky and sea. Big Pine Key is fishing headquarters for a laid-back community that swells with retirees in the winter. South of it, the dribble of islands can flash by in a blink of an eye if you don't take the time to stop at a roadside eatery or check out tours and charters at the little marinas. They include Little Torch Key, Middle Torch Key, Ramrod Key, Summerland Key, Cudjoe Key, Sugarloaf Keys, and Saddlebunch Key. Lying offshore of Little Torch Key, Little Palm Island once welcomed U.S. presidents and other notables to its secluded fishing camp. It was also the location for the movie *PT 109* about John F. Kennedy's celebrated World War II heroism. Today it still offers respite to the upper class in the form of an exclusive getaway resort accessible only by boat or seaplane.

ORIENTATION AND PLANNING

GETTING ORIENTED

In truth, the Lower Keys include Key West, but since it's *covered in its own section* and is as different from the rest of the Lower Keys as peanut butter is from jelly, this section covers just the keys between MM 37 and MM 9. The Seven Mile Bridge drops you into the lap of this homey, quiet part of the Keys.

Heed speed limits in these parts. They may seem incredibly strict, given that the traffic is lightest of anywhere in the

TOP REASONS TO GO

■ **Wildlife viewing.** The Lower Keys are populated with all kinds of animals. Watch especially for the Key deer but also other wildlife at the Blue Hole in National Key Deer Refuge.

■ **Bahia Honda Key State Park.** Explore the beach and trails, and then camp for the night at this gorgeous state park.

■ **Kayaking.** Get out in a kayak to spot birds in the Keys' backcountry wildlife refuges.

■ **Snorkeling.** Grab a mask and fins and head to Looe Key Reef to see amazing coral formations and fish so bright and animated they look like cartoons.

■ **Fishing.** All kinds of fishing are great in the Lower Keys. Cast from a bridge, boat, or shoreline flats for bonefish, tarpon, and other feisty catches.

Keys, but the purpose is to protect the resident Key deer population, and officers of the law pay strict attention.

PLANNING

GETTING HERE AND AROUND

To get to the Lower Keys, fly into either Miami International Airport or Key West International Airport. Key West is considerably closer, but there are far fewer flights coming in and going out. Rental cars are available at both airports. In addition, there is bus service from the Key West airport; $4 one-way with Key West Transit. *For detailed information on these services, see Air Travel in Travel Smart.*

HOTELS

Fishing lodges, dive resorts, and campgrounds are the most prevalent type of lodging in this part of the Keys. Rates are generally much lower than on other Keys, especially Key West, which makes this a good place to stay if you're on a budget.

Hotel reviews have been shortened. For full information, visit Fodors.com.

RESTAURANTS

Restaurants are fewer and farther between in the Lower Keys, and you won't find the variety of offerings in eateries closer to Miami and in Key West. Mostly you'll find seafood joints where dinner is fresh off the hook and license plates or dollar bills stuck to the wall count for decor. For a special occasion, hop aboard the ferry at Little Torch Key to experience the globetrotting cuisine of private Little Palm Island Resort & Spa. Restaurants may close for a two- to four-week vacation during the slow season—between mid-September and mid-November.

WHAT IT COSTS				
	$	$$	$$$	$$$$
Restaurants	Under $15	$16–$20	$21–$30	Over $30
Hotels	Under $200	$201–$300	$301–$400	Over $400

Prices in the restaurant reviews are the average cost of a main course at dinner or, if dinner isn't served, at lunch. Prices in the hotel reviews are the lowest cost of a standard double room in high season. Prices don't include taxes (6%, more in some counties, and 1%–5% tourist tax for hotel rooms).

BAHIA HONDA KEY

MM 38–36.

All of Bahia Honda Key is devoted to its eponymous state park, which keeps it in a pristine state. Besides the park's outdoor activities, it offers an up-close look of the original railroad bridge.

GETTING HERE AND AROUND
Bahia Honda Key lies a short distance from the southern terminus of the Seven Mile Bridge. A two-lane road travels its 2-mile length. It is 32 miles north of Key West and served by Key West Transit. *See Bus Travel in Travel Smart.*

EXPLORING

FAMILY **Fodor's Choice Bahia Honda State Park.** Most first-time visitors
★ to the region are dismayed by the lack of beaches—but then they discover Bahia Honda Key. The 524-acre park sprawls across both sides of the highway, giving it 2½ miles of fabulous sandy coastline. The snorkeling isn't bad, either; there's underwater life (soft coral, queen conchs, random little fish) just a few hundred feet offshore. Although swimming, kayaking, fishing, and boating are the main reasons to visit, you shouldn't miss biking along the 2½ miles of flat roads or hiking the Silver Palm Trail, with rare West

Indian plants and several species found nowhere else in the nation. Along the way you'll be treated to a variety of butterflies. Seasonal ranger-led nature programs take place at or depart from the Sand and Sea Nature Center. There are rental cabins, a campground, snack bar, gift shop, 19-slip marina, nature center, and facilities for renting kayaks and arranging snorkeling tours. Get a panoramic view of the island from what's left of the railroad—the Bahia Honda Bridge. ⊠ *MM 37 OS, 36850 Overseas Hwy.* ☎ *305/872–2353* ⊕ *www.floridastateparks.org/bahiahonda* 🖃 *$4.50 for single occupant vehicle, $9 for vehicle with 2–8 people.* ⊘ *Daily 8–sunset.*

WHERE TO STAY

$ 🏠 **Bahia Honda State Park Cabins.** *Rental.* Elsewhere you'd pay big bucks for the wonderful water views available at these cabins on Florida Bay. **Pros:** great bay-front views; beach-front camping; affordable rates. **Cons:** books up fast; area can be buggy. Ⓢ *Rooms from: $183* ⊠ *MM 37 OS, 36850 Overseas Hwy.* ☎ *305/872–2353, 800/326–3521* ⊕ *www. reserveamerica.com* 🛏 *6 cabins* ⊚ *No meals.*

SPORTS AND THE OUTDOORS

BEACHES

Sandspur Beach. Bahia Honda Key State Beach contains three beaches in all—on both the Atlantic Ocean and the Gulf of Mexico. Sandspur Beach, the largest, is regularly declared the best beach in the Florida Keys, and you'll be hard-pressed to argue. The sand is baby-powder soft, and the aqua water is warm, clear, and shallow. With their mild currents, the beaches are great for swimming, even with small fry. **Amenities:** food and drink, showers, toilets, water sports. **Best for:** snorkeling, swimming. ⊠ *MM 37 OS, 36850 Overseas Hwy.* ☎ *305/872–2353* ⊕ *www.floridastateparks. org/bahiahonda* ☎ *$4.50 for single occupant vehicle, $9 for vehicle with 2–8 people* ☉ *Daily 8–sunset.*

SCUBA DIVING AND SNORKELING

Bahia Honda Dive Shop. The concessionaire at Bahia Honda State Park manages a 19-slip marina; rents wet suits, snorkel equipment, and corrective masks; and operates twice-a-day offshore-reef snorkel trips. Park visitors looking for other fun can rent kayaks and beach chairs. ⊠ *MM 37 OS, 36850 Overseas Hwy.* ☎ *305/872–3210* ⊕ *www. bahiahondapark.com* ☉ *Kayak rentals from $10 per hr.; snorkel tours from $30.*

BIG PINE KEY

MM 32–30.

Welcome to the Keys' most natural holdout, where wildlife refuges protect rare and endangered animals. Here you have left behind the commercialism of the Upper Keys for an authentic backcountry atmosphere. How could things get more casual than Key Largo, you might wonder? Find out by exiting U.S. 1 to explore the habitat of the charmingly diminutive Key deer or cast a line from No Name Bridge. Tours explore the expansive waters of National Key Deer Refuge and Great White Heron National Wildlife Refuge, one of the first such refuges in the country. Along with Key West National Wildlife Refuge, it encompasses more than 200,000 acres of water and more than 8,000 acres of land on 49 small islands. Besides its namesake bird, the Great White Heron National Wildlife Refuge provides habitat for uncounted species of birds and three species of sea turtles. It is the only U.S. breeding site for the endangered hawksbill turtle.

GETTING HERE AND AROUND

Most people rent a car to get to Big Pine Key so they can also explore Key West and other parts of the chain.

VISITOR INFORMATION

Contact **Big Pine and the Lower Keys Chamber of Commerce** ☎ 305/872-2411, 800/872-3722 ⊕ www.lowerkeyschamber.com.

EXPLORING

National Key Deer Refuge. This 84,824-acre refuge was established in 1957 to protect the dwindling population of the Key deer, one of more than 22 animals and plants federally classified as endangered or threatened, including five that are found nowhere else on Earth. The Key deer, which stands about 30 inches at the shoulders and is a subspecies of the Virginia white-tailed deer, once roamed throughout the Lower and Middle Keys, but hunting, destruction of their habitat, and a growing human population caused their numbers to decline to 27 by 1957. The deer have made a comeback, increasing their numbers to approximately 750. The best place to see Key deer in the refuge is at the end of Key Deer Boulevard and on No Name Key, a sparsely populated island just east of Big Pine Key. Mornings and evenings are the best time to spot them. Deer may turn up along the road at any time of day, so drive slowly. They wander into nearby yards to nibble tender grass and bougainvillea blossom, but locals do not appreciate tourists driving into their neighborhoods after them. Feeding them is against the law and puts them in danger.

A quarry left over from railroad days, the **Blue Hole** is the largest body of freshwater in the Keys. From the observation platform and nearby walking trail, you might see the resident alligator, turtles, and other wildlife. There are two well-marked trails, recently revamped: the Jack Watson Nature Trail (0.6 mile), named after an environmentalist and the refuge's first warden; and the Fred Mannillo Nature Trail, one of the most wheelchair-accessible places to see an unspoiled pine-rockland forest and wetlands. The visitor center has exhibits on Keys biology and ecology. The refuge also provides information on the Key West National Wildlife Refuge and the Great White Heron National Wildlife Refuge. Accessible only by water, both are popular with kayak outfitters. ⊠ MM 30.5 BS, Visitor Center–Headquarters, Big Pine Shopping Center, 28950 Watson Blvd.

☎ *305/872–2239* ⊕ *www.fws.gov/nationalkeydeer* ✉ *Free*
⊙ *Daily sunrise–sunset; headquarters weekdays 8–5.*

WHERE TO EAT

$ ✕ **Good Food Conspiracy.** *Vegetarian.* Like good wine, this small natural-foods eatery and market, surrenders its pleasures a little at a time. Step inside to the aroma of brewing coffee, and then pick up the scent of fresh strawberries or carrots blending into a smoothie, the green aroma of wheatgrass juice, followed by the earthy odor of hummus. Order raw or cooked vegetarian and vegan dishes, organic soups and salads, and organic coffees and teas. Bountiful sandwiches include the popular tuna melt or hummus and avocado. Sit at the counter or in the back garden and mingle with the locals as folks have been doing since the early 1980s. Then stock up on healthful snacks like dried fruits, raw nuts, and carob-covered almonds and gluten-free items, too. ⑤ *Average main: $10* ⌂ *MM 30.2 OS, 30150 Overseas Hwy.* ☎ *305/872–3945* ⊕ *www.goodfoodconspiracy.com* ⌦ *Reservations not accepted* ⊙ *No dinner Sun.*

$ ✕ **No Name Pub.** *American.* This no-frills honky-tonk has been around since 1936, delighting inveterate locals and intrepid vacationers who come for the excellent pizza, cold beer, and *interesting* companionship. The decor, such as it is, amounts to the autographed dollar bills that cover every inch of the place. The full menu printed on place mats includes tasty conch chowder, a half-pound fried-grouper sandwich, spaghetti and meatballs, and seafood baskets. The lighting is poor, the furnishings are rough, and the music is oldies. This former brothel and bait shop is just before the No Name Key Bridge in the midst of a residential neighborhood. It's a bit hard to find, but worth the trouble if you want a singular Keys' experience. ⑤ *Average main: $15* ⌂ *MM 30 BS, 30813 Watson Blvd.* ⊹ *From U.S. 1, turn west on Wilder Rd., left on South St., right on Ave. B, right on Watson Blvd.* ☎ *305/872–9115* ⊕ *www.nonamepub.com* ⌦ *Reservations not accepted.*

WHERE TO STAY

$ ☷ **Big Pine Key Fishing Lodge.** *Hotel.* There's a congenial atmosphere at this lively family-owned lodge-campground-marina—a happy mix of tent campers (who have the fabulous waterfront real estate), RVers (who look pretty permanent), and motel dwellers who like to mingle at the rooftop pool and challenge each other to a game of poker.

Pros: local fishing crowd; nice pool; great price. **Cons:** RV park is too close to motel; deer will eat your food if you're camping. ⑤ *Rooms from: $114* ⊠ *MM 33 OS, 33000 Overseas Hwy.* ☎ *305/872–2351* ⊕ *www.big-pine-key.com/ fishinglodge.php* ⌿ *16 efficiencies* ⍟ *No meals.*

$$ ⚏ **Deer Run Bed & Breakfast.** *B&B/Inn.* Innkeepers Jen DeMaria and Harry Appel were way ahead of the green-lodging game when they opened in 2004, and guests love how Key deer wander the grounds of this beachfront B&B on a residential street lined with mangroves. **Pros:** quiet location; vegan, organic breakfasts; complimentary bikes, kayaks, and state park passes. **Cons:** price is a bit high; hard to find. ⑤ *Rooms from: $255* ⊠ *MM 33 OS, 1997 Long Beach Dr.* ☎ *305/872–2015* ⊕ *www.deerrunfloridabb.com* ⌿ *4 rooms* ⍟ *Breakfast.*

SPORTS AND THE OUTDOORS

BIKING

A good 10 miles of paved roads run from MM 30.3 BS, along Wilder Road, across the bridge to No Name Key, and along Key Deer Boulevard into the National Key Deer Refuge. Along the way you might see some Key deer. Stay off the trails that lead into wetlands, where fat tires can damage the environment.

Big Pine Bicycle Center. Owner Marty Baird is an avid cyclist and enjoys sharing his knowledge of great places to ride. He's also skilled at selecting the right bike for the journey, and he knows his repairs, too. His old-fashioned single-speed, fat-tire cruisers rent by the half or full day. Helmets, baskets, and locks are included. ⊠ *MM 30.9 BS, 31 County Rd.* ☎ *305/872–0130* ⊕ *www.bigpinebikes.com* ⌸ *From $8.*

FISHING

Cast from No Name Key Bridge or hire a charter to take you into backcountry or deep waters for fishing year-round.

Strike Zone Charters. Glass-bottom-boat excursions venture into the backcountry and Atlantic Ocean. The five-hour Island Excursion emphasizes nature and Keys history; besides close encounters with birds, sea life, and vegetation, there's a fish cookout on an island. Snorkel and fishing equipment, food, and drinks are included. This is one of the few nature outings in the Keys with wheelchair access. Deep-sea charter rates for up to six people can be arranged for a half or full day. It also offers flats fishing in the Gulf of Mexico. Dive excursions head to the wreck of the 110-foot *Adolphus Busch*, and scuba and snorkel trips to Looe Key Reef, prime scuba and snorkeling territory, aboard glass-bottom boats. ✉ *MM 29.6 BS, 29675 Overseas Hwy.* ☎ *305/872-9863, 800/654-9560* ⊕ *www. strikezonecharter.com* ⌨ *From $38.*

KAYAKING

There's nothing like the vast expanse of pristine waters and mangrove islands preserved by national refuges from here to Key West. The mazelike terrain can be confusing, so it's wise to hire a guide at least the first time out.

Big Pine Kayak Adventures. There's no excuse to skip a water adventure with this convenient kayak rental service, which delivers them to your lodging or anywhere between Seven Mile Bridge and Stock Island. The company, headed by *The Florida Keys Paddling Guide* author Bill Keogh, will rent you a kayak and then ferry you—called taxi-yakking—to remote islands with clear instructions on how to paddle back on your own. Rentals are by the half day or full day. Three-hour group kayak tours are the cheapest option and explore the mangrove forests of Great White Heron and Key Deer National Wildlife Refuges. More expensive four-hour custom tours transport you to exquisite backcountry areas teeming with wildlife. Kayak fishing charters are also popular. ✉ *Old Wooden Bridge Fishing Camp* ✛ *From MM 30, turn right at traffic light, continue on Wilder Rd. toward No Name Key; the fishing camp is just before the bridge with a big yellow kayak on the sign out front* ☎ *305/872-7474* ⊕ *www.keyskayaktours.com* ⌨ *From $50.*

SCUBA DIVING AND SNORKELING

Close to Looe Key Reef, this is prime scuba diving and snorkeling territory. Some resorts cater to divers with dive boats that depart from their own dock. Others can make arrangements for you.

LITTLE TORCH KEY

MM 29–10.

Little Torch Key and its neighbor islands, Ramrod Key and Summerland Key, are good jumping-off points for divers headed for Looe Key Reef. The islands also serve as a refuge for those who want to make forays into Key West but not stay in the thick of things.

The undeveloped backcountry at your door makes Little Torch Key an ideal location for fishing and kayaking. Nearby **Ramrod Key**, which also caters to divers bound for Looe Key, derives its name from a ship that wrecked on nearby reefs in the early 1800s.

Baby's Coffee. The aroma of rich, roasting coffee beans arrests you at the door of "the Southernmost Coffee Roaster." Buy it by the pound or by the cup along with sandwiches and sweets. ⊠ *MM 15 OS, 3178 Overseas Hwy.* ☎ *305/744–9866, 800/523–2326* ⊕ *www.babyscoffee.com.*

WHERE TO EAT

$$ ✕ **Geiger Key Smokehouse Bar & Grill.** *American.* There's a strong hint of the Old Keys at this ocean-side marina restaurant, which came under new management in 2010 by the same folks who own Hogfish Grill on Stock Island. "On the backside of paradise," as the sign says, its tiki structures overlook quiet mangroves at an RV park marina. Locals usually outnumber tourists. The all-day menu spans an ambitious array of sandwiches, tacos, and seafood. Local fishermen stop here for breakfast before heading out in search of the big one. Don't miss the Sunday barbecue from 4–9. ⑤ *Average main: $16* ⊠ *MM 10, 5 Geiger Key Rd., off Boca Chica Rd., Bay Point, Geiger Key* ☎ *305/296–3553, 305/294–1230* ⊕ *www.geigerkeymarina.com.*

$$$$ ✕ **Little Palm Island Restaurant.** *Eclectic.* The oceanfront setting calls to mind St. Barts and other high-end destinations of the Caribbean. Keep that in mind as you reach for the bill, which can also make you swoon. The restaurant at the exclusive Little Palm Island Resort—its dining room and adjacent outdoor terrace lit by candles and warmed by live music—is one of the most romantic spots in the Keys. The seasonal menu is a melding of French and Caribbean flavors, with exotic little touches. Think shrimp and yellowtail ceviche or coconut lobster bisque as a starter, followed by mahimahi with creamy cilantro polenta. The Sunday brunch buffet, the full-moon dinners with live entertainment, and the Chef's Table Dinner are very popular. The dining room is open to nonguests on a reservations-only basis. No children under 16 are allowed. ⑤ *Average main: $65* ⊠ *MM 28.5 OS, 28500 Overseas Hwy.* ☎ *305/872–2551* ⊕ *www.littlepalmisland.com* ⚓ *Reservations essential.*

$$ ✕ **Mangrove Mama's Restaurant.** *Seafood.* This could be the prototype for a Keys restaurant, given its shanty appearance, lattice trim, and roving sort of indoor-outdoor floor plan. Then there's the seafood, from the ubiquitous fish sandwich (fried, grilled, broiled, or blackened) to lobster Reubens, crab cakes, and coconut shrimp. Burgers, steaks, and ribs round out the menu. Hidden in a grove of banana and palm trees, the place opens for lunch, Sunday brunch, and dinner. ⑤ *Average main: $20* ⊠ *MM 20 BS, Sugarloaf Key* ☎ *305/745–3030* ⊕ *www.mangrovemamasrestaurant. com* ⊘ *Closed Sept.*

★ Fodor'sChoice × **Square Grouper.** *Seafood.* In an unassum-
$$$ ing warehouse-looking building right off U.S. 1, chef and owner Lynn Bell is creating seafood magic. Just ask the locals, who wait in line for a table along with visitors in the know. But don't let the exterior fool you: the dining room is surprisingly suave, with butcher paper–lined tables, mandarin-colored walls, and textural components through-out. While the restaurant earns rave reviews, its name still earns snickers. (A "square grouper" is slang for bales of marijuana dropped into the ocean during the drug-running 1970s.) The dishes here not only taste close-your-eyes-and-grin good, their presentation is lovely. For starters, try the flash-fried conch with wasabi drizzle or home-smoked fish dip. Then perhaps order the seafood pasta with key lime butter sauce. It's okay to drool. Upstairs, Chef Lynn has just opened a beatnik-style tapas bar. ⑤ *Average main: $25* ⊠ *MM 22.5 OS, Cudjoe Key* ☎ *305/745–8880* ⊕ *www. squaregrouperbarandgrill.com* ⊘ *Closed Sun., Sept., and several weeks in summer.*

WHERE TO STAY

★ Fodor'sChoice ☷ **Little Palm Island Resort & Spa.** *Resort. Haute*
$$$$ *tropicale* best describes this luxury retreat, and "second mortgage" might explain how some can afford the extrava-gant prices. **Pros:** secluded setting; heavenly spa; easy wild-life viewing. **Cons:** expensive; might be too quiet for some; only accessible by boat or seaplane. ⑤ *Rooms from: $1,590* ⊠ *MM 28.5 OS, 28500 Overseas Hwy.* ☎ *305/872–2524, 800/343–8567* ⊕ *www.littlepalmisland.com* ⇌ *30 suites* ⑩ *Some meals.*

$ ☷ **Looe Key Reef Resort & Dive Center.** *Hotel.* If your Keys vaca-tion is all about diving, you'll be well served at this scuba-obsessed operation—the closest place to stay to the stellar reef (and affordable to boot). **Pros:** guests get discounts on dive and snorkel trips; fun bar. **Cons:** small rooms; unheated pool; close to road. ⑤ *Rooms from: $89* ⊠ *MM 27.5 OS, 27340 Overseas Hwy., Ramrod Key* ☎ *305/872–2215,*

877/816–3483 ⊕ *www.diveflakeys.com* ⇆ *23 rooms, 1 suite* ⊚ *No meals.*

$ ⌁ **Parmer's Resort.** *Hotel.* Almost every room at this budget-friendly option has a view of South Pine Channel, with the lovely curl of Big Pine Key in the foreground. **Pros:** bright rooms; pretty setting; good value. **Cons:** a bit out of the way; housekeeping costs extra; little shade around the pool. ⑤ *Rooms from: $159* ⊠ *MM 28.7 BS, 565 Barry Ave.* ☏ *305/872–2157* ⊕ *www.parmersresort.com* ⇆ *18 rooms, 12 efficiencies, 15 apartments, 1 penthouse, 1 2-bedroom cottage* ⊚ *Breakfast.*

SPORTS AND THE OUTDOORS

AIR TOURS

Fantasy Dan's Airplane Rides. Departing from Sugarloaf Key Airport, passengers can spot sharks, stingrays, and other reef life on sightseeing rides for up to three people. ⊠ *Sugarloaf Key Airport, MM 17, 16855 Overseas Hwy.* ☏ *305/743–9100* ⊕ *www.floridaairplanetours.com* ⇲ *From $130.*

BOATING

Dolphin Marina. Dolphin Marina rents 19- and 22-foot boats with 150 horsepower for up to eight people by the half day and full day. ⊠ *28530 Overseas Hwy.* ☏ *305/872–2685* ⊕ *www.dolphinmarina.net* ⇲ *From $200 half day, from $250 full day.*

SCUBA DIVING AND SNORKELING

This is the closest you can get on land to Looe Key Reef, and that's where local dive operators love to head.

In 1744 the HMS *Looe,* a British warship, ran aground and sank on one of the most beautiful coral reefs in the Keys. Today the key owes its name to the ill-fated ship. The 5.3-square-nautical-mile reef, part of the **Florida Keys National Marine Sanctuary,** has strands of elkhorn coral on its eastern margin, purple sea fans, and abundant sponges and sea urchins. On its seaward side, it drops almost vertically 50 to 90 feet. In its midst, **Shipwreck Trail** plots the location of nine historic wreck sites in 14 to 120 feet of water. Buoys mark the sites, and underwater signs tell the history of each site and what marine life to expect. Snorkelers and divers will find the sanctuary a quiet place to observe reef life—except in July, when the annual Underwater Music Festival pays homage to Looe Key's beauty and promotes reef awareness with six hours of music broadcast via underwater speakers. Dive shops, charters, and private boats transport about 500 divers and snorkelers to hear the spectacle, which includes classical, jazz, New Age, and Caribbean music, as well as a little Jimmy Buffett. There are even underwater Elvis impersonators.

Looe Key Reef Resort & Dive Center. This center, the closest dive shop to Looe Key Reef, offers two affordable trips daily, 7:30 am or 12:15 pm (for divers, snorkelers, or bubble watchers). The maximum depth is 30 feet, so snorkelers and divers go on the same boat. On Wednesday and Sunday, it runs a trip for advanced divers that visits a wreck and a reef in the area. The dive boat, a 45-foot catamaran, is docked at the full-service Looe Key Reef Resort. ⊠ *Looe Key Reef Resort, MM 27.5 OS, 27340 Overseas Hwy., Ramrod Key* ☎ *305/872–2215, 877/816–3483* ⊕ *www. diveflakeys.com* ⊠ *From $39.*

WATER SPORTS

Reelax Charters. For a guided kayak tour, join Captain Andrea Paulson of Reelax Charters, who takes you to remote locations. Charters carry up to three people and can include snorkeling and beaching on a secluded island in the Keys backcountry. ⊠ *Sugarloaf Marina, MM 17 BS, 17015 Overseas Hwy., Sugarloaf Key* ☎ *305/304–1392* ⊕ *www.keyskayaking.com* ⊠ *From $240.*

Sugarloaf Marina. Rates for one-person kayaks are based on an hourly or daily rental Two-person kayaks are also available. Delivery is free for rentals of three days or more. The folks at the marina can also hook you up with an outfitter for a day of offshore or backcountry fishing. There's also a well-stocked ship store. ⊠ *MM 17 BS, 17015 Overseas Hwy., Sugarloaf Key* ☎ *305/745–3135* ⊕ *www. sugarloafkeymarina.com* ⊠ *From $15 per hr.*

KEY WEST

Updated
by Jill
Martin

SITUATED 150 MILES FROM MIAMI, 90 miles from Havana, and an immeasurable distance from sanity, this end-of-the-line community has never been like anywhere else. Even after it was connected to the rest of the country—by the railroad in 1912 and by the highway in 1938—it maintained a strong sense of detachment. The United States acquired Key West from Spain in 1821, along with the rest of Florida. The Spanish had named the island Cayo Hueso, or Bone Key, after the Native American skeletons they found on its shores. In 1823, President James Monroe sent Commodore David S. Porter to chase pirates away. For three decades, the primary industry in Key West was wrecking—rescuing people and salvaging cargo from ships that foundered on the nearby reefs. According to some reports, when pickings were lean the wreckers hung out lights to lure ships aground. Their business declined after 1849, when the federal government began building lighthouses.

In 1845, the army began construction on Fort Taylor, which kept Key West on the Union side during the Civil War. After the fighting ended, an influx of Cubans unhappy with Spain's rule brought the cigar industry here. Fishing, shrimping, and sponge gathering became important industries, as did pineapple canning. Throughout much of the 19th century and into the 20th, Key West was Florida's wealthiest city in per-capita terms. But in 1929, the local economy began to unravel. Cigar making moved to Tampa, Hawaii dominated the pineapple industry, and the sponges succumbed to blight. Then the Depression hit, and within a few years half the population was on relief.

Tourism began to revive Key West, but that came to a halt when a hurricane knocked out the railroad bridge in 1935. To help the tourism industry recover from that crushing blow, the government offered incentives for islanders to turn their charming homes—many of them built by shipwrights—into guesthouses and inns. That wise foresight has left the town with more than 100 such lodgings, a hallmark of Key West vacationing today. In the 1950s, the discovery of "pink gold" in the Dry Tortugas boosted the economy of the entire region. Catching Key West shrimp required a fleet of up to 500 boats and flooded local restaurants with some of the sweetest shrimp alive. The town's artistic community found inspiration in the colorful fishing boats.

Key West reflects a diverse population: Conchs (natives, many of whom trace their ancestry to the Bahamas), freshwater Conchs (longtime residents who migrated from somewhere else years ago), Hispanics (primarily Cuban immigrants), recent refugees from the urban sprawl of mainland Florida, military personnel, and an assortment of vagabonds, drifters, and dropouts in search of refuge. The island was once a gay vacation hot spot, and it remains a decidedly gay-friendly destination. Some of the once-renowned gay guesthouses, however, no longer cater to an exclusively gay clientele. Key Westers pride themselves on their tolerance of all peoples, all sexual orientations, and even all animals. Most restaurants allow pets, and it's not surprising to see stray cats, dogs, and even chickens roaming freely through the dining rooms. The chicken issue is one that government officials periodically try to bring to an end, but the colorful fowl continue to strut and crow, particularly in the vicinity of Old Town's Bahamian Village.

As a tourist destination, Key West has a lot to sell—an average temperature of 79°F, 19th-century architecture, and a laid-back lifestyle. Yet much has been lost to those eager for a buck. Duval Street is starting to resemble a shopping mall with name-brand storefronts, garish T-shirt shops, and tattoo shops with sidewalk views of the inked action. Cruise ships dwarf the town's skyline and fill the streets with day-trippers gawking at the hippies with dogs in their bike baskets, gay couples walking down the street holding hands, and the oddball lot of locals, some of whom bark louder than the dogs.

ORIENTATION AND PLANNING

WHEN TO GO

Key West has a growing calendar of festivals and artistic and cultural events—including the Conch Republic Celebration in April and the Halloween Fantasy Fest in October. December brings festivity in the form of a lighted boat parade at the Historic Seaport and New Year's Eve revelry that rivals any in the nation. Few cities of its size—a mere 2 miles by 4 miles—celebrate with the joie de vivre of this one.

GETTING HERE AND AROUND

AIR TRAVEL

You can fly directly to Key West on a limited number of flights, most of which connect at other Florida airports. But a lot of folks fly into Miami or Fort Lauderdale and drive down or take the bus.

BOAT TRAVEL

Key West Express operates air-conditioned ferries between the Key West Terminal (Caroline and Grinnell streets) and Marco Island, and Fort Myers Beach. The trip from Fort Myers Beach takes at least four hours each way and costs $86 one-way, $146 round-trip. Ferries depart from Fort Myers Beach at 8:30 am and from Key West at 6 pm. The Miami and Marco Island ferry costs $86 one-way and $146 round-trip, and departs at 8:30 am. A photo ID is required for each passenger. Advance reservations are recommended.

BUS AND SHUTTLE TRAVEL TO KEY WEST

Greyhound Lines runs a special Keys Shuttle twice a day (depending on the day of the week) from Miami International Airport (departing from Concourse E, lower level) and stops throughout the Keys. Fares run about $45 (Web fare) to $57 for Key West. Keys Shuttle runs scheduled service three times a day in 15-passenger vans between Miami Airport and Key West with stops throughout the Keys for $70 to $90 per person. SuperShuttle charges $102 per passenger for trips from Miami International Airport to the Upper Keys. To go farther into the Keys, you must book an entire 11-person van, which costs about $350 to Key West. You need to place your request for transportation back to the airport 24 hours in advance. *For detailed information on these services, see Air Travel in Travel Smart.*

BUS TRAVEL AROUND KEY WEST

Between mile markers 4 and 0, Key West is the one place in the Keys where you could conceivably do without a car, especially if you plan on staying around Old Town. If you've driven the 106 miles down the chain, you're probably ready to abandon your car in the hotel parking lot anyway. Trolleys, buses, bikes, scooters, and feet are more suitable alternatives. When your feet tire, catch a rickshaw-style pedicab ride, which will run you about $1.50 a minute. But to explore the beaches, New Town, and Stock Island, you'll need a car or taxi.

The City of Key West Department of Transportation has six color-coded bus routes traversing the island from 5:30 am to 11:30 pm. Stops have signs with the international bus symbol. Schedules are available on buses and at hotels, visitor centers, and shops, and online. The fare is $2 one-way. Its Lower Keys Shuttle bus runs between Marathon to Key West ($4 one-way), with scheduled stops along the way.

TOP REASONS TO GO

■ **The Dry Tortugas.** Do a day trip to Dry Tortugas National Park for snorkeling and hiking away from the crowds.

■ **Watching the sunset.** Revel in both the beautiful sunset and the gutsy performers at Mallory Square's nightly celebration.

■ **The Conch Tour Train.** Hop aboard for a narrated tour of the town's tawdry past and rare architectural treasures.

■ **Barhopping.** Nightlife rules in Key West. Do the "Duval Crawl," the local version of club hopping. But first fortify yourself at one of the town's exceptional restaurants.

■ **The Hemingway connection.** Visit Ernest Hemingway's historic home for a page out of Key West's literary past.

5

VISITOR INFORMATION

Contacts **Greater Key West Chamber of Commerce** ☎ *305/294–2587, 800/527–8539* ⊕ *www.keywestchamber.org.* **Gay & Lesbian Community Center** ✉ *513 Truman Ave.* ☎ *305/394–4603* ⊕ *www.gaykeywestfl.com.*

HOTELS

Key West's lodgings include historic cottages, restored Conch houses, and large resorts. Quaint guesthouses, the town's trademark, offer a true island experience in residential neighborhoods near Old Town's restaurants, shops, and clubs. A few rooms cost as little as $65 a night in the off-season, but most range from $100 to $300. Please note that certain guesthouses and inns do not welcome children under 16, and most do not permit smoking.

Hotel reviews have been shortened. For full information, visit Fodors.com.

RESTAURANTS

Keys restaurants get most exotic once you reach Key West, and you can pretty much find anything you want, though bargains are hard to come by. Pricier restaurants serve tantalizing fusion cuisine that reflects the influence of Cuba and other Caribbean islands. Tropical fruits and citrus figure prominently on the menus, and mango, papaya, and passion fruit are often featured in beverages. Of course, there are plenty of places that serve local seafood. Key West stays true to island character with a selection of hole-in-the-wall places that couldn't be any more colorful.

Key West

KEY

1 Exploring

① Hotels & Restaurants

Exploring

Fort East Martello Museum & Gardens, **1**

Key West Tropical Forest & Botanical Garden, **2**

Restaurants

HogFish Bar & Grill, **6**

Latitudes, **1**

Tavern N Town, **5**

Hotels

Best Western Key Ambassador Resort Inn, **7**

Key West Marriott Beachside Resort, **4**

Parrot Key Resort, **3**

Sunset Key, **2**

WHAT IT COSTS				
	$	$$	$$$	$$$$
Restaurants	Under $15	$16–$20	$21–$30	Over $30
Hotels	Under $200	$201–$300	$301–$400	Over $400

Prices in the restaurant reviews are the average cost of a main course at dinner or, if dinner isn't served, at lunch. Prices in the hotel reviews are the lowest cost of a standard double room in high season. Prices don't include taxes (6%, more in some counties, and 1%–5% tourist tax for hotel rooms).

TOURS

BIKE TOURS

Lloyd's Original Tropical Bike Tour. Explore the natural, non-commercial side of Key West at a leisurely pace, stopping on backstreets and in backyards of private homes to sample native fruits and view indigenous plants and trees with a 30-year Key West veteran. The behind-the-scenes tours run two hours and include a bike rental. ⊠ *Truman Ave. and Simonton St.* ☎ *305/304–4700, 305/294–1882* ⊕ *www. lloydstropicalbiketour.com* 🎫 *$39.*

BUS TOURS

City View Trolley Tours. In 2010, City View Trolley Tours began service, offering a little competition to the Conch Train and Old Town Trolley, which are owned by the same company. Purchase your tickets online or with your smartphone, but you pay double if you pay in person. Tours depart every 30 minutes from 9:30–4:30. Passengers can board and disembark at any of nine stops, and can reboard at will. ☎ *305/294–0644* ⊕ *www.cityviewtrolleys. com* 🎫 *From $19.*

Conch Tour Train. The Conch Tour Train is a 90-minute narrated tour of Key West, traveling 14 miles through Old Town and around the island. Board at Mallory Square or Angela Street and Duval Street depot every half hour (9–4:30 from Mallory Square). Discount tickets are available online. ☎ *305/294–5161, 888/916–8687* ⊕ *www. conchtourtrain.com* 🎫 *$30.45.*

Gay & Lesbian Trolley Tour. With its official motto being "One Human Family," Key West has long been a favorite of the gay and lesbian community. In fact, Key West wouldn't be the same without the gay community who renovated many of the ramshackle homes and guesthouses. The Gay & Lesbian Trolley Tour is a fun way to celebrate and learn more about the gay-specific activities Key West offers as well as the lesbian community's history on the Keys. Decorated with a rainbow, the 70-minute Gay and Lesbian Trolley Tour rumbles around the town beginning at 4 pm every Saturday afternoon. ✉ *513 Truman Ave.* ☎ *305/294–4603* ⊕ *www.gaykeywestfl.com* 🖬 *$25.*

Old Town Trolley. Old Town Trolley operates trolley-style buses, departing from the Mallory Square every 30 minutes from 9–4:30, for 90-minute narrated tours of Key West. The smaller trolleys go places the larger Conch Tour Train won't fit and you can ride a second consecutive day for free. You may disembark at any of 12 stops and reboard a later trolley. You can save $3 by booking online. It also offers package deals with Old Town attractions. ✉ *201 Front St.* ☎ *305/296–6688, 888/910–8687* ⊕ *www.trolleytours.com* 🖬 *$30.*

WALKING TOURS

Key West Promotions. If you're not entirely a do-it-yourselfer, Key West Promotions offers a variety of guided tours, including their famous pub crawl, a historic homes and gardens walking tour, Southernmost bike tour, a chilling ghost tour, and a palate-pleasing, Taste of Key West restaurant experience. ✉ *218 Whitehead St.* ☎ *305/294–7170* ⊕ *www.keywestwalkingtours.com.*

EXPLORING

Although the rest of the Keys are known for outdoor activities, Key West has something of a city feel and has a fair number of historic sights. Few open spaces remain, as promoters continue to churn out restaurants, galleries, shops, and museums to interpret the city's intriguing past.

OLD TOWN

The heart of Key West, the historic Old Town area runs from White Street to the waterfront. Beginning in 1822, wharves, warehouses, chandleries, ship-repair facilities, and eventually, in 1891, the U.S. Custom House, sprang up around the deep harbor to accommodate the navy's large ships and other sailing vessels. Wreckers, merchants, and sea captains built lavish houses near the bustling waterfront. A remarkable number of these fine Victorian and pre-Victorian structures have been restored to their original grandeur and now serve as homes, guesthouses, shops, restaurants, and museums. These, along with the dwellings of famous writers, artists, and politicians who've come to Key West over the past 175 years, are among the area's approximately 3,000 historic structures. Old Town also has the city's finest restaurants and hotels, lively street life, and popular nightspots.

TIMING

Allow two full days to see all the Old Town museums and homes, especially if you plan to peruse the shops. For a narrated trip on the tour train or trolley, budget an hour to ride the loop without getting off and an entire day if you plan to get off and on at some of the sights and restaurants.

TOP ATTRACTIONS

5

Audubon House and Tropical Gardens. If you've ever seen an engraving by ornithologist John James Audubon, you'll understand why his name is synonymous with birds. See his works in this three-story house, which was built in the 1840s for Captain John Geiger and filled with period furniture. It now commemorates Audubon's 1832 stop in Key West while he was traveling through Florida to study birds. After an introduction by a docent, you can do a self-guided tour of the house and gardens (or just the gardens). An art gallery sells lithographs of the artist's famed portraits. ⊠ *205 Whitehead St.* ☎ *305/294–2116, 877/294–2470* ⊕ *www. audubonhouse.com* ☜ *$7.50 gardens only; $12 house and gardens* ☉ *Daily 9:30–5 (last tour at 4:15).*

★ **Fodor's**Choice **Ernest Hemingway Home and Museum.** Amusing anecdotes spice up the guided tours of Ernest Hemingway's home, built in 1801 by the town's most successful wrecker. While living here between 1931 and 1942, Hemingway wrote about 70% of his life's work, including classics like *For Whom the Bell Tolls.* Few of his belongings remain aside from some books, and there's little about his actual work, but photographs help you visualize his day-to-day life. The famous six-toed descendants of Hemingway's cats—many named for actors, artists, authors, and even a hurricane—have free rein of the property. Tours begin every 10 minutes and take 30 minutes; then you're free to explore on your own. Be sure to find out why there is a urinal in the garden! ⊠ *907 Whitehead St.* ☎ *305/294–1136* ⊕ *www.hemingwayhome.com* ☜ *$13* ☉ *Daily 9–5.*

A GOOD TOUR

To cover many sights, take the Old Town Trolley, which lets you get off and reboard a later trolley, or the Conch Tour Train. Old Town is also manageable on foot, bicycle, moped, or electric car. The area is expansive, so you'll want either to pick and choose from the stops on this tour or break it into two or more days. Start on Whitehead Street at the **Ernest Hemingway Home and Museum**, then cross the street and climb to the top of the **Lighthouse Museum** for a spectacular view. Return to Whitehead Street and follow it north to Angela Street, where you'll turn right. At Margaret Street, the **City Cemetery** is worth a look for its aboveground vaults and unusual headstone inscriptions. Head north on Margaret Street, turn left onto Southard Street, and then right onto Simonton Street. Halfway up the block, **Nancy Forrester's Secret Garden** occupies Free School Lane. After wandering among the blossoms, return again to Southard Street, turn right, and follow it through Truman Annex to **Fort Zachary Taylor State Park**.

Walk west into Truman Annex to see the **Harry S. Truman Little White House Museum**, President Truman's vacation residence. Return east on Caroline and turn left on Whitehead to visit the **Audubon House and Gardens**, honoring the famed artist and naturalist. Follow Whitehead north to Greene Street and turn left to see the salvaged sea treasures of the **Mel Fisher Maritime Heritage Society Museum**. At Whitehead's northern end are the **Key West Aquarium** and the **Key West Museum of Art and History,** the former historic U.S. Custom House. By late afternoon you should be ready to cool off with a dip or catch a few rays at the beach. From the aquarium, head east two blocks to the end of Simonton Street, where you'll find the appropriately named **Simonton Street Beach**. Like all Key West beaches, it is man-made, with white sand imported from the Bahamas and north Florida. If you've brought your pet, stroll a few blocks east to **Dog Beach**, at the corner of Vernon and Waddell streets. A little farther east is **Higgs Beach–Astro Park**, on Atlantic Boulevard between White and Reynolds streets. As the sun starts to sink, return to the north end of Old Town and follow the crowds to Mallory Square, behind the aquarium, to watch Key West's nightly sunset spectacle. For dinner, head east on Caroline Street to **Historic Seaport at Key West Bight**.

Old Town Key West

| 0 | | 1/2 mile |
| 0 | | 1/2 km |

Wisteria Island

Fleming Key

Sunset Key

Key West Bight

9 Front St.

8
7 Greene St.

6

5 **3** Caroline St.

Eaton St.

10 **11**

Elizabeth St.
William St.
Margaret
Grinnell St.
Frances St.
White St.
Palm Ave.

Fleming St.
Key West Library
Nancy Forrester's Secret Garden
Southard St.

12

Thomas St.
Whitehead St.
Angela St.
Windsor Ln.
Virginia St.

17 Covington
Petronia St.
Emma St.
Olivia St. **2** **1** Truman Ave.
Fort St.
Julia St.
Virginia St.
Amelia St.
Whitehead St.
Duval St.
Simonton St.
Duncan St.
Margaret
William St.
Vernon
Reynolds
Grinnell St.
Varela St.
United St.
South St.
Flagler Ave.

13

16

Fort Zachary Taylor Beach

14 South Beach

Dog Beach

Higgs Beach–Astro City Playground

15 Casa Marina Ct.
White St.

ATLANTIC OCEAN

Audubon House and Gardens, **3**

City Cemetery, **12**

Dry Tortugas National Park The Bight Visitor Center, **11**

Eco-Discovery Center, **17**

Ernest Hemingway Home and Museum, **1**

Fort Zachary Taylor Historic State Park, **16**

Harry S Truman Little White House Museum, **5**

Historic Seaport at Key West Bight, **10**

Key West Aquarium, **8**

Key West Butterfly & Nature Conservatory, **13**

Key West Lighthouse Museum & Keeper's Quarters Museum, **2**

Key West Museum of Art & History in the Custom House, **6**

Key West Shipwreck Treasures Museum, **7**

Mallory Square and Pier, **9**

Mel Fisher Maritime Museum, **4**

The Southernmost Point, **14**

West Martello Tower, **15**

NEED A BREAK? **Key West Library.** Check out the pretty palm garden next to the Key West Library at 700 Fleming Street, just off Duval. This leafy, outdoor reading area, with shaded benches, is the perfect place to escape the frenzy and crowds of downtown Key West. There's free Internet access in the library, too. ⊠ *700 Fleming St.* ☎ *305/292–3595.*

Fort Zachary Taylor Historic State Park. Construction of the fort began in 1845 but was halted during the Civil War. Even though Florida seceded from the Union, Yankee forces used the fort as a base to block Confederate shipping. More than 1,500 Confederate vessels were detained in Key West's harbor. The fort, finally completed in 1866, was also used in the Spanish-American War. Take a 30-minute guided walking tour of the redbrick fort, a National Historic Landmark, at noon and 2, or self-tour anytime between 8 and 5. In February a celebration called Civil War Heritage Days includes costumed reenactments and demonstrations. From mid-January to mid-April the park serves as an open-air gallery for pieces created for Sculpture Key West. One of its most popular features is its man-made beach, a rest stop for migrating birds in the spring and fall; there are also picnic areas, hiking and biking trails and a kayak launch. ⊠ *Southard St., at the end of the street, through Truman Annex* ☎ *305/292–6713* ⊕ *www.floridastateparks. org/forttaylor* ⊠ *$4 for single occupant vehicles, $6 for 2–8 people in a vehicle, plus a 50¢ per person county surcharge.* ☉ *Daily 8–sunset.*

Harry S Truman Little White House Museum. Renovations to this circa-1890 landmark have restored the home and gardens to the Truman era, down to the wallpaper pattern. A free photographic review of visiting dignitaries and presidents—John F. Kennedy, Jimmy Carter, and Bill Clinton are among the chief executives who passed through here—is on display in the back of the gift shop. Engaging 45-minute tours begin every 20 minutes until 4:30. They start with an excellent 10-minute video on the history of the property and Truman's visits. On the grounds of **Truman Annex,** a 103-acre former military parade grounds and barracks, the home served as a winter White House for presidents Truman, Eisenhower, and Kennedy. ■ TIP→ **The house tour does require climbing steps. Visitors can do a free self-guided botanical tour of the grounds with a brochure from the museum store.** ⊠ *111 Front St.* ☎ *305/294–9911* ⊕ *www.trumanlittlewhitehouse. com* ⊠ *$16.13* ☉ *Daily 9–5, grounds 7–6.*

Historic Seaport at Key West Bight. What was once a funky—in some places even seedy—part of town is now an 8½-acre historic restoration of 100 businesses, including water-front restaurants, open-air bars, museums, clothing stores, bait shops, dive shops, docks, a marina, and water-sports concessions. It's all linked by the 2-mile waterfront **Harborwalk,** which runs between Front and Grinnell streets, passing big ships, schooners, sunset cruises, fishing charters, and glass-bottom boats. ⊠ *100 Grinnell St.* ☎ *305/293–8309* ⊕ *www.keywestseaport.com.*

NEED A BREAK? **Coffee Plantation.** Get your morning (or afternoon) buzz, and hook up to the Internet in the comfort of a homelike setting in a circa-1890 Conch house. Munch on sandwiches, wraps, and pastries, and sip a hot or cold espresso beverage. ⊠ *713 Caroline St.* ☎ *305/295–9808* ⊕ *www. coffeeplantationkeywest.com.*

FAMILY **Key West Butterfly & Nature Conservatory.** This air-conditioned refuge for butterflies, birds, and the human spirit gladdens the soul with hundreds of colorful wings—more than 45 species of butterflies alone—in a lovely glass-encased bubble. Waterfalls, artistic benches, paved pathways, birds, and lush, flowering vegetation elevate this above most butterfly attractions. The gift shop and gallery are worth a visit on their own. ⊠ *1316 Duval St.* ☎ *305/296–2988, 800/839–4647* ⊕ *www.keywestbutterfly.com* ☞ *$12* ⊙ *Daily 9–5, gallery and shop open until 5:30.*

Key West Lighthouse Museum & Keeper's Quarters Museum. For the best view in town, climb the 88 steps to the top of this 1847 lighthouse. The 92-foot structure has a Fresnel lens, which was installed in the 1860s at a cost of $1 million. The keeper lived in the adjacent 1887 clapboard house, which now exhibits vintage photographs, ship models, nautical charts, and lighthouse artifacts from all along the Keys' reefs. A kids' room is stocked with books and toys. ⊠ *938 Whitehead St.* ☎ *305/295–6616* ⊕ *www.kwahs.com* ☞ *$10* ⊙ *Daily 9:30–4:30.*

★ Fodor\$Choice **Key West Museum of Art & History in the Custom House.** When Key West was designated a U.S. port of entry in the early 1820s, a customhouse was established. Salvaged cargoes from ships wrecked on the reefs were brought here, setting the stage for Key West to become—for a time—the richest city in Florida. The imposing redbrick-and-terra-cotta Richardsonian Romanesque–style building reopened

CLOSE UP

Hemingway Was Here

In a town where Pulitzer Prize–winning writers are almost as common as coconuts, Ernest Hemingway stands out. Many bars and restaurants around the island claim that he ate or drank there.

Hemingway came to Key West in 1928 at the urging of writer John dos Passos and rented a house with his second wife, Pauline Pfeiffer. They spent winters in the Keys and summers in Europe and Wyoming, occasionally taking African safaris. Along the way, they had two sons, Patrick and Gregory. In 1931, Pauline's wealthy uncle Gus gave the couple the house at 907 Whitehead Street. Now known as the Ernest Hemingway Home & Museum, it's Key West's number-one tourist attraction. Renovations included the addition of a pool and a tropical garden.

In 1935, when the visitor bureau included the house in a tourist brochure, Hemingway promptly built the brick wall that surrounds it today. He wrote of the visitor bureau's offense in a 1935 essay for *Esquire,* saying, "The house at present occupied by your correspondent is listed as number eighteen in a compilation of the forty-eight things for a tourist to see in Key West. So there will be no difficulty in a tourist finding it or any other of the sights of the city, a map has been prepared by the local F.E.R.A. authorities to be presented to each arriving visitor. This is all very flattering to the easily bloated ego of your correspondent but very hard on production."

During his time in Key West, Hemingway penned some of his most important works, including *A Farewell to Arms, To Have and Have Not, Green Hills of Africa,* and *Death in the Afternoon.* His rigorous schedule consisted of writing almost every morning in his second-story studio above the pool, then promptly descending the stairs at midday. By afternoon and evening he was ready for drinking, fishing, swimming, boxing, and hanging around with the boys.

One close friend was Joe Russell, a craggy fisherman and owner of the rugged bar Sloppy Joe's, originally at 428 Greene Street but now at 201 Duval Street. Russell was the only one in town who would cash Hemingway's $1,000 royalty check. Russell and Charles Thompson introduced Hemingway to deep-sea fishing, which became fodder for his writing.

Hemingway stayed in Key West for 11 years before leaving Pauline for his third wife. Pauline and the boys stayed on in the house, which sold in 1951 for $80,000, ten times its original cost.

—Jim and Cynthia Tunstall

as a museum and art gallery in 1999. Smaller galleries have long-term and changing exhibits about the history of Key West, including a Hemingway room and a fine collection of folk artist Mario Sanchez's wood paintings. In 2011, to commemorate the 100th anniversary of the railroad's arrival to Key West in 1912, a new permanent Flagler exhibit opened. ✉ *281 Front St.* ☎ *305/295–6616* ⊕ *www. kwahs.com* ✉ *$9* ⊙ *Daily 9:30–4:30.*

Mallory Square and Pier. For cruise-ship passengers, this is the disembarkation point for an attack on Key West. For practically every visitor, it's the requisite venue for a nightly sunset celebration that includes street performers—human statues, sword swallowers, tightrope walkers, musicians, and more—plus craft vendors, conch fritter fryers, and other regulars who defy classification. (Wanna picture with my pet iguana?) With all the activity, don't forget to watch the main show: a dazzling tropical sunset. ✉ *Mallory Sq.*

The Southernmost Point. Possibly the most photographed site in Key West (even though the actual geographic southernmost point in the continental United States lies across the bay on a naval base, where you see a satellite dish), this is a must-see. Who wouldn't want his picture taken next to the big striped buoy that marks the southernmost point in the continental United States? A plaque next to it honors Cubans who lost their lives trying to escape to America and other signs tell Key West history. ✉ *Whitehead and South Sts.*

WORTH NOTING

City Cemetery. You can learn almost as much about a town's history through its cemetery as through its historic houses. Key West's celebrated 20-acre burial place may leave you wanting more, with headstone epitaphs such as "I told you I was sick," and, for a wayward husband, "Now I know where he's sleeping at night." Among the interesting plots are a memorial to the sailors killed in the sinking of the battleship USS *Maine,* carved angels and lambs marking graves of children, and grand aboveground crypts that put to shame many of the town's dwellings for the living. There are separate plots for Catholics, Jews, and refugees from Cuba. You're free to walk around the cemetery on your own, but the best way to see it is on a 90-minute tour given by the staff and volunteers of the Historic Florida Keys Foundation. Tours leave from the main gate, and reservations are required. ✉ *Margaret and Angela Sts.*

☎ *305/292–6718* ⊕ *www.historicfloridakeys.org* ☜ *Tours*
$15 ⊙ *Daily sunrise–6 pm; tours Tues. and Thurs. at 9:30*
year-round, call for additional times.

Dry Tortugas National Park The Bight Visitor Center. If you can't
see Fort Jefferson in the Dry Tortugas in person, this is
the next best thing. Opened in 2013, this free attraction
located in Key West's historic seaport has an impressive
(1:87) scale model of the fort; life-size figures including
the fort's most famous prisoner, Dr. Samuel Mudd; and
even a junior ranger station for little ones with hands-on
educational fun. The exhibits are housed in a historic site
as well, the old Thompson Fish House, where local fisherman would bring their daily catch for processing. History
lingers on within these walls but to get a whiff of the sea
and days gone past, you'll have to walk the docks out
front. Hours are 8:30 am to 5 pm daily. ✉ *240 Margaret*
St. ☎ *305/294–7009* ⊕ *www.nps.gov/drto/planyourvisit/*
the-bight-visitor-center.htm ⊙ *Daily 8:30–5.*

FAMILY **Eco-Discovery Center.** While visiting Fort Zachary Taylor Historic State Park, stop in at this 6,400-square-foot interactive
attraction, which encourages visitors to venture through
a variety of Florida Keys habitats from pinelands, beach
dunes, and mangroves to the deep sea. Walk through a
model of NOAA's (National Oceanic and Atmospheric
Administration) Aquarius, a unique underwater ocean
laboratory 9 miles off Key Largo, to virtually discover what
lurks beneath the sea. Touch-screen computer displays, a
dramatic movie, a 2,450-gallon aquarium, and live underwater cameras show off North America's only contiguous
barrier coral reef. ✉ *35 E. Quay Rd., at end of Southard*
St. in Truman Annex ☎ *305/809–4750* ⊕ *www.floridakeys.*
noaa.gov ☜ *Free (donations accepted)* ⊙ *Tues.–Sat. 9–4.*

FAMILY **Key West Aquarium.** Pet a nurse shark and explore the fasci-
nating underwater realm of the Keys without getting wet
at this historic aquarium. Hundreds of tropical fish and
enormous sea creatures live here—all locals. A touch tank
enables you to handle starfish, sea cucumbers, horseshoe
and hermit crabs, even horse and queen conchs—living
totems of the Conch Republic. Built in 1934 by the Works
Progress Administration as the world's first open-air aquarium, most of the building has been enclosed for all-weather
viewing. Guided tours, included in the admission price,
feature shark feedings. ✉ *1 Whitehead St.* ☎ *305/296–2051*

⊕ *www.keywestaquarium.com* 🖾 *$15.04* ☉ *Daily 10–8; tours at 11, 1, 2, 4:30, and 6:30.*

FAMILY **Key West Shipwreck Treasures Museum.** Much of Key West's history, early prosperity, and interesting architecture come from ships that ran aground on its coral reef. Artifacts from the circa-1856 *Isaac Allerton,* which yielded $150,000 worth of wreckage, make up the museum portion of this multifaceted attraction. Actors and films add a bit of Disney-esque drama. The final highlight is climbing to the top of the 65-foot lookout tower, a reproduction of the 20 or so towers used by Key West wreckers during the town's salvaging heydays. ⊠ *1 Whitehead St.* ☎ *305/292–8990* ⊕ *www.shipwreckhistoreum.com* 🖾 *$15.04* ☉ *Daily 9:40–5.*

Mel Fisher Maritime Museum. In 1622 two Spanish galleons laden with riches from South America foundered in a hurricane 40 miles west of the Keys. In 1985 diver Mel Fisher recovered the treasures from the lost ships, the *Nuestra Señora de Atocha* and the *Santa Margarita.* Fisher's incredible adventure tracking these fabled hoards and battling the state of Florida for rights is as amazing as the loot you'll see, touch, and learn about in this museum. Artifacts include a 77.76-carat natural emerald crystal worth almost $250,000. Exhibits on the second floor rotate and might cover slave ships, including the excavated 17th-century *Henrietta Marie,* or the evolution of Florida maritime history. ⊠ *200 Greene St.* ☎ *305/294–2633* ⊕ *www.melfisher. org* 🖾 *$12.50* ☉ *Weekdays 8:30–5, weekends 9:30–5.*

West Martello Tower. Among the arches and ruins of this redbrick Civil War–era fort, the Key West Garden Club maintains lovely gardens of native and tropical plants, fountains, and sculptures. It also holds art, orchid, and flower shows February through April and leads private garden tours one weekend in March. ⊠ *Atlantic Blvd. and White St.* ☎ *305/294–3210* ⊕ *www.keywestgardenclub.com* 🖾 *Donation welcome* ☉ *Daily 9:30–5.*

NEW TOWN

The Overseas Highway splits as it enters Key West, the two forks rejoining to encircle New Town, the area east of White Street to Cow Key Channel. The southern fork runs along the shore as South Roosevelt Boulevard (Route A1A) and skirts Key West International Airport. Part of New Town was created with dredged fill. The island would

THE CONCH REPUBLIC

Beginning in the 1970s, pot smuggling became a source of income for islanders who knew how to dodge detection in the maze of waterways in the Keys. In 1982, the U.S. Border Patrol threw a roadblock across the Overseas Highway just south of Florida City to catch drug runners and undocumented aliens. Traffic backed up for miles as Border Patrol agents searched vehicles and demanded that the occupants prove U.S. citizenship. Officials in Key West, outraged at being treated like foreigners by the federal government, staged a protest and formed their own "nation," the so-called Conch Republic. They hoisted a flag and distributed mock border passes, visas, and Conch currency. The embarrassed Border Patrol dismantled its roadblock, and now an annual festival recalls the city's victory.

have continued growing this way had the Army Corps of Engineers not determined in the early 1970s that it was detrimental to the nearby reef.

TIMING

Allow one to two hours to include brief stops at each attraction. If your interests lie in art, gardens, or Civil War history, you'll need three or four hours. Throw in time at the beach and make it a half-day affair.

Fort East Martello Museum & Gardens. This redbrick Civil War fort never saw a lick of action during the war. Today it serves as a museum, with historical exhibits about the 19th and 20th centuries. Among the latter are relics of the USS *Maine,* cigar factory and shipwrecking exhibits, and the citadel tower you can climb to the top. The museum, operated by the Key West Art and Historical Society, also has a collection of Stanley Papio's "junk art" sculptures inside and out, and a gallery of Cuban folk artist Mario Sanchez's chiseled and painted wooden carvings of historic Key West street scenes. ✉ *3501 S. Roosevelt Blvd.* ☎ *305/296–3913* ⊕ *www.kwahs.com* ✐ *$9* ☉ *Daily 9:30–4:30.*

Key West Tropical Forest & Botanical Garden. Established in 1935, this unique habitat is the only frost-free botanical garden in the continental United States. You won't see fancy topiaries and exotic plants, but you'll see a unique ecosystem that naturally occurs in this area and the Caribbean. There are paved walkways that take you past butterfly gardens, mangroves, Cuban palms, lots of birds like herons and ibis, and ponds where you can spy turtles and fish. It's a nice respite from the sidewalks and shops, and offers a natural slice of Keys paradise. ⊠ *5210 College Rd.* ☎ *305/296–1504* ⊕ *www.kwbgs.org* ⌑ *$7* ⊙ *Daily 10–4.*

BEACHES

OLD TOWN

Dog Beach. Next to Louie's Backyard, this tiny beach—the only one in Key West where dogs are allowed unleashed—has a shore that's a mix of sand and rocks. **Amenities:** none. **Best for:** walking. ⊠ *Vernon and Waddell Sts.* ⌑ *Free* ⊙ *Daily sunrise–sunset.*

FAMILY **Fort Zachary Taylor Beach.** The park's beach is the best and safest place to swim in Key West. There's an adjoining picnic area with barbecue grills and shade trees, a snack bar, and rental equipment, including snorkeling gear. A café serves sandwiches and other munchies. **Amenities:** food and drink; showers; toilets; water sports. **Best for:** swimming; snorkeling. ⊠ *Southard St., at the end of the street, through Truman Annex* ☎ *305/292–6713* ⊕ *www.floridastateparks. org/forttaylor* ⌑ *$4 for one-occupant vehicles, $6 for 2–8 people in a vehicle, plus 50¢ per person county surcharge* ⊙ *Daily 8–sunset, tours noon and 2.*

FAMILY **Higgs Beach–Astro City Playground.** This Monroe County park with its groomed pebbly sand is a popular sunbathing spot. A nearby grove of Australian pines provides shade, and the West Martello Tower provides shelter should a storm suddenly sweep in. Kayak and beach-chair rentals are available, as is a volleyball net. The beach also has a marker and cultural exhibit commemorating the gravesite of 295 enslaved Africans who died after being rescued from three South America–bound slave ships in 1860. Across the street, **Astro City Playground** is popular with young children. **Amenities:** parking; toilets; water sports. **Best for:** swimming; snorkeling. ⊠ *Atlantic Blvd., between White and Reynolds Sts.* ⌑ *Free* ⊙ *Daily 6 am–11 pm.*

South Beach. On the Atlantic, this stretch of sand, also known as City Beach, is popular with travelers staying at nearby motels. It is now part of the new Southernmost Hotel on the Beach resort but is open to the public with a fun beach bar and grill. There's little parking however, so most visitors walk or bike here. **Amenities:** food and drink;

parking; toilets. **Best for:** partiers; sunrise; sunset. ✉ *Duval St. at South St.* ▣ *Free* ☉ *Daily 7 am–11 pm.*

NEW TOWN

C.B. Harvey Memorial Rest Beach. This beach and park were named after Cornelius Bradford Harvey, former Key West mayor and commissioner. Adjacent to Higgs Beach, it has half a dozen picnic areas across the street, dunes, a pier, and a wheelchair and bike path. **Amenities:** none. **Best for:** walking. ✉ *Atlantic Blvd., east side of White St. Pier* ▣ *Free* ☉ *Daily 6 am–11 pm.*

Smathers Beach. This wide beach has nearly 1 mile of nice white sand, plus beautiful coconut palms, picnic areas, and volleyball courts, all of which make it popular with the spring-break crowd. Trucks along the road rent rafts, windsurfers, and other beach "toys." **Amenities:** parking; toilets; water sports. **Best for:** partiers. ✉ *S. Roosevelt Blvd.* ▣ *Free* ☉ *Daily 7 am–11 pm.*

WHERE TO EAT

Bring your appetite, a sense of daring, and a lack of pre-conceived notions about propriety. A meal in Key West can mean overlooking the crazies along Duval Street, watching roosters and pigeons battle for a scrap of food that may have escaped your fork, relishing the finest in what used to be the dining room of a 19th-century Victorian home, or gazing out at boats jockeying for position in the marina. And that's just the diversity of the setting. Seafood dominates local menus, but the treatment afforded that fish or crustacean can range from Cuban and New World to Asian and Continental.

OLD TOWN

$$ ✕ **Ambrosia.** *Japanese.* Ask any savvy local where to get the best sushi on the island and you'll undoubtedly be pointed to this bright and airy dining room with modern indoor waterfall literally steps from the Atlantic. Grab a seat at the sleek bar, where the back wall glows from purple to blue, or sit at the sushi bar and watch owner and head sushi chef Masa (albeit not the famous chef of the eponymous restaurants in New York and Las Vegas) prepare an impressive array of super fresh sashimi delicacies. Sushi lovers can't go wrong with the Ambrosia special: miso soup served with a sampler of 15 kinds of sashimi, seven pieces of sushi, and sushi rolls. There's an assortment of lightly fried tempura and teriyaki dishes and a killer bento box at lunch. Enjoy it all with a glass of premium sake or a cold glass of Sapporo beer. ⑤ *Average main: $20* ⊠ *Santa Maria Resort, 1401 Simonton St.* ☎ *305/293–0304* ⊕ *www. keywestambrosia.com* ⊗ *No lunch weekends. Closed 2 weeks after Labor Day.*

$$$ ✕ **Azur Restaurant.** *Eclectic.* Fuel up on the finest fare at this former gas station, now part of the Eden House complex. In a contemporary setting with indoor and outdoor seating, welcoming staff serves breakfast, lunch, and dinner that stand out from the hordes of Key West restaurants by virtue of originality. For instance, key lime-stuffed French toast and yellowtail snapper Benedict make breakfast a pleasant wake-up call. The crab cake BLT, duck *cubano* with fontina cheese, and charred marinated octopus command notice on the lunch menu. Four varieties of homemade gnocchi are a dinner-time specialty, along with tasting plates, "almost entrées" like braised lamb ribs over Moroccan-spiced chick peas, and main courses that include seafood risotto with chorizo and grilled sea bass. Sunday brunch served. ⑤ *Average main: $26* ⊠ *425 Grinnell St.* ☎ *305/292–2987* ⊕ *www. azurkeywest.com* ⟁ *Reservations essential.*

$$$ ✕ **Bistro 245.** *Seafood.* The sunset views alone are worth a visit, but the food here is stellar as well. Start upstairs at the bar with a key lime martini and watch the throngs below make Mallory Square a scene. Downstairs, you can choose between the open-air patio or the air-conditioned dining room with picture-window views. For dinner, try the lobster quesadilla or seafood cocktail as an appetizer before moving on to the shrimp and lobster fettuccine with asparagus and chèvre, seared mahimahi with tangerine butter, or pan-seared yellowtail in a white wine butter sauce. The breakfast menu features healthy options like fruit smoothies and smoked salmon, tofu, and avocado on a bagel. Creative salads and sandwiches make lunch an intriguing affair. ⑤ *Average main: $25* ⊠ *Westin Key West Resort, 245 Front St.* ☎ *305/294–4000* ⊕ *www.westin.com/ keywest.*

$$$ ✕ **Blue Heaven.** *Caribbean.* The outdoor dining area here is often referred to as "the quintessential Keys experience," and it's hard to argue. There's much to like about this historic restaurant where Hemingway refereed boxing matches and customers cheered for cockfights. Although these events are no more, the free-roaming chickens and cats add that "what-a-hoot" factor. Nightly specials include black bean

Old Town Key West Restaurants

Fleming Key

Key West Bight

Front St.
Greene St.
Caroline St.
Eaton St.
Fleming St.
Southard St.
Whitehead St.
Thomas St.
Angela St.
Petronia St.
Olivia St.
Julia St.
Virginia St.
Amelia St.
Fort St.
Geraldine St.
Emma St.
Duval St.
Simonton St.
William St.
Margaret
Grinnell St.
Frances St.
White St.
Windsor Ln.
Elizabeth St.
Truman Ave.
Duncan St.
Virginia St.
Varela St.
United St.
South St.
Reynolds
Flagler Ave.
Vernon
Palm Ave.
Casa Marina Ct.

0   1/2 mile
0   1/2 km

ATLANTIC OCEAN

Ambrosia, **27**
Azur Restaurant, **10**
Bistro 245, **2**
Blue Heaven, **20**
B. O.'s Fish Wagon, **8**
The Café, **17**
Café Marquesa, **15**
Café Solé, **12**
Camille's Restaurant, **4**
Conch Republic Seafood Company, **3**

Croissants de France, **21**
Dante's Key West Restaurant and Pool Bar, **7**
Deuce's off the Hook Grill, **22**
El Meson de Pepe, **1**
El Siboney, **26**
Finnegan's Wake Irish Pub and Eatery, **9**
Half Shell Raw Bar, **6**
Jimmy Buffett's Margaritaville Cafe, **14**
Lobo's Mixed Grill, **18**

Louie's Backyard, **28**
Mangia Mangia, **11**
Michaels Restaurant, **13**
Nine One Five, **24**
Pisces, **25**
Salute Ristorante at the Beach, **29**
Santiago's Bodega, **19**
Sarabeth's, **16**
Seven Fish, **23**
Turtle Kraals, **5**

soup, Caribbean BBQ shrimp, bison strip steak with black-berry salad, and jerk chicken. Desserts and breads are baked on the premises. The banana bread and shrimp and grits are hits during breakfast, but the signature meal here is the lobster Benedict with key lime hollandaise. Bring patience, as there is always a wait. ⑤ *Average main: $24* ✉ *729 Thomas St.* ☎ *305/296–8666* ⊕ *www.blueheavenkw. com* ⌁ *Reservations not accepted* ⊘ *Closed after Labor Day for 6 weeks.*

$ ✕ **B.O.'s Fish Wagon.** *Seafood.* What started out as a fish house on wheels appears to have broken down on the corner of Caroline and William streets and is today the cornerstone for one of Key West's junkyard-chic dining institutions. Step up to the wood-plank counter window and order the specialty: a grouper sandwich fried or grilled and topped with key lime sauce. Other choices include fish nuts (don't be scared, they're just fried nuggets), hot dogs, cracked-conch sandwich, and shrimp or soft-shell-crab sandwich. Talk sass with your host and find a picnic table or take a seat at the plank. Grab some paper towels off one of the rolls hanging around and busy yourself reading graffiti, license plates, and irreverent signs. It's a must-do Key West experience. ⑤ *Average main: $12* ✉ *801 Caroline St.* ☎ *305/294–9272* ⊕ *www.bosfishwagon.com* ▭ *No credit cards.*

$ ✕ **The Café.** *Vegetarian.* You don't have to be a vegetarian to love this New Age café decorated with bright artwork and a corrugated tin–fronted counter. Local favorites include homemade soup, veggie sandwiches and burgers (order them with a side of sweet potato fries), grilled portobello mushroom salad, seafood, vegan specialties, stir-fry din-ners, and grilled Gorgonzola pizza. There's also a nice selection of draft beer and wines by the glass, plus daily desserts (including vegan selections). ⑤ *Average main: $11* ✉ *509 Southard St.* ☎ *305/296–5515* ⊕ *www.thecafekw.com* ⌁ *Reservations not accepted* ⊘ *Closed Sun.*

★ Fodor'sChoice ✕ **Café Marquesa.** *European.* Chef Susan Ferry
$$$ presents seven or more inspired entrées on her changing menu each night; delicious dishes can include yellowtail snapper with pear, ricotta pasta purses with caponata, and Australian rack of lamb crusted with goat cheese and a port-fig sauce. End your meal on a sweet note with key lime napoleon with tropical fruits and berries. There's also a fine selection of wines and custom martinis such as the key limetini and the Irish martini. Adjoining the intimate Mar-quesa Hotel, the dining room is equally relaxed and elegant.

5

⑤ *Average main: $29* ✉ *600 Fleming St.* ☎ *305/292–1244*
⊕ *www.marquesa.com* ⚘ *Reservations essential* ⊘ *No lunch.*

$$$ ✕ **Café Solé.** *French.* This little corner of France hides behind a high wall in a residential neighborhood. Inside, French training intertwines with local ingredients, creating delicious takes on classics, including a must-try conch carpaccio, yellowtail snapper with mango salsa, and some of the best bouillabaisse that you'll find outside of Marseilles. Hog snapper, aka hogfish, is a house specialty here, prepared several ways by Chef John Correa, including with beurre blanc or red pepper custard sauce. From the land, there is filet mignon with a wild-mushroom demi-glace. Lunch is served from 11 to 2, dinner from 5 to 10. ⑤ *Average main: $27* ✉ *1029 Southard St.* ☎ *305/294–0230* ⊕ *www.cafesole. com* ⚘ *Reservations essential.*

$$$ ✕ **Camille's Restaurant.** *Modern American.* Break out the stretchy pants because everything on the menu at this affordable hot spot not only sounds scrumptious, it is. Start your day with a shrimp, lobster, or crab-cake Benedict—the latter was voted best in the Florida Keys. Lunch brings dishes like hand-pulled chicken salad or a mahimahi wrap. Evenings will have you swooning for the famous grilled stone-crab cakes with an addictive Captain Morgan spiced-rum mango sauce. Locals have tried to keep this place a secret for over 20 years, but the word is out. Line up beneath the bright pink awning and happily wait for your seat. Be sure to ask your server about the Barbie dolls—they have a most unique collection, many with Key West flair. ⑤ *Average main: $21* ✉ *1202 Simonton St., at Catherine St.* ☎ *305/296-4811* ⊕ *www.camilleskeywest.com* ⚘ *Reservations essential.*

$$$ ✕ **Conch Republic Seafood Company.** *Seafood.* Because of its location where the fast ferry docks, Conch Republic does a brisk business. It's huge, open-air, and on the water, so the place is hard to miss. The menu is ambitious, offering more than just standard seafood fare. The baked oysters callaloo (a spinach-like green), for instance, are a Caribbean-style twist on oysters Rockefeller. The grilled or fried shrimp basket comes with a trio of sauces, including the house mixture. Paella, plantain-crusted mahimahi, seafood stir-fry, and steaks are some other options. Live music adds to the decibel level. ⑤ *Average main: $25* ✉ *631 Greene St., at Elizabeth St.* ☎ *305/294-4403* ⊕ *www.conchrepublic-seafood.com* ⚘ *Reservations not accepted.*

$ ✕ **Croissants de France.** *French.* Pop into the bakery for something sinfully sweet or spend some time people-watching at the sidewalk café next door. Try the eggs brioche with mustard sauce for breakfast. Quiche and savory crêpes (shrimp and brie, for instance) are the standouts at lunch and dinner, but you can also get delicious burgers and paninis. Finish off your meal with a dessert crêpe or chocolate Grand Marnier mousse. Ⓢ *Average main: $14* ✉ *816 Duval St.* ☎ *305/294–2624* ⊕ *www.croissantsdefrance.com* ⊗ *Closed Wed. Easter to Thanksgiving.*

$$ ✕ **Dante's Key West Restaurant and Pool Bar.** *Seafood.* With the motto "come be an aquaholic," Dante's is as unique as Key West itself. Sun loungers, tiki bars, and tables with umbrellas and chairs surround a large free-form swimming pool. Servers bring you drinks poolside and the lunch and dinner menus offer a surprising array of fresh seafood dishes, from she-crab soup and tuna *tataki* (a Japanese technique of searing and marinating fish or meat) to stone crabs and lobster. Weekdays are tame; weekend pool parties are somewhat legendary. Some tables on the pool deck have a set food-and-drink minimum. Ⓢ *Average main: $18* ✉ *Conch Harbor Marina, 951 Caroline St.* ☎ *305/423–2001* ⊕ *www.danteskeywest.com.*

$$$ ✕ **Deuce's Off the Hook Grill.** *Modern American.* It's a tight fit with only six tables (and six counter seats), but if you don't mind sitting close to fellow diners, you will be rewarded with a made-from-scratch meal almost anytime of day. Battered chicken tenders with waffles and *huevos rancheros* will rev up your morning. Coconut-crusted mahimahi with mango salsa is the signature lunch dish, but the lobster pie (pizza with poached lobster, goat cheese, arugula, and shaved fig) is a close second. Dinners run the gamut with the likes of "The Gobbler" (freshly roasted turkey with bacon smashed potatoes on a sage-stuffed waffle) to grouper in bouillabaisse with fennel. A specials board lists plenty of tempting options, too, but be sure to ask the price since seafood risotto might *sound* great, but when the reality hits your bill, your wallet won't be happy. Ⓢ *Average main: $21* ✉ *728 Simonton St.* ☎ *305/414–8428* ⌔ *Reservations essential.*

$$ ✕ **El Meson de Pepe.** *Cuban.* If you want to get a taste of the island's Cuban heritage, this is the place. Perfect for after watching a Mallory Square sunset, you can dine alfresco or in the dining room on refined versions of Cuban classics. Begin with a megasized mojito while you enjoy the basket of bread and savory sauces. The expansive menu offers *tostones rellenos* (green plantains with different traditional fillings), ceviche (raw fish "cooked" in lemon juice), and

more. Choose from Cuban specialties such as roasted pork in a cumin mojo sauce and *ropa vieja* (shredded beef stew). At lunch, the local Cuban population and cruise-ship passengers enjoy Cuban sandwiches and smaller versions of dinner's most popular entrées. A Latin band performs outside at the bar during sunset celebration. ⑤ *Average main: $19* ⊠ *Mallory Sq., 410 Wall St.* ☎ *305/295–2620* ⊕ *www. elmesondepepe.com.*

$ ✕ **El Siboney.** *Cuban.* Dining at this family-style restaurant is like going to Mom's for Sunday dinner—if your mother is Cuban. The dining room is noisy, and the food is traditional *cubano.* There are well-seasoned black beans, a memorable paella, traditional *ropa vieja* (shredded beef), and local seafood served grilled, stuffed, and breaded. Dishes come with plantains and beans and rice or salad and fries. To make a good thing even better, the prices are very reasonable. ⑤ *Average main: $10* ⊠ *900 Catherine St.* ☎ *305/296–4184* ⊕ *www.elsiboneyrestaurant.com* ⚑ *Reservations not accepted.*

$ ✕ **Finnegan's Wake Irish Pub and Eatery.** *Irish.* "Come for the beer. Stay for the food. Leave with the staff," is the slogan of this popular pub. The pictures of Beckett, Shaw, Yeats, and Wilde on the walls and the creaky wood floors underfoot exude Irish country warmth. Traditional fare includes bangers and mash, chicken potpie, and "colcannonballs"— rich mashed potatoes with scallions, cabbage, and cheese sauce. Irish bread pudding topped with whiskey sauce and custard is a true treat. Live music on weekends and daily happy hours from 4 to 7 and midnight to 2 featuring more than 30 beers on tap make it popular with the spring-break and sometimes-noisy drinking crowd, but you can find quieter spots in the back room and on the porch. ⑤ *Average main: $13* ⊠ *320 Grinnell St.* ☎ *305/293–0222* ⊕ *www. keywestirish.com* ⚑ *Reservations not accepted.*

$$ ✕ **Half Shell Raw Bar.** *Seafood.* Smack-dab on the docks, FAMILY this legendary institution gets its name from the oysters, clams, and peel-and-eat shrimp that are a departure point for its seafood-based diet. It's not clever recipes or fine dining (or even air-conditioning) that packs 'em in; it's fried fish, po'boy sandwiches, and seafood combos. For a break from the deep fryer, try the fresh and light conch seviche "cooked" with lime juice. The potato salad is flavored with dill, and the "PamaRita" is a new twist in Margaritaville. ⑤ *Average main: $16* ⊠ *Lands End Village at Historic Seaport, 231 Margaret St.* ☎ *305/294–7496* ⊕ *www.halfshellrawbar.com* ⚑ *Reservations not accepted.*

$$ ╳**Jimmy Buffett's Margaritaville Cafe.** *American.* If you must have your cheeseburger in paradise, it may as well be here, where you can chew along with the songs playing on the sound system, TV monitors, and movie screen. The first of Buffett's line of chain eateries, it belongs here more than anywhere else, but quite frankly it's more about the name, music, and attitude (and margaritas) than the food. The menu has a Cajun-Caribbean flair, with such offerings as conch chowder (good and spicy!), blackened hot dog, grilled andouille sausage with red beans and rice, grilled mahimahi with pineapple-mango salsa, and barbecued ribs. Live bands pack the place come dinner and into the wee hours. Ⓢ *Average main: $16* ⊠ *500 Duval St.* ☎ *305/292–1435* ⊕ *www.margaritaville.com* ⊗ *Reservations not accepted.*

$$$ ╳**Latitudes.** *Eclectic.* For a special treat, take the short boat ride to lovely Sunset Key for lunch or dinner on the beach. Creativity and quality ingredients combine for dishes that are bound to impress as much as the setting. For lunch, the fish tacos with chipotle aioli and salsa are a fine example of the chef's use of local foods. At dinner, start with the crispy lobster-crab cakes or seared yellowfin tuna stacked with mango, then move on to one of the delightful entrées, such as yellowtail snapper with coconut-lime sauce, sweet potato–crusted grouper, or Wagyu skirt steak with mocha demi-glace. Choose a table inside looking out over the gulf or on the patio. The restaurant also serves breakfast. Ⓢ *Average main: $28* ⊠ *Sunset Village, 245 Front St.* ☎ *305/292–5300, 888/477–7786* ⊕ *www.westinsunsetkeycottages.com/latitudes-restaurant* ⊗ *Reservations essential.*

$ ╳**Lobo's Mixed Grill.** *American.* Famous for its selection of FAMILY wrap sandwiches, Lobo's has a reputation among locals for its 8-ounce, charcoal-grilled ground chuck burger—thick and juicy and served with lettuce, tomato, and pickle on a toasted bun. Mix it up with toppings like Brie, blue cheese, or portobello mushroom. The menu of 30 wraps includes rib eye, oyster, grouper, Cuban, and chicken Caesar. The menu includes salads and quesadillas, as well as a fried-shrimp-and-oyster combo. Beer and wine are served. This courtyard food stand closes around 5, so eat early. Most of Lobo's business is takeout (it has a half-dozen outdoor picnic tables), and it offers free delivery within Old Town. Ⓢ *Average main: $9* ⊠ *5 Key Lime Sq., east of intersection of Southard and Duval Sts.* ☎ *305/296–5303* ⊕ *www.lobosmixedgrill.com* ⊗ *Reservations not accepted* ⊗ *Closed Sun. Apr.–early Dec.*

$$$$ × **Louie's Backyard.** *Eclectic.* Feast your eyes on a steal-your-breath-away view and beautifully presented dishes prepared by executive chef Doug Shook. Once you get over sticker shock on the seasonally changing menu, settle in on the outside deck and enjoy dishes like grilled scallops with portobello relish, grilled king salmon with fried risotto, and mint-rubbed pork chop with salsa verde. A more affordable option upstairs is the Upper Deck, which serves tapas such as flaming ouzo shrimp, roasted olives with onion and feta, and Gruyère and duck confit pizza. If you come for lunch, the menu is less expensive but the view is just as fantastic. For night owls, the tin-roofed Afterdeck Bar serves cocktails on the water until the wee hours. ⑤ *Average main: $36* ⊠ *700 Waddell Ave.* ☎ *305/294–1061* ⊕ *www.louiesbackyard.com* ⌕ *Reservations essential* ⊗ *Closed Labor Day to mid-Sept. Upper Deck closed Sun. and Mon. No lunch at Upper Deck.*

$$ × **Mangia Mangia.** *Italian.* This longtime favorite serves large portions of homemade pastas that can be matched with any of their homemade sauces. Tables are arranged in a brick garden hung with twinkling lights and in a cozy, casual dining room in an old house. Everything out of the open kitchen is outstanding, including the *bollito misto di mare* (fresh seafood sautéed with garlic, shallots, white wine, and pasta) or the memorable spaghettini "schmappellini," homemade pasta with asparagus, tomatoes, pine nuts, and Parmesan. The wine list—with more than 350 offerings—includes old and rare vintages, and also has a good by-the-glass selection. ⑤ *Average main: $16* ⊠ *900 Southard St.* ☎ *305/294–2469* ⊕ *www.mangia-mangia.com* ⌕ *Reservations not accepted* ⊗ *No lunch.*

$$$ × **Michaels Restaurant.** *American.* White tablecloths, subdued lighting, and romantic music give Michaels the feel of an urban eatery. Garden seating reminds you that you are in the Keys. Chef-owner Michael Wilson flies in prime rib, cowboy steaks, and rib eyes from Allen Brothers in Chicago, which has supplied top-ranked steak houses for more than a century. Also on the menu is a melt-in-your-mouth grouper stuffed with jumbo lump crab, Kobe and tenderloin meat loaf, veal saltimbocca, and a variety of made-to-order fondue dishes (try the pesto pot, spiked with hot pepper and basil). To lighten up, smaller portions of many of the favorites are available until 7:30 Sunday through Thursday. The Hemingway (mojito-style) and the Third Degree (raspberry vodka and white crème de cacao) top the cocktail menu. ⑤ *Average main: $25* ⊠ *532*

Margaret St. ☎305/295–1300 ⊕*www.michaelskeywest.com* ⚹*Reservations essential* ⊘*No lunch.*

$$$ ✕**Nine One Five.** *Eclectic.* Twinkling lights draped along the lower- and upper-level outdoor porches of a 100-year-old Victorian mansion set an elegant—though unstuffy—stage here. If you like to sample and sip, you'll appreciate the variety of smaller plate selections and wines by the glass. Starters include a cheese platter, crispy duck confit, a tapas platter, and the signature "tuna dome" with fresh crab, lemon-miso dressing, and an ahi tuna–sashimi wrapping. There are also larger plates if you're craving something like seafood soup or steak au poivre frites. Dine outdoors and people-watch along upper Duval, or sit at a table inside while listening to light jazz. ⑤*Average main: $28* ⊠*915 Duval St.* ☎305/296–0669 ⊕*www.915duval.com* ⚹*Reservations essential* ⊘*No lunch.*

$$$$ ✕**Pisces.** *European.* In a circa-1892 former store and home, chef William Arnel and staff create a contemporary setting with a stylish granite bar, Andy Warhol originals, and glass oil lamps. Favorites include "lobster tango mango," flambéed in cognac and served with saffron butter sauce and sliced mangoes; filet mignon with bordelaise sauce; and yellowtail Atocha with lemon brown butter, shrimp, and scallops. ⑤*Average main: $35* ⊠*1007 Simonton St.* ☎*305/294–7100* ⊕*www.pisceskeywest.com* ⚹*Reservations essential* ⊘*No lunch.*

$$ ✕**Salute Ristorante at the Beach.** *Italian.* Sister restaurant to Blue Heaven, this colorful establishment sits on Higgs Beach, giving it one of the island's best lunch views—and a bit of sand and salt spray on a windy day. The intriguing menu is Italian with a Caribbean flair and will not disappoint. For dinner, popular dishes include linguine with mussels, lasagna, and white bean soup. At lunch the gazpacho refreshes with great flavor and texture, and the calamari marinara, antipasti sandwich, and yellowtail sandwich will having you singing *amore.* ⑤*Average main: $20* ⊠*1000 Atlantic Blvd., Higgs Beach* ☎*305/292–1117* ⊕*www.saluteonthebeach.com* ⚹*Reservations not accepted.*

★ Fodor'sChoice ✕**Santiago's Bodega.** *Tapas.* If you've ever won-
$ dered where chefs go for a great meal in the Lower Keys, this is their secret spot. Picky palates will be satisfied at this funky, dark, and sensuous corner house, which is well off the main drag. Dine on the front porch surrounded by fuchsia bougainvillea or inside amid eclectic paintings and mismatched chandeliers. Waiters recommend choosing three of the small plates per person, then sharing. That

number works. Cold tapas include dishes like yellowfin tuna seviche with large hunks of avocado and mango, and shaved beef carpaccio with smoked sea salt and truffle oil. Favorite hot tapas are filet mignon with creamy gorgonzola butter and cherry-hoisin-glazed beef short ribs. Dessert? The bread pudding is legendary. Reward yourself for finding this place with a fruit-filled glass of homemade red or white sangria. All bets say you'll eat here over and over again. ⑤ *Average main: $13* ✉ *Bahama Village, 207 Petronia St.* ☎ *305/296–7691* ⊕ *www.santiagosbodega.com* ⚲ *Reservations essential.*

$$ ✕ **Sarabeth's.** *American.* Named for the award-winning jam maker and pastry chef Sarabeth Levine, who runs the kitchen, it naturally is proclaimed for its all-morning, all-afternoon breakfast, best enjoyed in the picket-fenced front yard of this circa-1870 synagogue. Lemon ricotta pancakes, pumpkin waffles, omelets, and homemade jams make the meal. Lunch offerings range from a griddled smoked mozzarella sandwich to poached salmon "Cobb" salad. Start dinner with the signature velvety cream of tomato soup, or roasted red beets and Gorgonzola salad. The daily special augments the short entrée listing that includes meat loaf, green chili pepper macaroni with three cheeses, and grilled mahimahi with tomatillo sauce. In the mood for dessert? The warm orange-apricot bread pudding takes its cues from Sarabeth's most popular flavor of jam. ⑤ *Average main: $20* ✉ *530 Simonton St., at Souhard St .* ☎ *305/293–8181* ⊕ *www.sarabethskeywest.com* ⚲ *Reservations not accepted* ⊘ *Closed Mon.; Christmas through Easter, closed Tues.*

$$$ ✕ **Seven Fish.** *Seafood.* A local hot spot, this intimate, off-the-beaten-track eatery is good for an eclectic mix of dishes like tropical shrimp salsa, wild-mushroom quesadilla, seafood marinara, and old-fashioned meat loaf with real mashed potatoes. For dessert, the sweet potato pie provides an added measure of down-home comfort. Those in the know reserve for dinner early to snag one of the 20 or so tables clustered in the bare-bones dining room. ⑤ *Average main: $26* ✉ *632 Olivia St.* ☎ *305/296–2777* ⊕ *www.7fish.com* ⚲ *Reservations essential* ⊘ *Closed Tues. No lunch.*

$$ ✕ **Turtle Kraals.** *Seafood.* Named for the kraals, or corrals, FAMILY where sea turtles were once kept until they went to the cannery, this place calls to mind the island's history. The lunch/dinner menu offers an assortment of marine cuisine that includes seafood enchiladas, mesquite-grilled fish of the day, and mango crab cakes. The slow-cook wood smoker results in wonderfully tender ribs, brisket, mesquite-grilled oysters

with Parmesan and cilantro, and mesquite-grilled chicken sandwich. The open restaurant overlooks the marina at the Historic Seaport. Turtle races entertain during happy hour on Monday and Friday at 6 pm. ⑤ *Average main: $16* ✉ *231 Margaret St.* ☎ *305/294–2640* ⊕ *www.turtlekraals.com.*

NEW TOWN

$ ✕ **Hogfish Bar & Grill.** *Seafood.* It's worth a drive to Stock Island, just outside Key West, to sit along one of Florida's last surviving working waterfronts, watch the shrimpers and fishermen unloading their catch, and indulge in the freshness you're witnessing at this down-to-earth spot. Hogfish is of course the specialty. The "Killer Hogfish Sandwich" comes on Cuban Bread (you can also have it as a breakfast Benedict); sprinkle it with one of the house hot sauces. Other favorites include lobster BLT, pulled pork sandwich, hogfish tacos, gator bites, lobster potpie, and barbeque ribs. ⑤ *Average main: $13* ✉ *6810 Front St., Stock Island* ☎ *305/293–4041* ⊕ *www.hogfishbar.com.*

$$$ ✕ **Tavern N Town.** *Eclectic.* This handsome and warm restaurant has an open kitchen that adds lovely aromas from the wood-fired oven. The dinner menu offers a variety of options such as small plates of shrimp cocktail and Wagyu beef sliders and small pizzas for starters. For an entrée, try the coffee-crusted pork tenderloin with pine chutney or the prime rib. Bragging rights continue, as they've won the Master Chef's Classic at the Key West Food & Wine Festival for three years running. ⑤ *Average main: $26* ✉ *Key West Marriott Beachside Resort, 3841 N. Roosevelt Blvd.* ☎ *305/296–8100, 800/546–0885* ⊕ *www.beachsidekeywest. com* ⊗ *No lunch.*

WHERE TO STAY

Historic cottages, restored century-old Conch houses, and large resorts are among the offerings in Key West, the majority charging between $100 and $300 a night. In high season, Christmas through Easter, you'll be hard-pressed to find a decent room for less than $200, and most places raise prices considerably during holidays and festivals. Many guesthouses and inns do not welcome children under 16, and most do not permit smoking indoors. Most tariffs include an expanded Continental breakfast and, often, afternoon wine or snack.

LODGING ALTERNATIVES

The Key West Innkeepers Association is an umbrella organization for dozens of local properties. Vacation Rentals Key West lists historic cottages, homes, and condominiums for rent. Rent Key West Vacations specializes in renting vacation homes and condos for a week or longer. Vacation Key West lists all kinds of properties throughout Key West.

Key West Innkeepers Association ☎ *305/295–1334, 800/492–1911* ⊕ *www.keywestinns.com.*

Rent Key West Vacations ✉ *1075 Duval St., Ste. C11* ☎ *305/294–0990, 800/833–7368* ⊕ *www.rentkeywest.com.*

Vacation Key West ✉ *100 Grinnell St.* ☎ *305/295–9500, 800/595–5397* ⊕ *www.vacationkw.com.*

Vacation Rentals Key West ☎ *305/292–7997, 888/775–3993* ⊕ *www.keywestvacations.com.*

OLD TOWN

$$$ ⊡ **Ambrosia Key West.** *B&B/Inn.* If you desire personal attention, a casual atmosphere, and a dollop of style, stay at these twin inns spread out on nearly 2 acres. **Pros:** spacious rooms; poolside breakfast; friendly staff. **Cons:** on-street parking can be tough to come by; a little too spread out. ⑤ *Rooms from: $319* ✉ *615, 618, 622 Fleming St.* ☎ *305/296–9838, 800/535–9838* ⊕ *www.ambrosiakeywest.com* ⤳ *6 rooms, 3 town houses, 1 cottage, 10 suites* ⑩ *Breakfast.*

$ ⊡ **Angelina Guest House.** *B&B/Inn.* In the heart of Old Town, this home away from home offers simple, clean, attractively priced accommodations. **Pros:** good value; nice garden; friendly staff. **Cons:** thin walls; basic rooms; shared balcony. ⑤ *Rooms from: $109* ✉ *302 Angela St.* ☎ *305/294–4480, 888/303–4480* ⊕ *www.angelinaguesthouse.com* ⤳ *13 rooms* ⑩ *Breakfast.*

$$ ⊡ **Azul Key West.** *B&B/Inn.* The ultramodern—nearly minimalistic—redo of this classic circa-1903 Queen Anne mansion is a break from the sensory overload of Key West's other abundant Victorian guesthouses. **Pros:** lovely building; marble-floored baths; luxurious linens. **Cons:** on a busy street. ⑤ *Rooms from: $249* ✉ *907 Truman Ave.* ☎ *305/296–5152, 888/253–2985* ⊕ *www.azulhotels.us* ⤳ *10 rooms, 1 suite* ⑩ *Breakfast.*

$$$ ⊡ **Casa Marina Resort & Beach Club.** *Resort.* At any moment,
FAMILY you expect the landed gentry to walk across the oceanfront

Old Town Key West Hotels

Fleming Key

Key West Bight

TO SUNSET KEY →

ATLANTIC OCEAN

Ambrosia Key West, **6**
Angelina Guest House, **15**
Azul Key West, **22**
Casa Marina Resort & Beach Club, **29**
Courtney's Place, **17**
Crown Plaza Key West–La Concha, **14**
Eden House, **12**
The Gardens Hotel, **16**
Harborside Motel & Marina, **23**
Heron House Court, **11**

Hyatt Key West Resort & Spa, **3**
Island City House Hotel, **9**
Island House, **13**
Key Lime Inn, **19**
Key West Bed and Breakfast/The Popular House, **8**
La Pensione, **21**
Marquesa Hotel, **7**
Merlin Guesthouse, **18**
Mermaid & the Alligator, **20**
Ocean Breeze Inn, **26**

Ocean Key Resort & Spa, **1**
Pier House Resort and Caribbean Spa, **2**
The Reach Resort, **28**
Santa Maria Suites , **27**
Simonton Court, **5**
Southernmost Hotel , **25**
Speakeasy Inn, **24**
Westin Key West Resort & Marina, **4**
Westwinds Inn, **10**

lawn of this luxurious resort, just as they did when this 13-acre resort was built back in the 1920s. **Pros:** nice beach; historic setting; away from the crowds. **Cons:** long walk to central Old Town; expensive resort fee. ⑤ *Rooms from: $359* ✉ *1500 Reynolds St.* ☎ *305/296–3535, 866/203–6392* ⊕ *www.casamarinaresort.com* ⤢ *241 rooms, 70 suites* ⓘ *No meals.*

$$ ⊡ **Courtney's Place.** *B&B/Inn.* If you like kids, cats, and dogs, you'll feel right at home in this collection of accommodations ranging from cigar-maker cottages to shotgun houses. **Pros:** near Duval Street; fairly priced. **Cons:** small parking lot; small pool, minimum-stay requirements. ⑤ *Rooms from: $249* ✉ *720 Whitmarsh Ln., off Petronia St.* ☎ *305/294–3480, 800/869–4639* ⊕ *www. courtneysplacekeywest.com* ⤢ *6 rooms, 2 suites, 2 efficiencies, 8 cottages* ⓘ *Breakfast.*

$$ ⊡ **Crowne Plaza Key West–La Concha.** *Hotel.* History and franchises can mix, as this 1920s-vintage hotel proves with its handsome faux-palm atrium lobby and sleep-conducive rooms. **Pros:** restaurant and Starbucks in-house; close to downtown attractions; free Wi-Fi. **Cons:** high-traffic area; confusing layout; expensive valet-only parking. ⑤ *Rooms from: $199* ✉ *430 Duval St.* ☎ *305/296–2991* ⊕ *www. laconchakeywest.com* ⤢ *160 rooms, 8 rooms with balconies, 10 suites* ⓘ *No meals.*

$ ⊡ **Eden House.** *Hotel.* From the vintage metal rockers on the street-side porch to the old neon hotel sign in the lobby, this 1920s rambling Key West mainstay hotel is high on character, low on gloss. **Pros:** free parking; hot tub is actually hot; daily happy hour around the pool; discount at excellent Azur restaurant. **Cons:** pricey; a bit of a musty smell in some rooms; no TV in some rooms. ⑤ *Rooms from: $200* ✉ *1015 Fleming St.* ☎ *305/296–6868, 800/533–5397* ⊕ *www.edenhouse.com* ⤢ *36 rooms, 8 suites* ⓘ *No meals.*

★ **Fodor's**Choice ⊡ **The Gardens Hotel.** *Hotel.* Built in 1875, this **$$$** gloriously shaded, award-winning property was a labor of love from the get-go, and it covers a third of a city block in Old Town. **Pros:** luxurious bathrooms; secluded garden seating; free domestic phone calls and Wi-Fi. **Cons:** hard to get reservations; expensive; nightly secure parking fee. ⑤ *Rooms from: $385* ✉ *526 Angela St.* ☎ *305/294–2661, 800/526–2664* ⊕ *www.gardenshotel.com* ⤢ *17 rooms* ⓘ *Breakfast.*

$ ⊡ **Harborside Motel & Marina.** *Hotel.* This little motel neatly packages three appealing characteristics—affordability, safety, and a pleasant location between Old Town and

New Town at Garrison Bight. **Pros:** grills for cookouts; friendly fishing atmosphere; boat slips. **Cons:** more than a mile from Duval Street; cash deposit for keys required. ⑤*Rooms from: $139* ⊠*903 Eisenhower Dr.* ☎*305/294–2780, 800/501–7823* ⊕*www.keywestharborside.com* ⇋*7 rooms, 5 efficiencies, 4 houseboats* ⓞ*No meals.*

$$ ☑ **Heron House Court.** *B&B/Inn.* Conch-style architecture harks back to this property's circa-1900 origins as a boarding house and cigar-maker cottages. **Pros:** charming; fluffy bathrobes. **Cons:** faces noisy Eaton Street; owner's suite smells musty. ⑤*Rooms from: $219* ⊠*412 Frances St.* ☎*305/296–4719, 888/265–2395* ⊕*www.heronhousecourt. com* ⇋*2 suites, 14 rooms* ⓞ*Breakfast.*

$$ ☑ **Hyatt Key West Resort and Spa.** *Resort.* With its own man-
FAMILY made beach, the Hyatt Key West is one of few resorts where you can dig your toes in the sand, then walk a short distance away to the streets of Old Town. **Pros:** a little bit away from the bustle of Old Town; plenty of activities. **Cons:** beach is small; cramped-feeling property. ⑤*Rooms from: $290* ⊠*601 Front St.* ☎*305/809–1234* ⊕*www.keywest.hyatt. com* ⇋*118 rooms* ⓞ*No meals.*

$$ ☑ **Island City House Hotel.** *B&B/Inn.* A private garden with brick walkways, tropical plants, and a canopy of palms sets this convivial guesthouse apart from the pack. **Pros:** lush gardens; knowledgeable staff. **Cons:** spotty Wi-Fi service; no front-desk staff at night; some rooms are small. ⑤*Rooms from: $295* ⊠*411 William St.* ☎*305/294–5702, 800/634–8230* ⊕*www.islandcityhouse.com* ⇋*24 suites* ⓞ*No meals.*

$$ ☑ **Island House.** *Hotel.* Geared specifically toward gay men, this hotel features a health club, a video lounge, a café and bar, and rooms in historic digs. **Pros:** lots of privacy; just the place to get that all-over tan; free happy hour for guests. **Cons:** no women allowed; some shared baths. ⑤*Rooms from: $235* ⊠*1129 Fleming St.* ☎*305/294–6284, 800/890–6284* ⊕*www.islandhousekeywest.com* ⇋*34 rooms, 3 with shared bath* ⓞ*No meals.*

$ ☑ **Key Lime Inn.** *B&B/Inn.* This 1854 Grand Bahama–style house on the National Register of Historic Places succeeds by offering amiable service, a great location, and simple rooms with natural-wood furnishings. **Pros:** free parking; some rooms have private outdoor spaces. **Cons:** standard rooms are pricey; pool faces a busy street; mulch-covered paths. ⑤*Rooms from: $179* ⊠*725 Truman Ave.* ☎*305/294–5229, 800/549–4430* ⊕*www.keylimeinn.com* ⇋*37 rooms* ⓞ*Breakfast.*

$ ⊠ **Key West Bed and Breakfast/The Popular House.** *B&B/Inn.* There are accommodations for every budget, but the owners reason that budget travelers deserve as pleasant an experience (and lavish a tropical Continental breakfast) as their well-heeled counterparts. **Pros:** lots of art; tiled outdoor shower; hot tub and sauna area is a welcome hangout. **Cons:** some rooms are small. ⑤*Rooms from: $99* ⊠*415 William St.* ☎*305/296–7274, 800/438–6155* ⊕*www.keywestbandb.com* ✏*10 rooms, 6 with private bath* ⦿*Breakfast.*

$$ ⊠ **La Pensione.** *B&B/Inn.* Hospitality and period furnishings make this 1891 home, once owned by a cigar executive, a wonderful glimpse into Key West life in the late 19th century. **Pros:** pine-paneled walls; off-street parking; some rooms have wraparound porches. **Cons:** street-facing rooms are noisy. ⑤*Rooms from: $258* ⊠*809 Truman Ave.* ☎*305/292–9923, 800/893–1193* ⊕*www.lapensione.com* ✏*9 rooms* ⦿*Breakfast.*

★ **Fodor's**Choice ⊠ **Marquesa Hotel.** *Hotel.* In a town that prides **$$$** itself on its laid-back luxury, this complex of four restored 1884 houses stands out. **Pros:** elegant setting; romantic atmosphere; turndown service. **Cons:** street-facing rooms can be noisy; expensive rates. ⑤*Rooms from: $345* ⊠*600 Fleming St.* ☎*305/292–1919, 800/869–4631* ⊕*www. marquesa.com* ✏*27 rooms* ⦿*No meals.*

$$ ⊠ **Merlin Guesthouse.** *B&B/Inn.* Key West guesthouses don't usually welcome families, but this laid-back jumble of rooms and suites is an exception. **Pros:** good location near Duval Street; good rates. **Cons:** neighbor noise; street parking. ⑤*Rooms from: $279* ⊠*811 Simonton St.* ☎*305/296–3336, 800/642–4753* ⊕*www.merlinguesthouse.com* ✏*10 rooms, 6 suites, 4 cottages* ⦿*Breakfast.*

$$ ⊠ **Mermaid & the Alligator.** *B&B/Inn.* An enchanting combination of flora and fauna makes this 1904 Victorian house a welcoming retreat. **Pros:** hot plunge pool; massage pavilion; island-getaway feel. **Cons:** minimum stay required (length depends on season); dark public areas; plastic lawn chairs. ⑤*Rooms from: $268* ⊠*729 Truman Ave.* ☎*305/294–1894, 800/773–1894* ⊕*www.kwmermaid. com* ✏*9 rooms* ⦿*Breakfast.*

$ ⊠ **Ocean Breeze Inn.** *B&B/Inn.* What this simple South Beach area motel lacks in style it makes up for in value. **Pros:** early (2 pm) check-in; clean and spacious rooms; staff remembers your name. **Cons:** bland decor; small pool; no staff after 6 pm. ⑤*Rooms from: $200* ⊠*625 South St.*

☎ *305/296–2829, 877/879–2362* ⊕ *www.oceanbreezeinn. com* ⇆ *15 rooms* ❍ *Breakfast.*

★ **Fodor's**Choice 🏨 **Ocean Key Resort & Spa.** *Resort.* A pool and
$$$$ lively open-air bar and restaurant sit on Sunset Pier, a
popular place to watch the sun sink into the horizon. **Pros:**
well-trained staff; lively pool scene; best spa on the island.
Cons: $20 per night valet parking; too bustling for some;
pricey. ⑤ *Rooms from: $450* ⊠ *Zero Duval St.* ☎ *305/296–
7701, 800/328–9815* ⊕ *www.oceankey.com* ⇆ *64 rooms,
36 suites* ❍ *No meals.*

$$$$ 🏨 **Pier House Resort and Caribbean Spa.** *Resort.* The location—on a quiet stretch of beach at the foot of Duval—is
ideal as a buffer from and gateway to the action. **Pros:**
beautiful beach; good location; nice spa. **Cons:** lots of
conventions; poolside rooms are small; not really suitable
for children under 16. ⑤ *Rooms from: $460* ⊠ *1 Duval St.*
☎ *305/296–4600, 800/327–8340* ⊕ *www.pierhouse.com*
⇆ *116 rooms, 26 suites* ❍ *No meals.*

$$ 🏨 **The Reach Resort.** *Resort.* Embracing Key West's only natu-
ral beach, this full-service, luxury resort offers sleek rooms
with modern amenities as well as shared access to its sister
Casa Marina resort nearby. **Pros:** removed from Duval
hubbub; great sunrise views; pullout sofas in most rooms.
Cons: expensive resort fee; high rates. ⑤ *Rooms from: $300*
⊠ *1435 Simonton St.* ☎ *305/296–5000, 888/318–4316*
⊕ *www.reachresort.com* ⇆ *72 rooms, 78 suites* ❍ *No meals.*

★ **Fodor's**Choice 🏨 **Santa Maria Suites.** *Rental.* It's odd to call this
$$$ a hidden gem when it sits on a prominent corner just one
block off Duval, but you'd never know the luxury that
awaits behind its concrete facade. **Pros:** amenities galore;
front desk concierge services; private parking lot. **Cons:**
daily resort fee; beds low to the ground. ⑤ *Rooms from:
$350* ⊠ *1401 Simonton St.* ☎ *866/726–8259, 305/296–5678*
⊕ *www.santamariasuites.com* ⇆ *34 suites* ❍ *No meals.*

$$ 🏨 **Simonton Court.** *B&B/Inn.* A small world all its own, this
adult lodging makes you feel deliciously sequestered from
Key West's crasser side, but close enough to get there on
foot. **Pros:** lots of privacy; well-appointed accommodations;
friendly staff. **Cons:** minimum stays required in high season.
⑤ *Rooms from: $275* ⊠ *320 Simonton St.* ☎ *305/294–6386,
800/944–2687* ⊕ *www.simontoncourt.com* ⇆ *17 rooms, 6
suites, 6 cottages* ❍ *Breakfast.*

$$$ 🏨 **Southernmost Hotel.** *Hotel.* This hotel's location on the
quiet end of Duval means you don't have to deal with
the hustle and bustle of downtown unless you want to—
it's within a 20-minute walk (but around sunset, this end

of town gets its share of car and foot traffic). **Pros:** pool attracts a lively crowd; access to nearby properties and beach; free parking and Wi-Fi. **Cons:** can get crowded around the pool and public areas; expensive nightly resort fee. ⑤ *Rooms from: $359* ✉ *1319 Duval St.* ☎ *305/296–6577, 800/354–4455* ⊕ *www.southernmostresorts.com* ⌁ *124 rooms* ⎮⚪⎮ *No meals.*

$ ⌘ **Speakeasy Inn.** *B&B/Inn.* During Prohibition, Raul Vasquez made this place popular by smuggling in rum from Cuba; today its reputation is for having reasonably priced rooms within walking distance of the beach. **Pros:** good location; reasonable rates; kitchenettes. **Cons:** no pool; on busy Duval. ⑤ *Rooms from: $169* ✉ *1117 Duval St.* ☎ *305/296–2680* ⊕ *www.speakeasyinn.com* ⌁ *4 suites* ⎮⚪⎮ *Breakfast.*

★ **Fodor'sChoice** ⌘ **Sunset Key.** *Resort.* This private island retreat $$$$ with its own sandy beach feels completely cut off from the world, yet you're just minutes away from the action. **Pros:** peace and quiet; roomy verandas; free 24-hour shuttle; free Wi-Fi. **Cons:** luxury doesn't come cheap. ⑤ *Rooms from: $695* ✉ *245 Front St.* ☎ *305/292–5300, 888/477–7786* ⊕ *www.westinsunsetkeycottages.com* ⌁ *40 cottages* ⎮⚪⎮ *Breakfast.*

$$$$ ⌘ **Westin Key West Resort & Marina.** *Resort.* This waterfront resort's two three-story, Keys-style buildings huddle around its 37-slip marina in the middle of Old Town. **Pros:** good location; bar and restaurant overlook Mallory Square; access to Sunset Key; free Wi-Fi. **Cons:** feels too big for Key West; often crowded; conference clientele. ⑤ *Rooms from: $409* ✉ *245 Front St.* ☎ *305/294–4000* ⊕ *www.westin.com/keywest* ⌁ *146 rooms, 32 suites* ⎮⚪⎮ *No meals.*

$ ⌘ **Westwinds Inn.** *B&B/Inn.* This cluster of historic gingerbread-trimmed houses has individually decorated rooms that make you feel right at home, if your home has standard white wicker furniture and inexpensive art on the walls. **Pros:** away from Old Town's bustle; lots of character; affordable rates. **Cons:** small lobby; confusing layout; a long walk from Duval Street. ⑤ *Rooms from: $200* ✉ *914 Eaton St.* ☎ *305/296–4440, 800/788–4150* ⊕ *www.westwindskeywest.-com* ⌁ *21 rooms, 4 suites* ⎮⚪⎮ *Breakfast.*

THE HOLIDAYS KEY WEST STYLE

On New Year's Eve, Key West celebrates the turning of the calendar page with three separate ceremonies that parody New York's dropping-of-the-ball drama. Here they let fall a 6-foot conch shell from Sloppy Joe's Bar, a pirate wench from the towering mast of a tall ship at the Historic Seaport, and a drag queen (elegantly decked out in a ball gown and riding an oversize red high-heel shoe) at Bourbon Street Pub. You wouldn't expect any less from America's most outrageous city.

Key West is one of the nation's biggest party towns, so the celebrations here take on a colorful hue. In keeping with Key West's rich maritime heritage, its month-long Bight Before Christmas begins Thanksgiving Eve at Key West Bight. The Lighted Boat Parade creates a quintessential Florida spectacle with live music and decorated vessels of all shapes and sizes.

Some years, Tennessee Williams Theatre hosts a Key West version of the Nutcracker. In this unorthodox retelling, the heroine sails to a coral reef and is submerged in a diving bell. (What? No sugarplum fairies?) Between Christmas and New Year's Day, the Holiday House and Garden Tour is another yuletide tradition.

NEW TOWN

$ ☷**Best Western Key Ambassador Resort Inn.** *Hotel.* You know what to expect from this chain hotel: well-maintained rooms, predictable service, and competitive prices. **Pros:** big pool area; popular tiki bar. **Cons:** airport noise; lacks personality. Ⓢ*Rooms from: $200* ✉*3755 S. Roosevelt Blvd., New Town* ☎*305/296–3500, 800/432–4315* ⊕*www.keyambassador.com* ⬆*101 rooms* ❍*Breakfast.*

$$$ ☷**Key West Marriott Beachside Hotel.** *Hotel.* This hotel vies for convention business with the biggest ballroom in Key West, but it also appeals to families with its spacious condo units decorated with impeccable good taste. **Pros:** private beach; poolside cabanas. **Cons:** small beach; long walk to Old Town; cookie-cutter facade. Ⓢ*Rooms from: $340* ✉*3841 N. Roosevelt Blvd., New Town* ☎*305/296–8100, 800/546–0885* ⊕*www.keywestmarriottbeachside.com* ⬆*93 rooms, 93 1-bedroom suites, 10 2-bedroom suites, 26 3-bedroom suites* ❍*No meals.*

$$$ ☷**Parrot Key Resort.** *Hotel.* This revamped destination resort feels like an old-fashioned beach community with picket

fences and rocking-chair porches. **Pros:** four pools; finely appointed units; access to marina and other facilities at three sister properties in Marathon. **Cons:** outside walking distance to Old Town; no transportation provided; hefty resort fee. ⑤ *Rooms from: $329* ✉ *2801 N. Roosevelt Blvd., New Town* ☎ *305/809–2200* ⊕ *www.parrotkeyresort.com* ⌁*74 rooms, 74 suites, 74 3-bedroom villas* ⊚*No meals.*

NIGHTLIFE AND PERFORMING ARTS

NIGHTLIFE

Rest up: Much of what happens in Key West occurs after dark. Open your mind and take a stroll. Scruffy street performers strum next to dogs in sunglasses. Characters wearing parrots or iguanas try to sell you your photo with their pet. Brawls tumble out the doors of Sloppy Joe's. Drag queens strut across stages in Joan Rivers garb. Tattooed men lick whipped cream off women's body parts. And margaritas flow like a Jimmy Buffett tune.

Best of the Bars. Southernmost Scavenger Hunt's "Best of the Bars" challenge has teams of two to five touring the bars of Key West for clues, libations, and prizes. It hosts the event at 7 pm most Fridays, Saturdays, and Sundays, starting at Sloppy Joe's. The cost is $20 per person. For information, call ☎ *305/292–9994* or visit ⊕ *www.keywesthunt.com.*

BARS AND LOUNGES

Capt. Tony's Saloon. When it was the original Sloppy Joe's in the mid-1930s, Hemingway was a regular. Later, a young Jimmy Buffett sang here and made this watering hole famous in his song "Last Mango in Paris." Captain Tony was even voted mayor of Key West. Yes, this place is a beloved landmark. Stop in and take a look at the "hanging tree" that grows through the roof, listen to live music seven nights a week, and play some pool. ✉ *428 Greene St.* ☎ *305/294–1838* ⊕ *www.capttonyssaloon.com.*

Cowboy Bill's Honky Tonk Saloon. Ride the mechanical bucking bull, listen to live bands croon cry-in-your-beer tunes, and grab some pretty decent chow at the indoor-outdoor spread known as Cowboy Bill's Honky Tonk Saloon. There's live music from Tuesday through Saturday. Wednesday brings—we kid you not—sexy bull riding. ✉ *610½ Duval St.* ☎ *305/295–8219* ⊕ *www.cowboybillskw.com.*

Durty Harry's. This megasize entertainment complex is home to eight different bars and clubs, both indoor and outdoor. Their motto is, "Eight Famous Bars, One Awesome Night," and they're right. You'll find pizza, dancing, live music, a martini bar, and the infamous Red Garter strip club. ✉ *208 Duval St.* ☎ *305/296–5513.*

The Garden of Eden. Perhaps one of Duval's more unusual and intriguing watering holes, The Garden of Eden sits atop the Bull & Whistle saloon and has a clothing-optional policy. Most drinkers are looky-lous, but some actually bare it all, including the barmaids. ✉ *Bull & Whistle Bar, 224 Duval St.* ☎ *305/396–4565* ⊕ *www.bullkeywest.com.*

Green Parrot Bar. Pause for a libation in the open-air and breathe in the spirit of Key West. Built in 1890 as a grocery store, this property has been many things to many people over the years. It's touted as the oldest bar in Key West and the sometimes-rowdy saloon has locals outnumbering out-of-towners, especially on nights when bands play. ✉ *601 Whitehead St., at Southard St.* ☎ *305/294–6133* ⊕ *www. greenparrot.com.*

Hog's Breath Saloon. Belly up to the bar for a cold mug of the signature Hog's Breath Lager at this infamous joint, a must-stop on the Key West bar crawl. Live bands play daily 1 pm–2 am (except when the game's on TV). You never know who'll stop by and perhaps even jump on stage for an impromptu concert. ✉ *400 Front St.* ☎ *305/296–4222* ⊕ *www.hogsbreath.com.*

Margaritaville Café. A youngish, touristy crowd mixes with aging Parrot Heads. It's owned by former Key West resident and recording star Jimmy Buffett, who has been known to perform here. The drink of choice is, of course, a margarita, made with Jimmy's own brand of Margaritaville tequila. There's live music nightly, as well as lunch and dinner. ✉ *500 Duval St.* ☎ *305/292–1435* ⊕ *www.margaritaville.com.*

Pier House. The party here begins with a steel-drum band to celebrate the sunset on the beach (on select Thursdays and Fridays), then moves indoors to the Wine Galley piano bar for live jazz. ✉ *1 Duval St.* ☎ *305/296–4600, 800/327–8340* ⊕ *www.pierhouse.com.*

Schooner Wharf Bar. This open-air waterfront bar and grill in the historic seaport district retains its funky Key West charm and hosts live entertainment daily. Its margaritas rank among Key West's best, as does the bar itself, voted

Best Local's Bar six years in a row. For great views, head up to the second floor and be sure to order up some fresh seafood and fritters and Dark and Stormy cocktails. ✉ *202 William St.* ☎ *305/292–3302* ⊕ *www.schoonerwharf.com.*

Sloppy Joe's. There's history and good times at the successor to a famous 1937 speakeasy named for its founder, Captain Joe Russell. Decorated with Hemingway memorabilia and marine flags, the bar is popular with travelers and is full and noisy all the time. A Sloppy Joe's T-shirt is a de rigueur Key West souvenir, and the gift shop sells them like crazy. Grab a seat (if you can) and be entertained by the bands and by the parade of people in constant motion. ✉ *201 Duval St.* ☎ *305/294–5717* ⊕ *www.sloppyjoes.com.*

The Top. On the seventh floor of the Crowne Plaza Key West La Concha, this is one of the best places in town to view the sunset and enjoy live entertainment on Friday and Saturday nights. ✉ *430 Duval St.* ☎ *305/296–2991* ⊕ *www.laconchakeywest.com.*

Two Friends Patio Lounge. Love karaoke? Get it out of your system at Two Friends Patio Lounge, where your performance gets a live Internet feed via the bar's Karaoke Cam. The singing starts at 8:30 pm most nights. ✉ *512 Front St.* ☎ *305/296–3124* ⊕ *www.twofriendskeywest.com.*

Virgilio's Martini Bar. In the best traditions of a 1950s cocktail lounge, this bar serves chilled martinis to the soothing tempo of live jazz and blues. Locals love the late night dancing and $5 Martini Mondays. ✉ *524 Duval St.* ☎ *305/296–8118* ⊕ *www.virgilioskeywest.com.*

GAY AND LESBIAN BARS

Aqua. Key West's largest gay bar, Aqua hosts drag shows, karaoke contests, dancing, and live entertainment at three bars, including one outside on the patio. ✉ *711 Duval St.* ☎ *305/294–0555* ⊕ *www.aquakeywest.com.*

Bourbon Street Complex. Pick your entertainment at the Bourbon Street Complex, a club within an all-male guesthouse. There are 10 video screens along with dancers grooving to the latest music spun by DJs at the Bourbon Street Pub. ✉ *724 Duval St.* ☎ *305/293–9800* ⊕ *www.bourbonstpub.com.*

Island House Café + Bar. Part of a men's resort, Island House Café + Bar serves frozen and other cocktails along with creative cuisine in tropical gardens with a pool where clothing is optional. It is open 24 hours. ⊠ *Island House, 1129 Fleming St.* ☎ *305/294–6284, 800/890–6284* ⊕ *www. islandhousekeywest.com.*

La Te Da Hotel and Bar. This venue hosts female impersonators (catch Christopher Peterson when he's on stage) and riotously funny cabaret shows nightly in the Crystal Room Cabaret Lounge. There is also live entertainment nightly, including the popular local singer Lenore Troia in the Terrace Garden Bar and smooth jazz and pricey martinis in the ultracool piano bar. ⊠ *1125 Duval St.* ☎ *305/296–6706* ⊕ *www.lateda.com.*

PERFORMING ARTS

Red Barn Theatre. With more than 30 years' experience, the Red Barn Theatre, a small professional theater, performs dramas, comedies, and musicals, including works by new playwrights. Big things happen in this little theater; it's well worth a visit while you're here. ⊠ *319 Duval St.* ☎ *305/296–9911, 866/870–9911* ⊕ *www.redbarntheatre.com.*

South Florida Symphony. Key West native and nationally recognized conductor, Sebrina Maria Alfonso, directs the South Florida Symphony (formerly the Key West Symphony). Now in its 15th season, this traveling group of symphonic musicians (based in Fort Lauderdale) is as talented a bunch as you'll find anywhere. They perform at the Tennessee Williams Theatre while in Key West. ☎ *305/292–1774* ⊕ *www.southfloridasymphony.org.*

Tennessee Williams Fine Arts Center. On Stock Island, the Tennessee Williams Fine Arts Center presents chamber music, dance, jazz concerts, and dramatic and musical plays with major stars, as well as other performing arts events. You can also see the South Florida Symphony Orchestra perform here. ⊠ *Florida Keys Community College, 5901 College Rd.* ☎ *305/296–1520 administration, 305/295–7676 box office* ⊕ *www.tennesseewilliamstheatre.com.*

Tropic Cinema. Catch the classics and the latest art, independent, and foreign films shown daily in this four-screen theater. A newly upgraded café enhances the complex. ⊠ *416 Eaton St.* ☎ *305/295–9493, 877/761–3456* ⊕ *www. tropiccinema.com.*

Waterfront Playhouse. Home to the Key West Players, the community-run Waterfront Playhouse is an 1880s ice warehouse that was converted into a 180-seat regional theater presenting comedy and drama from December to May. The troupe first banded together in 1940, counting Tennessee Williams among its members. ⊠*Mallory Sq.* ☎*305/294–5015* ⊕*www.waterfrontplayhouse.org.*

SHOPPING

On these streets, you'll find colorful local art of widely varying quality, key limes made into everything imaginable, and the raunchiest T-shirts in the civilized world. Browsing the boutiques—with frequent pub stops along the way—makes for an entertaining stroll down Duval Street. Cocktails certainly help the appreciation of some goods, such as the figurine of a naked man blowing bubbles out his backside or the swashbuckling pirate costumes that are no longer just for Halloween.

Sculpture Key West. Key West bursts with art, especially every year between January and April, when artists unveil their latest works at two exhibitions in Fort Zachary Taylor State Park and West Martello Tower. More than 30 artists from around the country are selected to bring their contemporary sculpture for outdoor exhibitions. In years past, sculptures have ranged from a dinosaur surfacing in a pond and a giant Key West chicken to heads floating in the water and abstract formations suggesting sea and seaside vegetation.

ARTS AND CRAFTS

Key West is filled with art galleries, and the variety is truly amazing. Most of them congregate around the south end of Duval Street. The town's large artist community locally produces much of the art, but many galleries carry international artists from as close as Haiti and as far away as France. Local artists do a great job of preserving the island's architecture and spirit.

Alan S. Maltz Gallery. The owner, declared the state's official wildlife photographer by the Wildlife Foundation of Florida, captures the state's nature and character in stunning portraits. Spend four figures for large-format images on canvas or save on small prints and closeouts. ⊠*1210 Duval St.* ☎*305/294–0005* ⊕*www.alanmaltz.com.*

Art@830. This inviting gallery carries a little bit of everything, from pottery to paintings and jewelry to sculptures. Most outstanding is its selection of glass art, particularly the jellyfish lamps. Take time to admire all that is here. ⊠*830*

Caroline St., Historic Seaport ☎*305/295–9595* ⊕*www.
art830.com.*

Gallery on Greene. This is the largest gallery–exhibition space
in Key West and it showcases 37 museum-quality artists.
They pride themselves on being the leader in the field of
representational fine art, painting, sculptures, and repro-
ductions from the Florida Keys and Key West. You can see
the love immediately from gallery curator Nancy Frank,
who aims to please everyone, from the casual buyer to the
established collector. ✉*606 Greene St.* ☎*305/294–1669*
⊕*www.galleryongreene.com.*

Gingerbread Square Gallery. The oldest private art gallery in
Key West represents local and internationally acclaimed
artists on an annually changing basis, in mediums ranging
from graphics to art glass. ✉*1207 Duval St.* ☎*305/296–
8900* ⊕*www.gingerbreadsquaregallery.com.*

Glass Reunions. Find a collection of wild and impressive
fine-art glass here. It's worth a stop in just to see the imagi-
native and over-the-top glass chandeliers, jewelry, dishes,
and platters. ✉*825 Duval St.* ☎*305/294–1720* ⊕*www.
glassreunions.com.*

Haitian Art Company. Haitian-art connoisseurs will love the
bright colors in the paintings, the bead-and-sequin work in
the handicrafts, and fine metal sculptures. ✉*605 Simonton
St.* ☎*305/735–4664* ⊕*www.haitian-art-co.com.*

Key West Pottery. You won't find any painted coconuts here,
but you will find a collection of contemporary tropical
ceramics. Wife and husband owners Kelly Lever and Adam
Russell take real pride in this working studio that, in addition to their own creations, features artists from around
the country. This is one of the island's only specialty galleries. ✉*929 Truman Avenue* ☎*305/900–8303* ⊕*www.
keywestpottery.com.*

KW Light Gallery at Island Arts. Historian, photographer, and
painter Sharon Wells opened this gallery to showcase her
own fine-art photography, painted tiles, and canvases. She
also offers private tours of Key West. ✉*1128 Duval St.*
☎*305/923–5133* ⊕*www.keywesttiles.com.*

Lucky Street Gallery. High-end contemporary paintings are
the focus at this gallery with over 30 years of experience and
a passionate staff. There are also a few pieces of jewelry by
internationally recognized Key West–based artists. Chang-

ing exhibits, artist receptions, and special events make this a lively venue. ✉ *1130 Duval St.* ☎ *305/294–3973* ⊕ *www. luckystreetgallery.com.*

Pelican Poop Shoppe. Caribbean art sells in a historic building (with Hemingway connections, of course). For $2 admission or a $10 purchase, you can stroll the tropical courtyard garden. The owners buy directly from the artisans every year, so the prices are very attractive. ✉ *314 Simonton St.* ☎ *305/292–9955.*

BOOKS

Key West Island Bookstore. This home away from home for the large Key West writers' community carries new, used, and rare titles. It specializes in Hemingway, Tennessee Williams, and South Florida mystery writers. ✉ *513 Fleming St.* ☎ *305/294–2904* ⊕ *www.keywestislandbooks.com.*

CLOTHING AND FABRICS

Fairvilla Megastore. Don't leave town without a browse through the legendary shop, where you'll find an astonishing array of fantasy wear, outlandish costumes (check out the pirate section), and other "adult" toys. ✉ *520 Front St.* ☎ *305/292–0448* ⊕ *www.fairvilla.com.*

Kino Sandals. A pair of Kino Sandals was once a public declaration that you'd been to Key West. The attraction? You can watch these inexpensive items being made. The factory has been churning out several styles since 1966. Walk up to the counter, grab a pair, try them on, and lay down some cash. It's that simple. ✉ *107 Fitzpatrick St.* ☎ *305/294–5044* ⊕ *www.kinosandalfactory.com* ☉ *Closed Sun. in off-season.*

Seam Shoppe. Take home a shopping bag full of scarlet hibiscus, fuchsia heliconias, blue parrot fish, and even pink flamingo fabric, selected from the city's widest selection of tropical-print fabrics. ✉ *1114 Truman Ave.* ☎ *305/296–9830* ⊕ *www.tropicalfabricsonline.com.*

Towels of Key West. Wrap yourself in colorful, island comfort with Towels of Key West, the longest-running retail shop on Duval Street (since the mid-1970s). There are more than 60 unique towel designs to get you beach ready; some you'd expect, others are more whimsical. All are hand-sewn on the island. ✉ *806 Duval St.* ☎ *305/292–1120, 800/927–0316* ⊕ *shop.towelsofkeywest1.net.*

FOOD AND DRINK

Fausto's Food Palace. Since 1926 Fausto's has been the spot to catch up on the week's gossip and to chill out in summer—it has groceries, organic foods, marvelous wines, a sushi chef on duty 8 am–3 pm, and box lunches to go. There are two locations you can shop at in Key West (the other is at 1105 White St.), plus a recently opened online store. ⊠ *522 Fleming St.* ☎ *305/296–5663* ⊕ *www.faustos.com.*

★ Fodor'sChoice **Kermit's Key West Lime Shoppe.** You'll see Kermit himself standing on the corner every time a trolley passes, pie in hand. Besides pie, his shop carries a multitude of key lime products from barbecue sauce to jellybeans. His prefrozen pies, dressed with a special long-lasting whipped cream instead of meringue, travels well. This is a must-stop shop while in Key West. The key lime pie is the best on the island; once you try it frozen on a stick, dipped in chocolate, you may consider quitting your job and moving here. Savor every bite on their outdoor patio/garden area. Heaven. ⊠ *200 Elizabeth St., Historic Seaport* ☎ *305/296–0806, 800/376–0806* ⊕ *www.keylimeshop.com.*

Key West Winery. You'll be pleasantly surprised with the fruit wines sold here. Display crates hold bottles of wines made from blueberries, blackberries, pineapples, cherries, mangoes, watermelons, passion fruit, and, of course, key limes. Stop in for a free tasting. ⊠ *103 Simonton St.* ☎ *305/292–1717, 866/880–1717* ⊕ *www.thekeywestwinery.com.*

Peppers of Key West. If you like it hot, you'll love this collection of hundreds of sauces, salsas, and sweets guaranteed to light your fire. ⊠ *602 Greene St.* ☎ *305/295–9333, 800/597–2823* ⊕ *www.peppersofkeywest.com.*

GIFTS AND SOUVENIRS

Cayo Hueso y Habana. Part museum, part shopping center, this circa-1879 warehouse includes a hand-rolled cigar shop, one-of-a-kind souvenirs, a Cuban restaurant, and exhibits that tell of the island's Cuban heritage. Outside, a memorial garden pays homage to the island's Cuban ancestors. ⊠ *410 Wall St., Mallory Sq.* ☎ *305/293–7260.*

Cocktails! Key West. Could there possibly be a better location to celebrate the art of the drink than Key West? This celebratory shop carries everything you need for cocktails including beautiful hand-painted stemware, highball, martini, and shot glasses, mugs, accessories, and art that blends perfectly. Most of the designs are made on the island. ⊠ *808 Duval St.* ☎ *305/292–1190* ⊕ *www.cocktailskeywest.com.*

Montage. For that unique (but slightly overpriced) souvenir of your trip to Key West head here, where you'll discover hundreds of handcrafted signs of popular Key West guest-houses, inns, hotels, restaurants, bars, and streets. If you can't find what you're looking for, they'll make it for you. ⊠ *291 Front St.* ☎ *305/395–9101, 877/396–4278* ⊕ *www. montagekeywest.com.*

HEALTH AND BEAUTY

Key West Aloe. This shop produces hundreds of soap, candle, sunscreen, and skin-care products for men and women. ⊠ *416 Greene St., at Simonton St.* ☎ *305/735-4927, 800/445–2563* ⊕ *www.keywestaloe.com.*

SHOPPING CENTERS

Bahama Village. Where to start your shopping adventure? This cluster of spruced-up shops, restaurants, and vendors is responsible for the restoration of the colorful historic district where Bahamians settled in the 19th century. The village lies roughly between Whitehead and Fort streets and Angela and Catherine streets. Hemingway frequented the bars, restaurants, and boxing rings in this part of town. ⊠ *Between Whitehead and Fort streets and Angela and Catherine streets.*

SPORTS AND THE OUTDOORS

Unlike the rest of the region, Key West isn't known primarily for outdoor pursuits. But everyone should devote at least half a day to relaxing on a boat tour, heading out on a fishing expedition, or pursuing some other adventure at sea. The ultimate excursion is a boat or seaplane trip to Dry Tortugas National Park for snorkeling and exploring Fort Jefferson. Other excursions cater to nature lovers, scuba divers, and snorkelers, and folks who just want to get out in the water and enjoy the scenery and sunset. For those who prefer land-based recreation, biking is the way to go. Hiking is limited, but walking the streets of Old Town provides plenty of exercise.

AIR TOURS

Conch Republic Air Force. Up to two passengers can fly in a 1942 Waco; tours range from a 15–18 minute Best of Key West to a 30–35 minute Island and Reef excursion. ⊠ *Key West Airport, 3469 S. Roosevelt Blvd.* ☎ *305/851–8359* ⊕ *www.keywestbiplanes.com* ⊠ *From $175.*

BIKING

Key West was practically made for bicycles, but don't let that lull you into a false sense of security. Narrow and one-way streets along with car traffic result in several bike accidents a year. Some hotels rent or lend bikes to guests; others will refer you to a nearby shop and reserve a bike for you. Rentals usually start at about $12 a day, but some places also rent by the half day. △ **Lock up; bikes—and porch chairs!—are favorite targets for local thieves.**

A&M Rentals. Rent beach cruisers with large baskets or scooters. Look for the huge American flag on the roof, or call for free airport, ferry, or cruise ship pickup. ⊠ *523 Truman Ave.* ☎ *305/294–0399* ⊕ *www.amscooterskeywest. com* ⊠ *Bicycles from $15, scooters from $35.*

Eaton Bikes. Tandem, three-wheel, and children's bikes are available in addition to the standard beach cruisers and hybrid bikes. Delivery is free for all Key West rentals. ⊠ *830 Eaton St.* ☎ *305/294–8188* ⊕ *www.eatonbikes.com* ⊠ *From $18 per day.*

Moped Hospital. This outfit supplies balloon-tire bikes with yellow safety baskets for adults and kids, as well as scooters and even double-seater scooters. ⊠ *601 Truman Ave.* ☎ *305/296–3344, 866/296–1625* ⊕ *www.mopedhospital. com* ⊠ *Bicycles from $12 per day, scooters from $35 per day.*

BOATING

Key West is surrounded by marinas, so it's easy to find what you're looking for, whether it's sailing with dolphins or paddling in the mangroves. In addition to its popular kayaking trips, Key West Eco-Tours offers sunset sails and private charters. (*See Kayaking.*)

Classic Harbor Line. In the morning, noon, or night, boarding one of these classic vessels is a mariner's dream. The Gatsby-style Yacht Beacon with a handsome mahogany bar offers a Mangrove and Mimosa morning cruise, Snorkel,

Kayak & Dolphin Adventure, or Sunset Cocktail Cruise. The *Schooner America 2.0* is refined and elegant, and her comfortable seating makes her a favorite when she sails Key West each November–April. Two-hour sunset champagne cruises are an island highlight. ⊠ *202-R Williams St.* ☎ *305/293–7245* ⊕ *www.sail-keywest.com* ☎ *From $45.*

Dancing Dolphin Spirit Charters. Victoria Impallomeni, a wilderness guide and environmental marine science expert, invites up to six nature lovers—especially children—aboard the *Imp II*, a 25-foot Aquasport, for four-hour and seven-hour ecotours that frequently include encounters with wild dolphins. While island hopping, you visit underwater gardens, natural shoreline, and mangrove habitats. For her Dolphin Day for Humans tour, Impallomeni pulls you through the water, equipped with mask and snorkel, on a specially designed "dolphin water massage board" that simulates dolphin swimming motions. Sometimes dolphins follow the boat and swim among participants. All equipment is supplied. ⊠ *MM 5 OS, Murray's Marina, 5710 Overseas Hwy.* ☎ *305/304–7562, 888/822–7366* ⊕ *www. captainvictoria.com* ☎ *From $500.*

Sunset Culinaire Tours. This tour operator serves a full menu of gourmet meals with fine wine and beer aboard a sleek cruising yacht every evening at sunset; however, you must have a group of six or more. ⊠ *5555 College Rd.* ☎ *305/296–0982* ⊕ *www.sunsetculinaire.com* ☎ *$85.*

White Knuckle Thrill Boat Ride. For something with an adrenaline boost, book with this specially designed jet boat. It holds up to 10 people and does amazing maneuvers like 360s, fishtails, and other water stunts. The cost includes a pickup shuttle from your hotel. ⊠ *Sunset Marina, 555 College Rd.* ☎ *305/797–0459* ⊕ *www.whiteknucklethrillboatride. com* ☎ *$59.*

FISHING

Any number of local fishing guides can take you to where the big ones are biting, either in the backcountry for snapper and snook or to the deep water for the marlins and shark that lured Hemingway here.

Key West Bait & Tackle. Prepare to catch a big one with the live bait, frozen bait, and fishing equipment provided here. They even offer rod and reel rentals (starting at $15 for 24 hours). Stop by their on-site Live Bait Lounge where you can sip ice-cold beer while telling fish tales. ⊠ *241 Margaret St.* ☎ *305/292–1961* ⊕ *www.keywestbaitandtackle.com.*

Key West Pro Guides. This outfitter offers only private charters, and you pay by the half day. Trips include flats and backcountry fishing and reef and offshore fishing. ⊠ *G-31 Miriam St.* ☎ *866/259–4205* ⊕ *www.keywestproguides. com* ⊠ *From $400.*

GOLFING

Not in the least a golfing destination, Key West does have one course on Stock Island. Make your tee times early in season.

Key West Golf Club. Key West isn't a major golf destination, but there is one course on Stock Island designed by Rees Jones that will downright surprise you with its water challenges and tropical beauty. It's also the only "Caribbean" golf course in the United States, boasting 200 acres of unique Florida foliage and wildlife. Hole 8 is the famous "Mangrove Hole," which will give you stories to tell. It's a 143-yard, par 3 that is played completely over a mass of mangroves with their gnarly roots and branches completely intertwined. Bring extra balls and book your tee time early in season. Nike rental clubs are available. ⊠ *6450 E. College Rd.* ☎ *305/294–5232* ⊕ *www.keywestgolf.com* ⊠ *$52–$97* ⚐ *18 holes. 6500 yards. Par 70.*

KAYAKING

Key West Eco-Tours. Key West is surrounded by marinas, so it's easy to find a water-based activity or tour, whether it's sailing with dolphins or paddling in the mangroves. These sail-kayak-snorkel excursions take you into backcountry flats and mangrove forests without the crowds. The 4½-hour trip includes lunch. Private sunset sails and private charters are also available. ⊠ *Historic Seaport, 100 Grinnell St.* ☎ *305/294–7245* ⊕ *www.keywestecotours.com* ⊠ *From $115.*

Lazy Dog Kayak Guides. Take a two- or four-hour guided sea kayak–snorkel tour around the mangrove islands just east of Key West. Costs include transportation, bottled water, a snack, and supplies, including snorkeling gear. Paddleboard tours are also available, as are rentals for self-touring. ⊠ *5114 Overseas Hwy.* ☎ *305/295–9898* ⊕ *www.lazydog. com* ⊠ *From $40.*

SCUBA DIVING AND SNORKELING

The Florida Keys National Marine Sanctuary extends along Key West and beyond to the Dry Tortugas. Key West National Wildlife Refuge further protects the pristine waters. Most divers don't make it this far out in the Keys, but if you're looking for a day of diving as a break from the nonstop party in Old Town, expect to pay about $65 and upward for a two-tank dive. Serious divers can book dive trips to the Dry Tortugas. The USS *Vandenberg* is another popular dive spot, known for its world's first underwater transformative art exhibit on an artificial reef.

Captain's Corner. This PADI–certified dive shop has classes in several languages and twice-daily snorkel and dive trips to reefs and wrecks aboard the 60-foot dive boat *Sea Eagle*. Use of weights, belts, masks, and fins is included. ✉ *125 Ann St.* ☎ *305/296–8865* ⊕ *www.captainscorner. com* ⌐ *From $40.*

Dive Key West. Operating over 40 years, Dive Key West is a full-service dive center that has charters, instruction, gear rental, sales, and repair. You can take either snorkel excursions or regular scuba trips. ✉ *3128 N. Roosevelt Blvd.* ☎ *305/296–3823* ⊕ *www.divekeywest.com* ⌐ *Snorkeling from $59, scuba from $75.*

Snuba of Key West. Safely dive the coral reefs without getting a scuba certification. Ride out to the reef on a catamaran, then follow your guide underwater for a one-hour tour of the coral reefs. You wear a regulator with a breathing hose that is attached to a floating air tank on the surface. No prior diving or snorkeling experience is necessary, but you must know how to swim. The price includes beverages. ✉ *Garrison Bight Marina, Palm Ave., between Eaton St. and N. Roosevelt Blvd.* ☎ *305/292–4616* ⊕ *www.snubakeywest. com* ⌐ *From $99.*

STAND-UP PADDLEBOARDING

SUP Key West. This ancient sport from Hawaii involves a surfboard and a paddle and has quickly become a favorite Florida water sport known as SUP (stand-up paddleboarding). SUP Key West gives lessons and tours of the estuaries. What's more, your tour guides are experts (one's even a PhD) in marine biology and ecology. Call ahead to make arrangements. ✉ *110 Grinnell St.* ☎ *305/240–1426* ⊕ *www. supkeywest.com* ⌐ *From $45.*

EXCURSION TO DRY TORTUGAS NATIONAL PARK

70 miles southwest of Key West.

The Dry Tortugas lie in the Central Time Zone. Key West Seaplane pilots like to tell their passengers that they land 15 minutes before they take off. If you can't do the time-consuming and (by air, at least, expensive) trip, the national park operates an interpretive center in the Historic Seaport at Old Key West Bight.

GETTING HERE AND AROUND

For now, the ferryboat *Yankee Freedom III* departs from a marina in Old Town and does day trips to Garden Key. Key West Seaplane Adventures has half- and full-day trips to the Dry Tortugas, where you can explore Fort Jefferson, built in 1846, and snorkel on the beautiful protected reef. Departing from the Key West airport, the flights include soft drinks and snorkel equipment for $265 half-day, $465 full-day, plus there's a $5 park fee (cash only). If you want to explore the park's other Keys, look into renting a boat or hiring a private charter. The Dry Tortugas National Park and Fort Jefferson Interpretive Center at 240 Margaret St. is a way to experience it for free. *See Exploring in Key West.*

Key West Seaplane Adventures. The 35- to 40-minute trip to the Dry Tortugas skims above the trademark windowpane-clear waters of the Florida Keys. The seaplane perspective provides an awesome experience that could result in a stiff neck from craning to look out the window and down from 500 feet above. In the Flats that edge Key West, you can spot stingrays, sea turtles, and sharks in the shallow water. In the area dubbed The Quicksands, water plunges to 30-foot depths and sand undulates in dune-like formations. Shipwrecks also festoon these waters; here's where Mel Fisher harvested treasure from the *Atocha* and *Margarita.* His 70-foot work ship, the *Arbutus,* deteriorated and eventually sank at the northern edge of the treasure sites. With its mast poking out above water, it's easy to spot and fun to photograph. From there, the water deepens from emerald hues to shades of deep blue as depths reach 70 feet. Seaplanes of Key West's most popular trip is the half-day option, where you spend about 2½ hours on Garden Key. The seaplanes leave during your stay, so be prepared to carry all your possessions with you. The morning trip beats the ferries to the island, so you'll have it to yourself until the others arrive. Snorkeling equipment, soft drinks, and birding lists are supplied. ⊠ *Key West International Airport, 3471 S. Roosevelt Blvd., Key West* ☎ *305/293–9300* ⊕ *www. keywestseaplanecharters.com* ⊡ *From $295.*

Yankee Freedom III. The fast, sleek, 110-foot catamaran *Yankee Freedom III* travels to the Dry Tortugas in 2¼ hours. The time passes quickly on the roomy vessel equipped with four restrooms, three warm freshwater showers, and two bars. Stretch out on two decks that are both air-conditioned, with cushioned seating. There is also an open sundeck with sunny and shaded seating. Continental breakfast and lunch are included. On arrival, a naturalist leads a 45-minute guided tour, which is followed by lunch and a free afternoon for swimming, snorkeling (gear included), and exploring. The vessel is ADA–certified for visitors using wheelchairs. ■TIP→ **The Dry Tortugas lies in the central time zone.** ⊠ *Lands End Marina, 240 Margaret St., Key West* ☎ *305/294–7009, 800/634–0939* ⊕ *www.yankeefreedom.com* ⊡ *$170, parking $5* ⊙ *Trips daily at 8 am; check in 7:15 am.*

EXPLORING

Dry Tortugas National Park. This park, 70 miles off the shores of Key West, consists of seven small islands. Tour the fort; then lay out your blanket on the sunny beach for a picnic before you head out to snorkel on the protected reef. Many people like to camp here ($3 per person per night, eight sites plus group site and overflow area; first come, first served), but note that there's no freshwater supply and you must carry off whatever you bring onto the island.

The typical visitor from Key West, however, makes it no farther than the waters of Garden Key. Home to 19th-century Fort Jefferson, it is the destination for seaplane and fast ferry tours out of Key West. With 2½ to 6½ hours to spend on the island, visitors have time to tour the mammoth fort-cum-prison and then cool off with mask and snorkel along the fort's moat wall.

History buffs might remember long-deactivated Fort Jefferson, the largest brick building in the Western Hemisphere, as the prison that held Dr. Samuel Mudd, who unwittingly set John Wilkes Booth's leg after the assassination of Abraham Lincoln. Three other men were also held there for complicity in the assassination. Original construction on the fort began in 1846 and continued for 30 years, but was never completed because the invention of the rifled cannon made it obsolete. That's when it became a Civil War prison and later a wildlife refuge. In 1935 President Franklin Roosevelt declared it a national monument for its historic and natural value.

The brick fort acts as a gigantic, almost 16-acre reef. Around its moat walls, coral grows and schools of snapper, grouper, and wrasses hang out. To reach the offshore coral heads requires about 15 minutes of swimming over sea-grass beds. The reef formations blaze with the color and majesty of brain coral, swaying sea fans, and flitting tropical fish. It takes a bit of energy to swim the distance, but the water depth pretty much measures under 7 feet all the way, allowing for sandy spots to stop and rest. (Standing in sea-grass meadows and on coral is detrimental to marine life.)

Serious snorkelers and divers head out farther offshore to epic formations, including Palmata Patch, one of the few surviving concentrations of elkhorn coral in the Keys. Day-trippers congregate on the sandy beach to relax in the sun and enjoy picnics. Overnight tent campers have use of restroom facilities and achieve a total getaway from noise, lights, and civilization in general. Remember that no matter how you get here, the park's $5 admission fee must be paid in cash.

The park has set up with signage a self-guided tour that takes about 45 minutes. You should budget more time if you're into photography, because the scenic shots are hard to pass up. Ranger-guided tours are also available at certain times. Check in at the visitor center for a schedule. The small office also shows an orientation video, sells books and other educational materials, and, most important, provides a blast of air-conditioning on hot days.

Birders in the know bring binoculars to watch some 100,000 nesting sooty terns at their only U.S. nesting site, Bush Key, adjacent to Garden Key. Noddy terns also nest in the spring. During winter migrations, birds fill the airspace so thickly they literally fall from the sky to make their pit stops, birders say. Nearly 300 species have been spotted in the park's seven islands, including frigatebirds, boobies, cormorants, and broad-winged hawks. Bush Key is closed to foot traffic during nesting season, January through September. ✉ *Key West* ⊕ *www.nps.gov/drto* ◪ *$5.*

GATEWAYS TO
THE KEYS

ALTHOUGH IT'S POSSIBLE TO FLY INTO KEY WEST, many people don't because of the expense and limited number of flights. Furthermore, if you are visiting the Upper or Middle Keys, there is a drive, regardless of which airport you fly into. This means that many visitors flying into Florida to visit the Keys will pass through Miami. In some cases, people choose to stay a while to absorb some of the new luxe hotels, hot nightlife, and stylish restaurants, not to mention the expansive beaches, of which the Keys do not have in abundance. But, travelers on more of a budget may want to look a bit farther afield to either Homestead or Florida City, both south of Miami, the two major gateways to both the Keys and the Everglades.

PLANNING

See Travel Smart for information on flights and car rentals in Miami.

HOTELS

If you are looking for the hot spots, then you need look no farther than Miami's South Beach, which is awash with both new high-rises and restored art deco gems. The choices in Homestead and Florida City are more pedestrian, but also friendlier to the wallet and closer to the Keys. Given the driving distance, if you arrive late in Miami, you may just want to sleep before getting an early start to drive down to the Keys; in that case, a basic room may be just what the travel agent ordered.

Hotel reviews have been shortened. For full information, visit Fodors.com.

RESTAURANTS

Miami has a vibrant dining scene, with prices to match, but you can still find reasonably priced local restaurants and chains, mostly outside the trendy South Beach area. Most restaurants south of Miami are small, mom-and-pop establishments serving homey food or local specialties such as alligator, fish, stone crab, frogs' legs, and fresh Florida lobster from the Keys. There are plenty of chain restaurants and fast-food establishments, especially in the Homestead and Florida City areas.

Gateways to the Keys

	$	$$	$$$	$$$$
Restaurants	Under $15	$16–$20	$21–$30	Over $30
Hotels	Under $200	$201–$300	$301–$400	Over $400

Prices in the restaurant reviews are the average cost of a main course at dinner or, if dinner isn't served, at lunch. Prices in the hotel reviews are the lowest cost of a standard double room in high season. Prices don't include taxes (6%, more in some counties, and 1%–5% tourist tax for hotel rooms).

MIAMI

Updated by Paul Rubio

In the 1950s, Miami was best known for alligator wrestlers and "U-pick" strawberry fields and citrus groves. Well, things have changed. Mainland Miami is now South Florida's commercial hub, while its sultry sister, Miami Beach (America's Riviera), encompasses 17 islands in Biscayne Bay. Seducing winter refugees with its sunshine, beaches, palms, and nightlife, Miami Beach is what most people envision when they think of Miami. Exploring the city will require a car if you intend to go beyond South Beach.

EXPLORING

TOP ATTRACTIONS

FAMILY Fodor'sChoice **Fairchild Tropical Botanic Garden.** With 83 acres
★ of lakes, sunken gardens, a 560-foot vine pergola, orchids, bellflowers, coral trees, bougainvillea, rare palms, and flowering trees, Fairchild is the largest tropical botanical garden in the continental United States. The tram tour highlights the best of South Florida's flora; then you can set off exploring on your own. A 2-acre rain-forest exhibit showcases tropical plants from around the world complete with a waterfall and stream. The conservatory, Windows to the Tropics, is home to rare tropical plants, including the Titan Arum (*Amorphophallus titanum*), a fast-growing variety that attracted thousands of visitors when it bloomed in 1998. (It was only the sixth documented bloom in this country in the 20th century.) The Keys Coastal Habitat, created in a marsh and mangrove area in 1995 with assistance from the Tropical Audubon Society, provides food and shelter to resident and migratory birds. Check out the Montgomery Botanical Center, a research facility devoted to palms and cycads. Spicing up Fairchild's calendar are plant sales, afternoon teas, and genuinely special events year-round, such as the International Mango Festival the second weekend in July. The excellent bookstore–gift shop carries books on gardening and horticulture, and the Garden Café serves sandwiches and, seasonally, smoothies made from the garden's own crop of tropical fruits. ✉ *10901 Old Cutler Rd., Coral Gables* ☎ *305/667–1651* ⊕ *www.fairchildgarden.org* ☑ *$25* ⊗ *Daily 7:30–4:30.*

FAMILY **Jungle Island.** Originally located deep in south Miami and known as Parrot Jungle, South Florida's original tourist attraction opened in 1936 and moved closer to Miami Beach in 2003. Located on Watson Island, a small stretch of land off I–395 between Downtown Miami and South Beach, Jungle Island is far more than a park where cockatoos ride tricycles; this interactive zoological park is home to just about every unusual and endangered species you would want to see, including a rare albino alligator, a liger (lion and tiger mix), and myriad exotic birds. The most intriguing offerings are the VIP animal tours, including the Lemur Experience ($79.95), in which the highly social primates make themselves at home on your lap or shoulders. Jungle Island offers complimentary shuttle service to most Downtown Miami and South Beach hotels. ✉ *Watson Island, 1111 Parrot Jungle Trail, off MacArthur Causeway (I–395), Downtown* ☎ *305/400–7000* ⊕ *www. jungleisland.com* ⊴ *$34.95, plus $8 parking* ⊗ *Weekdays 10–5, weekends 10–6.*

FAMILY **Fodor's**Choice **Lincoln Road Mall.** This open-air pedestrian mall
★ flaunts some of Miami's best people-watching. The eclectic interiors of myriad fabulous restaurants, colorful boutiques, art galleries, lounges, and cafés are often upstaged by the bustling outdoor scene. It's here among the prolific alfresco dining enclaves that you can pass the hours easily beholding the beautiful people. Indeed, outdoor restaurant and café seating take center stage along this wide pedestrian road adorned with towering date palms, linear pools, and colorful broken-tile mosaics. Some of the shops on Lincoln Road are owner-operated boutiques carrying a smart variety of clothing, furnishings, jewelry, and decorative elements. You'll also find typical upscale chain stores— H & M, American Eagle Outfitters, Forever 21, and so on. Lincoln Road is fun, lively, and friendly for people–old, young, gay, and straight—and their dogs.

Two landmarks worth checking out at the eastern end of Lincoln Road are the massive 1940s keystone building at 420 Lincoln Road, which has a 1945 Leo Birchanky mural in the lobby, and the 1921 mission-style Miami Beach Community Church, at Drexel Avenue. The Lincoln Theatre (No. 541–545), at Pennsylvania Avenue, is a classical four-story art deco gem with friezes, which now houses H &M. At Euclid Avenue there's a monument to Morris Lapidus, the brains behind Lincoln Road Mall, who in his 90s watched the renaissance of his whimsical South Beach creation. At Lenox Avenue, a black-and-white art deco movie house with a Mediterranean barrel-tile roof is now the Colony Theater (1040 Lincoln Rd.), where live theater and experimental films are presented. ✉ *Lincoln Rd., between Washington Ave. and Alton Rd., South Beach, Miami Beach* ⊕ *www.lincolnroadmall.com.*

FAMILY **Venetian Pool.** Sculpted from a rock quarry in 1923 and fed by artesian wells, this 820,000-gallon municipal pool had a major face-lift in 2010. It remains quite popular because of its themed architecture—a fantasy version of a water-

Miami

KEY

1 Exploring

1 Hotels & Restaurants

South Beach

West Ave. · Alton Rd. · Lenox Ave. · Michigan Ave. · Jefferson Ave. · Meridian Ave. · Euclid Ave. · Pennsylvania Ave. · Washington Ave. · Collins Ave. · Ocean Dr.

Lincoln Rd. Mall

16th St. · 15th St. · Española Way · 14th Pl. · 14th St. · 13th St. · 12th St. · 11th St. · 10th St. · 9th St. · 8th St. · 7th St. · 6th St. · 5th St. · 4th St. · 3rd St. · 2nd St. · 1st St. · Biscayne St.

Flamingo Park

Lummus Park

Atlantic Ocean

Exploring

Art Deco Welcome Center, **3**
Bass Museum of Art, **1**
Cuban Memorial Boulevard, **6**
Fairchild Tropical Botanic Garden, **8**
Jungle Island, **4**
Lincoln Road Mall, **2**
Venetian Pool, **5**
Vizcaya Museum and Gardens, **7**

Restaurants

Azul, **14**
Big Pink, **10**
Havana Harry's, **16**
Joe's Stone Crab Restaurant, **11**
News Café, **7**
Perricone's Marketplace and Café, **15**
Pubbelly, **12**
Yardbird Southern Table & Bar, **4**

Hotels

Angler's Hotel, **9**
Circa 39 Hotel, **1**
National Hotel, **3**

Park Central, **8**
The Standard Miami Beach, **13**
Surfcomber Miami, South Beach, **2**
The Tides South Beach, **6**
Villa Paradiso, **5**

CORAL GABLES

CORAL GABLES

COCONUT GROVE

MIAMI

ATLANTIC OCEAN

Biscayne Bay

Virginia Key

Fisher Island

KEY BISCAYNE

Marine Stadium

Grove Isle

Julia Tuttle Causeway

Venetian Causeway

MacArthur Causeway

Rickenbacker Causeway

Cruise Ship Terminal

see inset

0   2 mile
0   2 kilometer

front Italian village—created by Denman Fink. The pool has earned a place on the National Register of Historic Places and showcases a nice collection of vintage photos depicting 1920s beauty pageants and swank soirées held long ago. Paul Whiteman played here, Johnny Weissmuller and Esther Williams swam here, and you should, too (but no kids under three). A snack bar, lockers, and showers make this must-see user-friendly as well. ⊠ *2701 De Soto Blvd., at Toledo St., Coral Gables* ☎ *305/460–5306* ⊕ *www.gablesrecreation.com* ☒ *$11; free parking across De Soto Blvd.* ☉ *Usually open Tues.–Sun. 11–4:30, but best to call ahead.*

★ **Fodor's**Choice **Vizcaya Museum and Gardens.** Of the 10,000 people living in Miami between 1912 and 1916, about 1,000 of them were gainfully employed by Chicago industrialist James Deering to build this European-inspired residence. Once comprising 180 acres, this National Historic Landmark now occupies a 30-acre tract that includes a rockland hammock (native forest) and more than 10 acres of formal gardens with fountains overlooking Biscayne Bay. The house, open to the public, contains 70 rooms, 34 of which are filled with paintings, sculpture, antique furniture, and other fine and decorative arts. The collection spans 2,000 years and represents the Renaissance, baroque, rococo, and neoclassical periods. The 90-minute self-guided Discover Vizcaya Audio Tour is available in multiple languages for an additional $5. Moonlight tours, offered on evenings that are nearest the full moon, provide a magical look at the gardens; call for reservations. ⊠ *3251 S. Miami Ave., Coconut Grove* ☎ *305/250–9133* ⊕ *www.vizcayamuseum. org* ☒ *$18* ☉ *Daily 9:30–4:30* ☉ *Closed Tues.*

WORTH NOTING

Art Deco Welcome Center. Run by the Miami Design Preservation League, the center provides information about the buildings in the district. An improved gift shop sells 1930s–50s art deco memorabilia, posters, and books on Miami's history. Several tours—covering Lincoln Road, Española Way, North Beach, and the entire Art Deco District, among others—start here. You can choose from a self-guided iPod audio tour or join one of the regular morning walking tours at 10:30 every day. On Thursday a second tour takes place at 6:30 pm. Arrive at the center 15 minutes beforehand and pre-purchase tickets online. All the options provide detailed histories of the art deco hotels as well as an introduction to the art deco, Mediterranean revival, and Miami Modern

(MiMo) styles found within the Miami Beach Architectural Historic District. Don't miss the special boat tours during Art Deco Weekend, in early January. *(⇨ For a map of the Art Deco District and info on some of the sites there, see the "A Stroll Down Deco Lane" in-focus feature.)* ✉ *1001 Ocean Dr., South Beach, Miami Beach* ☏ *305/672–2014* ⊕ *www.mdpl.org* ✇ *Tours $20* ⊙ *Daily 9:30–7.*

Bass Museum of Art. Special exhibitions join a diverse collection of European art at this museum whose original building is constructed of keystone and has unique Maya-inspired carvings. An expansion designed by Japanese architect Arata Isozaki houses another wing and an outdoor sculpture garden. Works on permanent display include *The Holy Family,* a painting by Peter Paul Rubens; *The Tournament,* one of several 16th-century Flemish tapestries; and works by Albrecht Dürer and Henri de Toulouse-Lautrec. Docent tours are by appointment but free with entry. ✉ *2100 Collins Ave., South Beach, Miami Beach* ☏ *305/673–7530* ⊕ *www.bassmuseum.org* ✇ *$8* ⊙ *Wed.–Sun. noon–5.*

Cuban Memorial Boulevard. Four blocks in the heart of Little Havana are filled with monuments to Cuba's freedom fighters. South of *Calle Ocho* (8th Street), S.W. 13th Ave. becomes a ceiba tree–lined parkway known as Cuban Memorial Boulevard, divided at the center by a narrow grassy mall with a walking path through the various memorials. Among them is the *Eternal Torch of the Brigade 2506,* blazing with an endless flame and commemorating those who were killed in the failed Bay of Pigs invasion of 1961. Another is a bas-relief map of Cuba depicting each of its *municipios.* There's also a bronze statue in honor of Nestory (Tony) Izquierdo, who participated in the Bay of Pigs invasion and served in Nicaragua's Somozan forces. ✉ *S.W. 13th Ave., between S.W. 8th and S.W.12th Sts., Little Havana.*

BEACHES

Almost every east–west side street in Miami Beach dead-ends at the ocean. Sandy shores also stretch along the southern side of the Rickenbacker Causeway to Key Biscayne, where you'll find more popular beaches. Greater Miami is best known for its ocean beaches, but there's freshwater swimming here, too, in pools and lakes. Below are the highlights for the get-wet set.

CORAL GABLES

FAMILY **Matheson Hammock Park and Beach.** Kids love the gentle waves and warm water of this beach in Coral Gables suburbia, near Fairchild Tropical Botanic Garden. But the beach is only part of the draw—the park includes a boardwalk trail, a playground, and a golf course. Plus the park is a prime spot for kiteboarding. The man-made lagoon, or "atoll pool," is perfect for inexperienced swimmers, and it's one of the best places in mainland Miami for a picnic. ■TIP➔ **Nevertheless, the water can be a bit murky, and with the emphasis on families, it's not the best place for singles.** The park also offers a full-service marina. **Amenities:** parking (fee); toilets. **Best for:** swimming. ✉ *9610 Old Cutler Rd.* ☎ *305/665–5475* ⊕ *www.miamidade.gov/parks/parks/matheson_beach.asp* ✉ *$5 per vehicle weekdays, $6 weekends* ⊙ *Daily sunrise–sunset.*

KEY BISCAYNE

★ **Fodor's** Choice **Bill Baggs Cape Florida State Park.** Thanks to inviting beaches, sunsets, and a tranquil lighthouse, this park at Key Biscayne's southern tip is worth the drive. In fact, the 1-mile stretch of pure beachfront has been named several times in Dr. Beach's revered America's Top 10 Beaches list. It has 18 picnic pavilions available as daily rentals, two cafés that serve light lunches (Lighthouse Café, overlooking the Atlantic Ocean, and the Boater's Grill, on Biscayne Bay) , and plenty of space to enjoy the umbrella and chair rentals. A stroll or ride along walking and bicycle paths provides wonderful views of Miami's dramatic skyline. From the southern end of the park you can see a handful of houses rising over the bay on wooden stilts, the remnants of Stiltsville, built in the 1940s and now protected by the Stiltsville Trust. The nonprofit group was established in 2003 to preserve the structures, because they showcase the park's rich history. Bill Baggs has bicycle rentals, a playground, fishing piers, and guided tours of the **Cape Florida Lighthouse,** South Florida's oldest structure. The lighthouse was erected in 1845 to replace an earlier one damaged in an 1836 Seminole attack, in which the keeper's helper was killed. Free tours are offered at the restored cottage and lighthouse at 10 am and 1 pm Thursday to Monday. Be there a half hour beforehand. **Amenities:** food and drink, lifeguards, parking, showers, toilets. **Best for:** solitude, sunsets, walking. ✉ *1200 S. Crandon Blvd., Key Biscayne* ☎ *305/361–5811* ⊕ *www.floridastateparks.org/*

6

capeflorida ⌑*$8 per vehicle; $2 per pedestrian* ☉*Daily 8–sunset.*

SOUTH BEACH

★ Fodor'sChoice **South Beach.** A 10-block stretch of white sandy beach hugging the turquoise waters along Ocean Drive—from 5th to 15th streets—is one of the most popular in America, known for drawing unabashedly modelesque sunbathers and posers. With the influx of new luxe hotels and hotspots from 1st to 5th and 16th to 25th streets, the South Beach stand-and-pose scene is now bigger than ever and stretches yet another dozen plus blocks. The beaches crowd quickly on the weekends with a blend of European tourists, young hipsters, and sun-drenched locals offering Latin flavor. Separating the sand from the traffic of Ocean Drive is palm-fringed **Lummus Park**, with its volleyball nets and chickee huts (huts made of palmetto thatch over a cypress frame) for shade. The beach at **12th Street** is popular with gays, in a section often marked with rainbow flags. Locals hang out on 3rd Street beach, in an area called **SoFi** (South of Fifth) where they watch fit Brazilians play foot volley, a variation of volleyball that uses everything but the hands. Because much of South Beach leans toward skimpy sunning—women are often in G-strings and casually topless—many families prefer the tamer sections of Mid- and North Beach. Metered parking spots next to the ocean are a rare find. Instead, opt for a public garage a few blocks away and enjoy the people-watching as you walk to find your perfect spot on the sand. **Amenities:** food and drink; lifeguards; parking (fee); showers; toilets. **Best for:** partiers; sunrise; swimming; walking. ⌑*Ocean Dr., from 5th to 15th Sts., then Collins Ave. to 25th St., South Beach, Miami Beach.*

WHERE TO EAT

Because Miami dining is a part of the trendy nightlife scene, most dinners don't start until 8 or 9 pm and may go well into the night. To avoid a long wait among the late-night partiers at hot spots, arrive before 7 or make reservations. Attire is usually casual chic, but patrons like to dress to impress. When you get your bill, check whether a gratuity is already included; most restaurants add between 15% and 20% (ostensibly for the convenience of, and protection from, the many Latin American and European tourists who are used to this practice in their homelands), but supplement it depending on your opinion of the service.

$$$$ ╳**Azul.** *Eclectic.* A restaurant known for producing celebrity chefs and delivering dining fantasies of Food Network proportions, Azul is a Miami foodie institution. With its Forbes five-star, award-winning team, Azul offers a haute-cuisine experience on par with a two- or three-Michelin-star restaurant. Chefs fuse disparate ingredients, merging as decadent, gastronomic art. Headliners include Tuna Poke with white soy, scallion, and macadamia nuts and the Basil "Sous-Vide" Salmon with ratatouille and fine herbs. Dine here and you'll undoubtedly experience bold new taste sensations while enjoying one of the finest wine lists in the city and an incomparable skyline view. ⑤ *Average main: $48* ⊠ *Mandarin Oriental, Miami, 500 Brickell Key Dr., Downtown, Miami* ☎ *305/913–8358* ⊕ *www.mandarinoriental. com/miami* ⚑ *Reservations essential.*

$ ╳**Big Pink.** *American.* The decor in this innovative, super-popular diner may remind you of a roller-skating rink—everything is pink Lucite, stainless steel, and campy (think sports lockers as decorative touches)—and the menu is 3 feet tall, complete with a table of contents. Food is solidly all-American, with dozens of tasty sandwiches, pizzas, turkey or beef burgers, and side dishes, each and every one composed with gourmet flair. Big Pink also makes a great spot for brunch. ⑤ *Average main: $14* ⊠ *157 Collins Ave., South Beach, Miami Beach* ☎ *305/532–4700* ⊕ *www. mylesrestaurantgroup.com.*

$ ╳**Havana Harry's.** *Cuban.* When Cuban families want an affordable home-cooked meal with a twist but don't want to cook it themselves or go supercheap at the Cuban fast-food joint, Pollo Tropical, they come to this big, unassuming restaurant. In fact, you're likely to see whole families here representing multiple generations. The fare is traditional Cuban: long thin steaks known as *bistec palomilla* (a panfried steak), roast chicken with citrus marinade, and fried pork chunks; contemporary flourishes—mango sauce and guava-painted pork roast—are kept to a minimum. Most dishes come with white rice, black beans, and a choice of ripe or green plantains. The sweet ripe ones offer a good contrast to the savory dishes. Start with the $5.25 *mariquitas* (plantain chips) with mojo. Finish with the acclaimed flan. ⑤ *Average main: $14* ⊠ *4612 Le Jeune Rd., Coral Gables* ☎ *305/661–2622* ⊕ *www.havanaharrys.net.*

★ **Fodor's**Choice ╳**Joe's Stone Crab Restaurant.** *Seafood.* In South

$$$$ Beach's decidedly new-money scene, the stately Joe's Stone Crab is an old-school testament to good food and good service. South Beach's most storied restaurant started as a turn-of-the-century eating house when Joseph Weiss discovered succulent stone crabs off the Florida coast. A century later, the restaurant stretches a city block and serves 2,000 dinners a day to local politicians and moneyed patriarchs. Stone crabs, served with legendary mustard sauce, crispy hash browns, and creamed spinach, remain the staple. Though stone-crab season runs from October 15 to May 15, Joe's remains open year-round (albeit with a limited schedule) serving other phenomenal seafood dishes. Finish your meal with tart key lime pie, baked fresh daily. ■TIP→ **Joe's famously refuses reservations, and weekend waits can be three hours long—yes, you read that correctly—so come early or order from Joe's Take Away next door.** ⑤ *Average main: $45* ✉ *11 Washington Ave., South Beach, Miami Beach* ☎ *305/673–0365, 305/673–4611 for takeout* ⊕ *www. joesstonecrab.com* ⚓ *Reservations not accepted* ⊗ *No lunch Sun. and Mon. and mid-May–mid-Oct.*

$$ ╳ **News Café.** *American.* No trip to Miami is complete without a stop at this Ocean Drive landmark, though the food is nothing special. The 24-hour café attracts a crowd with snacks, light meals, drinks, periodicals, and the people-parade on the sidewalk out front. Most prefer sitting outside, where they can feel the salt breeze and gawk at the human scenery. Sea-grape trees shade a patio where you can watch from a quiet distance. Offering a little of this and a little of that—bagels, pâtés, chocolate fondue, sandwiches, and a terrific wine list—this joint has something for everyone. Although service can be indifferent to the point of laissez-faire and the food is mediocre at best, News Café is just one of those places visitors love. ⑤ *Average main: $16* ✉ *800 Ocean Dr., South Beach, Miami Beach* ☎ *305/538–6397* ⊕ *www.newscafe.com* ⚓ *Reservations not accepted.*

$$$ ╳ **Perricone's Marketplace and Café.** *Italian.* Brickell Avenue south of the Miami River is a haven for Italian restaurants, and this lunch place for local bigwigs is the biggest and most popular among them. It's housed partially outdoors and partially indoors in an 1880s Vermont barn. Recipes were handed down from generation to generation, and the cooking is simple and good. Buy your wine from the on-premises deli, and enjoy it (for a small corking fee) with homemade minestrone; a generous antipasto; linguine with a sauté of jumbo shrimp, scallops, and calamari; or gnocchi with four cheeses. The homemade tiramisu and cannoli are top-notch. ⑤ *Average main: $22* ✉ *Mary Brickell Village, 15 S.E. 10th St., Downtown, Miami* ☎ *305/374–9449* ⊕ *www. perricones.com.*

★ Fodor'sChoice ✕ **Pubbelly.** *Eclectic.* Five years after opening,
$$$ South Beach's favorite neighborhood gastropub still packs the house nightly. The petite eatery, located on a residential street in SoBe's western reaches, attracts the who's who of beach socialites, hipsters, and the occasional tourist coming to chow down on inventive Asian-Latin small plates, dumplings, charcuterie, and seasonal large plates by executive chef/owner Jose Mendin. From bay scallops *Bourguignon* to short-rib tartare to *huitlacoche* (corn truffle) dumplings in squid ink black butter, Pubbelly constantly pushes the envelope on inventive cuisine, and locals simply can't get enough. Expect deservedly long wait times, especially on weekends. But not to worry, after a few rounds of craft beers, sake cocktails, and eclectic wines from the awesome drink menu, your table will be ready in no time! Ⓢ *Average main: $28* ⌂ *1418 20th St., South Beach, Miami Beach* ☎ *305/532-7555* ⊕ *www.pubbelly.com.*

$$$ ✕ **Yardbird Southern Table & Bar.** *Southern.* There's a helluva lot of Southern lovin' from the Lowcountry at this lively and funky South Beach spot. Miami's A-list puts calorie counting aside for decadent nights filled with comfort foods and innovative drinks. The family-style menu is divided between "small plates," "the bird," "plates," and "fixin's," but have no doubt the "the bird" takes center stage (or plate) here. You'll rave about Mama's chicken biscuits, the chicken 'n' watermelon 'n' waffles, and Llewellyn's fine fried chicken, which requires a 27-hour marination and slow-cooking process. Oh, and then there are the sides, like house-cut fries with a buttermilk dipping sauce and bacon salt or the supercreamy macaroni and cheese. Don't plan on hitting the beach in a bikini the next day. Ⓢ *Average main: $28* ⌂ *1600 Lenox Ave., South Beach, Miami Beach* ☎ *305/538-5220* ⊕ *www.runchickenrun.com.*

WHERE TO STAY

South Beach is the center of the action in Miami Beach, but it's also expensive. If you are looking for a budget-conscious hotel, you'll almost certainly have to choose one that's a few blocks from the beach rather than one located right across the street.

$$$ ▨ **Angler's Hotel.** *Hotel.* Miami's newest addition to the Kimpton portfolio has an air of serenity and privacy that pervades this discreet little oasis of personality-driven villas (built in 1930 by architect Henry Maloney) and modern tower units, together capturing the feel of a sophisticated private Mediterranean villa community. **Pros:** gardened private retreat; excellent service; daily complimentary wine hour. **Cons:** on busy Washington Avenue; not directly on beach. ⑤ *Rooms from: $339* ✉ *660 Washington Ave., South Beach, Miami Beach* ☎ *305/534–9600* ⊕ *www. anglershotelmiami.com* ⤳ *24 rooms, 20 suites* ⦿| *No meals.*

$ ⊡ **Circa 39 Hotel.** *Hotel.* Located in the heart of Mid-Beach, this stylish yet affordable 100-guest room boutique hotel pays attention to every detail and gets them all right, with amenities that include a swimming pool and sundeck complete with cabanas and umbrella-shaded chaises that invite all-day lounging. **Pros:** affordable; chic; intimate; beach chairs provided; art deco fireplace. **Cons:** not on the beach side of Collins Avenue. ⑤ *Rooms from: $187* ✉ *3900 Collins Ave., Mid-Beach, Miami Beach* ☎ *305/538–4900, 877/824–7223* ⊕ *www.circa39.com* ⤳ *96 rooms* ⦿| *No meals.*

$$$$ ⊡ **National Hotel.** *Hotel.* The National Hotel has maintained its distinctive art deco heritage (the chocolate- and ebony-hued pieces in the lobby date back to the 1930s, and the baby grand piano headlines the throwback Blues Bar) while also keeping up with SoBe's glossy newcomers with its renovated cabana wing and art deco tower. **Pros:** stunning pool; perfect location. **Cons:** street noise on the weekends; rooms don't have the finesse of neighbors. ⑤ *Rooms from: $405* ✉ *1677 Collins Ave., South Beach, Miami Beach* ☎ *305/532–2311, 800/327–8370* ⊕ *www.nationalhotel. com* ⤳ *143 rooms, 9 suites* ⦿| *No meals.*

$$ ⊡ **Park Central.** *Hotel.* This seven-story, oft-photographed 1937 archetypal art deco building on Ocean Drive offers a wide range of somewhat dated, Old Florida–style rooms complete with wicker chairs and black-and-white photos of old beach scenes. **Pros:** spacious rooftop sundeck; comfy beds; good location. **Cons:** dated furnishings; small bathrooms; most rooms have limited views. ⑤ *Rooms from: $289* ✉ *640 Ocean Dr., South Beach, Miami Beach* ☎ *305/538–1611* ⊕ *www.theparkcentral.com* ⤳ *113 rooms, 12 suites* ⦿| *No meals.*

$$ ⊡ **The Standard Miami Beach.** *Resort.* An extension of André Balazs's trendy and hip yet budget-conscious hotel chain, the shabby-chic Standard is a mile from South Beach on an island just over the Venetian Causeway and boasts one of South Florida's most renowned spas and hottest pool scenes. **Pros:** free bike and kayak rentals; swank pool scene; great spa; inexpensive. **Cons:** slight trek to South Beach; small rooms with no views. ⑤ *Rooms from: $299* ✉ *40*

Island Ave., Belle Isle, Miami ☎*305/673–1717* ⊕*www.standardhotel.com* ⚓*104 rooms, 1 suite* ⫶⊙⫶*No meals.*

★ **Fodor's**Choice ⌁ **Surfcomber Miami, South Beach.** *Hotel.* In 2012
$$ the legendary Surfcomber joined the hip Kimpton Hotel group, spawning a fantastic nip-and-tuck that's rejuvenated the rooms and common spaces to reflect vintage luxe and ocean-side freshness, and offering a price point that packs the place with a young, sophisticated, yet unpretentious crowd. **Pros:** stylish but not pretentious; pet-friendly; on the beach. **Cons:** small bathrooms; front desk often busy. ⑤*Rooms from: $299* ⊠*1717 Collins Ave., South Beach, Miami Beach* ☎*305/532–7715* ⊕*www.surfcomber.com* ⚓*182 rooms, 4 suites* ⫶⊙⫶*No meals.*

$$$ ⌁ **The Tides South Beach.** *Hotel.* Formerly the crown jewel of the Viceroy Hotel Group, the Tides South Beach is an exclusive Ocean Drive art deco hotel of just 45 ocean-facing suites adorned with soft pinks and corals, gilded accents, and marine-inspired decor. **Pros:** superior service; great beach location; ocean views from all suites plus the terrace restaurant. **Cons:** tiny elevators; mediocre restaurant. ⑤*Rooms from: $396* ⊠*1220 Ocean Dr., South Beach, Miami Beach* ☎*305/604–5070* ⊕*www.tidessouthbeach.com* ⚓*45 suites* ⫶⊙⫶*No meals.*

$ ⌁ **Villa Paradiso.** *B&B/Inn.* One of South Beach's best deals for budget travelers, Paradiso has huge rooms with kitchens and a charming tropical courtyard with benches for hanging out at all hours. **Pros:** great hangout spot in courtyard; good value; great location. **Cons:** no pool; no restaurant; not trendy. ⑤*Rooms from: $174* ⊠*1415 Collins Ave., South Beach, Miami Beach* ☎*305/532–0616* ⊕*www.villaparadisohotel.com* ⚓*17 studios* ⫶⊙⫶*No meals.*

NIGHTLIFE

One of Greater Miami's most popular pursuits is barhopping. Bars range from intimate enclaves to showy see-and-be-seen lounges to loud, raucous frat parties. There's a New York–style flair to some of the newer lounges, which are increasingly catering to the Manhattan party crowd who escape to South Beach for long weekends. Undoubtedly, Miami's pulse pounds with nonstop nightlife that reflects the area's potent cultural mix. On sultry, humid nights with the huge full moon rising out of the ocean and fragrant night-blooming jasmine intoxicating the senses, who can resist Cuban salsa with some disco and hip-hop thrown in for good measure? When this place throws a party, hips shake, fingers snap, and bodies touch. It's no wonder many clubs are still rocking at 5 am. If you're looking for a relatively nonfrenetic evening, your best bet is one of the chic hotel bars on Collins Avenue.

How to get past the velvet ropes at the hottest South Beach nightspots? First, if you're staying at a hotel, use the concierge. Decide which clubs you want to check out (consult *Ocean Drive* magazine's celebrity pages if you want to be among the glitterati), and the concierge will email, fax, or call in your names to the clubs so you'll be on the guest list when you arrive. This means much easier access and usually no cover charge (which can be upward of $20) if you arrive before midnight. Guest list or no guest list, follow these pointers: Make sure there are more women than men in your group. Dress up—casual chic is the dress code. For men this means no sneakers, no shorts, no sleeveless vests, and no shirts unbuttoned past the top button. For women, provocative and seductive is fine; overly revealing is not. Black is always right. At the door: don't name-drop—no one takes it seriously. Don't be pushy while trying to get the doorman's attention. Wait until you make eye contact, and then be cool and easygoing. If you decide to tip him (which most bouncers don't expect), be discreet and pleasant, not big-bucks obnoxious—a $10 or $20 bill quietly passed will be appreciated, however.

SHOPPING

If you're over the climate-controlled slickness of shopping malls and can't face one more food-court "meal," you've got choices in Miami. Head out into the sunshine and shop the city streets, where you'll find big-name retailers and local boutiques alike. Take a break at a sidewalk café to power up on some Cuban coffee or fresh-squeezed OJ and enjoy the tropical breezes.

Give your plastic a workout by shopping the many high-profile tenants on the densely packed two-block stretch of **Collins Avenue** between 5th and 10th streets. Think Club Monaco, MAC, Kenneth Cole, Barney's Co-Op, and A/X Armani Exchange. Sprinkled amid the upscale vendors are hair salons, spas, cafés, and such familiar stores as the Gap, Urban Outfitters, and Banana Republic. Be sure to head over one street east and west to catch the shopping on Ocean Drive and Washington Avenue.

The eight-block-long **Lincoln Road Mall** is the trendiest place on Miami Beach. Home to more than 150 shops, 20-plus art galleries and nightclubs, about 50 restaurants and cafés, and the renovated Colony Theatre, Lincoln Road is like a larger, more sophisticated cousin of Ocean Drive. The "see and be seen" theme is furthered by outdoor seating at every restaurant, where well-heeled patrons lounge and discuss the people (and pet) parade passing by. An 18-screen movie theater anchors the west end of the street, which is where most of the worthwhile shops are; the far-east end is mostly discount and electronics shops. Sure, there's a Pottery Barn, a Gap, and a Williams-Sonoma, but the emphasis is on art galleries and emporia with unique personalities, like En Avance, Chroma, Base, and Jonathan Adler.

HOMESTEAD

30 miles southwest of Miami.

Updated by Lynne Helm

In recent years, Homestead has redefined itself as a destination for tropical agro- and ecotourism. At a crossroads between Miami and the Keys as well as Everglades and Biscayne national parks, the area has the added dimension of shopping centers, residential development, hotel chains, and the Homestead–Miami Speedway—when car races are scheduled, hotels hike up their rates and require minimum stays. The historic downtown has become a preservation-driven Main Street. Krome Avenue, where it cuts through the city's heart, is lined with restaurants, an arts complex, antiques shops, and low-budget, sometimes undesirable accommodations. West of north–south Krome Avenue, miles of fields grow fresh fruits and vegetables. Some are harvested commercially, and others beckon with "U-pick" signs. Stands selling farm-fresh produce and nurseries that grow and sell orchids and tropical plants abound. In addition to its agricultural legacy, the town has an eclectic flavor, attributable to its population mix: descendants of pioneer Crackers, Hispanic growers and farm workers, professionals escaping the Miami hubbub, and latter-day Northern retirees.

EXPLORING

ArtSouth. This groundbreaking project centered on a 3½-acre complex includes the historic First Baptist Church, 30 artist studios, galleries, workshops, a sculpture garden, and stage. Watch artists at work and enjoy concert performances. Check out Second Saturdays—events happen from 3–7 pm on the second Saturday of every month—which include free live entertainment, art demonstrations, and self-guided tours. ⊠ *240 N. Krome Ave.* ☎ *305/247-9406* ⊕ *www.artsouthhomestead.org* ⊠ *Free* ⊙ *Mon.–Fri. 10–6, Sat. noon–6.*

FAMILY   **Coral Castle.** Driven by unrequited love, 100-pound Latvian immigrant Ed Leedskalnin (1887–1951) fashioned this attraction along Dixie Highway in the early 1900s out of massive slabs of coral rock, a feat he likened to building the pyramids. You can learn how he peopled his fantasy world with his imaginary wife and three children, studied astronomy, and created a simple home and elaborate courtyard without formal engineering education and with mostly hand-made tools. Highlights of this National Register of Historic Places site, originally named Rock Gate, include a working sundial, and a banquet table shaped like Florida. ⊠ *28655 S. Dixie Hwy.* ☎ *305/248-6345* ⊕ *www. coralcastle.com* ⊠ *$15* ⊙ *Daily 8–6.*

FAMILY   **Dante Fascell Visitor Center.** Go outside on the wide veranda to soak up views across mangroves and Biscayne Bay at this Convoy Point visitor center. Inside the museum, artistic vignettes and on-request videos including the 11-minute *Spectrum of Life* explore the park's four ecosystems, while the Touch Table gives both kids and adults a feel for bones, feathers, and coral. Facilities include the park's canoe and tour concession, restrooms with showers, a ranger information area, gift shop with books, and vending machines. Various ranger programs take place daily during busy fall and winter seasons. On the second Sunday monthly (December through April), the free Family Fun Fest offers hands-on activities. Rangers also give informal tours on Boca Chita Key; arrange in advance. A short trail and boardwalk lead to a jetty, and there are picnic tables and grills. This is the only area of the park accessible without a boat. ⊠ *9700 S.W. 328th St.* ☎ *305/230-7275* ⊕ *www.nps. gov/bisc* ⊠ *Free* ⊙ *Daily 9–5.*

WHERE TO EAT

$ ✕ **Bobbie Jo's Diner.** *Southern.* For Southern home-style cooking, head to Bobbie Jo's, once upon a time known as Sam's Kitchen. Breakfast is served all day. Dinners—including chicken livers, chicken and dumplings, and fried clams—come with fresh-baked corn bread and a daily selection of sides such as okra with tomatoes, turnip greens, pickled beets, or onion rings. Burgers come with fries and cole slaw, while other sandwiches, including a tasty egg salad for under five bucks, come with pickles and chips. Don't miss out on the changing line-up of homemade soups and desserts. All this goodness comes cheap, but at the expense of anything-but-glamorous dining environs and often slow (albeit friendly) service. ⑤ *Average main: $10* ✉ *1320 N. Krome Ave.* ☎ *305/246–2990* ⊗ *No dinner Sun.*

$ ✕ **NicaMex.** *Mexican.* Among the local Latin population this 68-seat eatery is a low-budget favorite for Nicaraguan and Mexican flavors. It helps if you know Spanish, but the menu is bilingual and some staffers speak English. Although they term it *comidas rapidas* (fast food), the cuisine is not Americanized. Try authentic huevos rancheros or *chilaquiles* (corn tortillas cooked in red-pepper sauce) for breakfast. Specialties include *chicharron en salsa verde* (fried pork skin in hot-green-tomato sauce). Hearty beef soups are top sellers. If you want (or dare), Mexican plates from tacos to tostadas can be made with beef tongue. Choose among domestic or imported beers, and escape south of the border. ⑤ *Average main: $10* ✉ *32 N.W. 1st St., across from Krome Ave. bandstand* ☎ *305/247–0727.*

SPORTS AND THE OUTDOORS ⊗

AUTO RACING

Homestead-Miami Speedway. The speedway buzzes more than 280 days each year with racing, manufacturer testing, car-club events, driving schools, and ride-along programs. The facility has 65,000 grandstand seats, club seating eight stories above racing action, and two tracks—a 2.21-mile continuous road course and a 1.5-mile oval. A packed schedule includes GRAND-AM and NASCAR events. Two tunnels on the grounds are below sea level. ✉ *One Speedway Blvd.* ☎ *866/409–7223* ⊕ *www. homesteadmiamispeedway.com.*

BOATING

Homestead Bayfront Park. Boaters, anglers, and beachgoers give high ratings to facilities at this recreational area adjacent to Biscayne National Park. The 174-slip marina, accommodating up to 50-foot vessels, has a ramp, dock, bait-and-tackle shop, fuel station, ice, and dry storage. The park also has a snack bar, tidal swimming area, a beach with lifeguards, playground, ramps for people with disabilities, and a picnic pavilion with grills, showers, and restrooms. ✉ *9698 S.W. 328th St.* ☎ *305/230–3033* ⌚ *$6 per passenger vehicle; $12 per vehicle with boat Mon.–Thurs., $15 Fri.–Sun.; $15 per RV or bus* ☉ *Daily sunrise–sunset.*

SHOPPING

Krome Avenue. In the heart of Old Homestead, this popular shopping street with a brick sidewalk has art galleries and antiques stores, including Jacobsen's Antique Mall, with multiple dealers. ✉ *144 N. Krome Ave.*

FLORIDA CITY

2 miles southwest of Homestead.

Updated by Lynne Helm

Florida's Turnpike ends in Florida City, the southernmost town of the peninsula, spilling thousands of vehicles onto U.S. 1 and eventually west to Everglades National Park, east to Biscayne National Park, or south to the Florida Keys. Florida City and Homestead run into each other, but the difference couldn't be more noticeable. As the last outpost before 18 miles of mangroves and water, this stretch of U.S. 1 is lined with fast-food eateries, service stations, hotels, bars, dive shops, and restaurants. Hotel rates increase significantly during NASCAR races at the nearby Homestead–Miami Speedway. Like Homestead, Florida City is rooted in agriculture, with hundreds of acres of farmland west of Krome Avenue and a huge farmers' market that processes produce shipped nationwide.

WHERE TO EAT

$$ ✕ **Capri Restaurant.** *Italian.* This friendly family-owned enterprise has been a magnet for affordable Italian-American classics since 1958. Dine amid redbrick walls at round tables, or at sunny courtyard tables with umbrellas. Options range from the all-you-care-to-eat pasta on Tuesdays ($8) to crunchy-crust pizza or paninis, or steak, prime rib, and a multitude of seafood-pasta combos. Tuesday is also lobster night. Daily early birds (4:30–6:30) include soup or salad and potato or spaghetti. Specialty martinis and fruity cocktails supplement an extensive wine list. ⑤ *Average main: $16* ✉ *935 N. Krome Ave.* ☎ *305/247–1542* ⊕ *www. dinecapri.com* ☉ *No lunch Sun.*

$ ✕**Farmers' Market Restaurant.** *Seafood.* Although this eatery is within the farmers' market on the edge of town and is big on serving fresh vegetables, seafood figures prominently on the menu. A family of anglers runs the place, so fish and shellfish are only hours from the sea, and there's a fish fry on Friday nights. Catering to farmers, the restaurant opens at 5:30 am, serving pancakes, jumbo eggs, and fluffy omelets with home fries or grits in a pleasant dining room with red and green checked tablecloths. For lunch or dinner, choose among fried shrimp or conch, seafood pasta, country-fried steak, and roast turkey, as well as salads, burgers and sandwiches. $ *Average main: $13* ✉*300 N. Krome Ave.* ☎*305/242–0008.*

$$ ✕**Mutineer Wharf Restaurant.** *Seafood.* Families and older couples flock to this kitschy roadside outpost with a fish-and-duck pond. Built in 1980 to look like a ship—back when Florida City barely got on maps—etched glass divides bi-level dining rooms, with velvet-upholstered chairs, an aquarium, and nautical antiques. Florida lobster tails, stuffed grouper, shrimp, and snapper top the menu, along with another half-dozen daily seafood specials. Add to that steaks, ribs, and chicken. Yellowfin tuna wraps and grouper sandwiches are filling items for lunch, especially before a trip into Everglades Park. You also can relax for dinner in the restaurant's Wharf Lounge. Friday and Saturday nights feature live entertainment and dancing. $ *Average main: $18* ✉*11 S.E. 1st Ave. (U.S. 1), at Palm Dr.* ☎*305/245–3377* ⊕*www.mutineerrestaurant.com.*

$ ✕**Rosita's Restaurante.** *Mexican.* As a growing local Mexican population can attest, this delightful hole-in-the-wall boasts authenticity you just don't get in Tex-Mex chains. Order à la carte specialties or dinners and combos with salad, beans, and rice. Breakfast, lunch, and dinner entrées, served all day, range from Mexican eggs, enchiladas, and taco salad to stewed beef and fried pork chops. Food is spicy, but for more fire, avail yourself of the fresh-tasting salsa, pickled jalapeños, or bottled habanero sauce on tables. Spiffy, with an open kitchen and take-out counter, Rosita's is a favorite with guests at the Everglades International Hostel across the street. $ *Average main: $11* ✉*199 W. Palm Dr.* ☎*305/246–3114.*

6

WHERE TO STAY

$ ☷ **Best Western Gateway to the Keys.** *Hotel.* For easy access to Everglades and Biscayne national parks as well as the Keys, you'll be well-situated at this sprawling, two-story lodging spot two blocks off Florida's Turnpike. **Pros:** convenient to parks, outlet shopping, and dining; business services; attractive pool area. **Cons:** traffic noise; fills up fast in high season. ⑤*Rooms from: $135* ⊠*411 S. Krome Ave.* ☎*305/246–5100, 888/981–5100* ⊕*www.bestwestern. com/gatewaytothekeys* ➾*114 rooms* ⑩*Breakfast.*

$ ☷ **Quality Inn.** *Hotel.* Amid an asphalt complex of hotels, gas stations, and eateries just off U.S. 1, this two-story Quality Inn (previously a Comfort Inn) with exterior corridors has a friendly front desk staff offering tips on Everglades or Keys adventures, or action at the nearby track. **Pros:** close to restaurants and services. **Cons:** no elevator; noisy location. ⑤*Rooms from: $89* ⊠*333 S. E. 1st Ave.* ☎*305/248–4009, 888/352–2489* ⊕*www.qualityinn.com* ➾*123 rooms* ⑩*Breakfast.*

$ ☷ **Fairway Inn.** *Hotel.* With a waterfall pool, this two-story motel with exterior room entry has some of the area's lowest chain rates, and it's next to the Chamber of Commerce visitor center so you'll have easy access to reading and planning material. **Pros:** affordable; convenient to restaurants, parks, and raceway. **Cons:** plain, small rooms; no-pet policy. ⑤*Rooms from: $89* ⊠*100 S.E. 1st Ave.* ☎*305/248–4202, 888/340–4734* ➾*160 rooms* ⑩*Breakfast.*

$ ☷ **Ramada Inn.** *Hotel.* If you're looking for an uptick from other chains, this pet-friendly property offers more amenities and comfort, such as 32-inch flat-screen TVs, duvet-covered beds, closed closets, and stylish furnishings. **Pros:** extra room amenities; convenient location. **Cons:** chain anonymity. ⑤*Rooms from: $99* ⊠*124 E. Palm Dr.* ☎*305/247–8833* ⊕*www.hotelfloridacity.com* ➾*123 rooms* ⑩*Breakfast.*

$ ☷ **Travelodge.** *Hotel.* This bargain motor lodge is close to Florida's Turnpike, Everglades and Biscayne national parks, and Homestead-Miami Speedway. **Pros:** convenience to track and U.S. 1; nice pool; complimentary breakfast. **Cons:** busy location; some small rooms; no pets. ⑤*Rooms from: $89* ⊠*409 S.E. 1st Ave.* ☎*305/248–9777, 800/758–0618* ⊕*www.tlflcity.com* ➾*88 rooms* ⑩*Breakfast.*

SHOPPING

FAMILY **Robert Is Here.** Want take-home gifts? This remarkable fruit stand sells more than 100 types of jams, jellies, honeys, and salad dressings along with its vegetables, juices, fresh-fruit milk shakes (try the key lime), and some 30 kinds of tropical fruits, including (in season) carambola, lychee, egg fruit, monstera, sapodilla, dragonfruit, genipa, sugar apple, and tamarind. Back in 1960, the stand got started when seven-year-old Robert sat at this spot hawking his father's bumper cucumber crop. Now Robert (still on the scene daily with his wife and kids) ships nationwide and donates seconds to needy area families. An assortment of animals out back—goats to iguanas and emus, along with a splash pool—creates entertainment value for kids. Picnic tables, benches, and a waterfall with a koi pond add serenity. On the way to Everglades National Park, Robert opens at 8 am, operating until at least 7, and shutting down from Labor Day until November. ⊠ *19200 S.W. 344th St.* ☎ *305/246–1592.*

6

TRAVEL SMART
FLORIDA KEYS

GETTING HERE AND AROUND

Key West International Airport is the only airport in the Keys that accommodates commercial flights, and five major airlines and a few small companies serve the airport. Most visitors fly into Miami International Airport and either drive to their destination in the Keys or take an air shuttle to Key West. The drive is long and slow. It can be done in a half day, but it's better to break up the drive and spend some time exploring the Keys outside of Key West.

■TIP→ Ask the local tourist board about hotel and local transportation packages that include tickets to major museum exhibits or other special events.

▌ AIR TRAVEL

About 450,000 passengers use the Key West International Airport (EYW) each year; its most recent renovation includes a beach where travelers can catch their last blast of rays after clearing security. Because flights are few, many prefer flying into Miami International Airport (MIA) and driving the 110-mile Overseas Highway (aka U.S. 1).

AIRPORTS

The fittingly tiny, laid-back Key West International Airport (EYW) has greeted domestic passengers and overseas private planes since 1957. In 2009, the airport completed its four-year renovation, which includes a beach where travelers can catch their last blast

of rays after clearing security. The new McCoy Terminal sits atop a 475-car parking ramp.

The airport is a short drive from Old Town, so should your flight get delayed (it happens often enough), jump in a taxi and enjoy a few more hours of Key West freedom. Note that ⊕ *www.keywestinternationalairport.com* is not the official airport site; it is operated by an outside travel agency.

Contacts **Key West International Airport** (EYW). ✉ *3491 S. Roosevelt Blvd., Key West* ☎ *305/296–5439* ⊕ www.monroecounty-fl.gov/index.aspx?NID=105. **Miami International Airport** (MIA). ✉ *Miami* ☎ *305/876–7000* ⊕ www.miami-airport.com.

GROUND TRANSPORTATION

Airporter operates scheduled van and bus pickup service from all Miami International Airport (MIA) baggage areas to wherever you want to go in Key Largo ($50) and Islamorada ($55). Groups of three or more passengers receive discounts. There are three departures daily; reservations are required 48 hours in advance. There's no website, so reservations need to be made by phone.

Greyhound Lines runs a special Keys shuttle twice a day (depending on the day of the week) from Miami International Airport (departing from Concourse E, lower level) and stops throughout the Keys. Fares run from around $25 for Key Largo (MM 99.6) or Islamorada (Burger King, MM 82) to around $45 for Key West (⊠ *3535 S. Roosevelt, Key West International Airport*).

Keys Shuttle runs scheduled service six times a day in 15-passenger vans (nine passengers maximum) between Miami and Fort Lauderdale airports and Key West with stops throughout the Keys for $60 to $90 per person sharing rides.

SuperShuttle charges about $165 for two passengers for trips to the Upper Keys; to go farther, you must book an entire 11-person van, which costs $250 to Marathon or $350 to Key West. For a trip to the airport, place your request 24 hours in advance.

Contacts Airporter ☏ *305/852–3413, 800/830–3413*. **Greyhound** ☏ *800/231–2222* ⊕ *www.greyhound. com*. **Keys Shuttle** ☏ *305/289–9997, 888/765–9997* ⊕ *www.keysshuttle. com*. **SuperShuttle** ☏ *305/871–2000* ⊕ *www.supershuttle.com*.

FLIGHTS

American Airlines, Cape Air, Delta (Express Jet), United (Silver Air), and US Airways provide service between Key West International Airport and Miami, Fort Lauderdale/Hollywood, Fort Myers, West Palm Beach, Orlando, Tampa, Atlanta, and Charlotte, NC (seasonally).

Flying time from Miami is 50 minutes, from Orlando just over an hour, from Atlanta about 2 hours.

Contacts AirTran. AirTran flies to Miami, Fort Lauderdale, Fort Myers,

Jacksonville, Key West, Orlando, Pensacola, Sarasota, Tampa, and West Palm Beach. ☏ *800/247–8726* ⊕ *www.airtran.com*. **American Airlines.** AA flies to Fort Lauderdale, Fort Myers, Fort Walton Beach, Gainesville, Jacksonville, Key West, Miami, Orlando, Pensacola, Tallahassee, Tampa, and West Palm Beach. ☏ *800/433–7300* ⊕ *www.aa.com*. **United.** United flies to Daytona, Fort Lauderdale, Fort Myers, Fort Walton Beach, Gainesville, Jacksonville, Key West, Miami, Orlando, Pensacola, Sarasota/Bradenton, Tallahassee, Tampa, and West Palm Beach. ☏ *800/864–8331 for U.S. reservations, 800/538–2929 for international reservations* ⊕ *www.united. com*. **Delta.** Delta flies to Daytona Beach, Fort Lauderdale, Fort Myers, Fort Walton Beach, Gainesville, Jacksonville, Key West, Melbourne, Miami, Orlando, Panama City, Pensacola, Sarasota, Tallahassee, Tampa, and West Palm Beach. ☏ *800/221–1212 for U.S. reservations, 800/241–4141 for international reservations* ⊕ *www.delta.com*. **US Airways.** US Airways, which recently merged with American Airlines, flies to Daytona Beach, Fort Lauderdale, Fort Myers, Fort Walton Beach, Gainesville, Jacksonville, Key West, Melbourne, Miami, Orlando, Pensacola, Sarasota, Tallahassee, Tampa, and West Palm Beach. ☏ *800/428–4322 for U.S. and Canadian reservations, 800/622–1015 for international reservations* ⊕ *www.usairways.com*.

▌ BOAT TRAVEL

Boaters can travel to and through the Keys either along the Intracoastal Waterway (5-foot draft limitation) through Card, Barnes, and Blackwater sounds and into Florida Bay, or along the deeper Atlantic Ocean route through Hawk Channel, a buoyed passage. Refer to NOAA Nautical Charts Numbers 11451, 11445, and 11441. The Keys are full of marinas that welcome transient visitors, but they don't have enough slips for everyone. Make reservations in advance, and ask about channel and dockage depth—many marinas are quite shallow.

For non-emergency information, contact the Coast Guard Group Key West on VHF-FM Channel 16. Safety and weather information is broadcast at 7 am and 5 pm Eastern Standard Time on VHF-FM Channels 16 and 22A. There are stations in Islamorada and Marathon.

Key West Express operates air-conditioned ferries between the Key West Terminal (Caroline and Grinnell streets) and Marco Island and Fort Myers Beach. The trip from Fort Myers Beach takes at least four hours each way and costs $86 one-way, $146 round-trip. Ferries depart from Fort Myers Beach at 8:30 am and from Key West at 6 pm. The Marco Island ferry costs $86 one-way and $146 round-trip, and departs at 8:30 am (the return trip leaves Key West at 5 pm). A photo ID is required for each passenger. Advance reservations are recommended.

Contacts Key West Express ⊠ *100 Grinnell St., Key West* ☎ *888/539–2628* ⊕ *www.seakeywestexpress. com.*

▌ BUS TRAVEL

The City of Key West Department of Transportation has six color-coded bus routes traversing the island from 6:30 am to 11:30 pm. Stops have signs with the international bus symbol. Schedules are available on buses and at hotels, visitor centers, and shops. The fare is $2 one-way.

The Lower Keys Shuttle bus runs from Marathon to Key West ($4 one-way), with scheduled stops along the way.

Miami Dade Transit provides daily bus service from MM 50 in Marathon to the Florida City Wal-Mart Supercenter on the mainland. The bus stops at major shopping centers as well as on-demand anywhere along the route during daily round trips on the hour from 6 am to 10 pm. The cost is $2 one-way, exact change required.

Contact City of Key West Department of Transportation ☎ *305/809–3910* ⊕ *www.kwtransit. com.*

▌ CAR TRAVEL

By car, from Miami International Airport, follow signs to Coral Gables and Key West, which puts you on LeJeune Road, then Route 836 west. Take the Homestead Extension of Florida's Turnpike south (toll road), which ends at Florida City and connects to the Overseas Highway (U.S. 1). Tolls from the airport run approximately $3. Payment is collected via **Sun Pass,** a prepaid toll program, or with **Toll-By-Plate,** a system that photographs each vehicle's license plate and mails a monthly bill for tolls, plus a $2.50 administrative fee, to the vehicle's registered owner.

You can also buy a mini-window transponder for your personal vehicle (and add value to the account) online for $4.99, and this will allow you to get the best rates on tolls. A regular transponder costs $25 and can also be purchased and recharged online.

For visitors renting cars in Florida, most major rental companies have programs allowing customers to use the Toll-By-Plate system, but this can be expensive. Tolls, plus varying service fees, are automatically charged to the credit card used to rent the vehicle. Under no circumstances should motorists attempt to stop in high-speed electronic tolling lanes. Travelers can contact Florida's Turnpike Enterprise for more information about the all-electronic tolling on Florida's Turnpike.

The alternative from Florida City is Card Sound Road (Route 905A), which has a bridge toll of $1 (cash only). Continue to the only stop sign and turn right on Route 905, which rejoins U.S. 1 31 miles south of Florida City.

Except in Key West, a car is essential for visiting the Keys. The best Keys road map, published by the Homestead–Florida City Chamber of Commerce, can be obtained for $5.50 from the Tropical Everglades Visitor Association (*see ⇨ Visitor Information*).

Avis, Budget, Enterprise, and Hertz serve Marathon Airport. Avis, Alamo, Budget, Dollar, Enterprise, Hertz, National, and Thrifty serve Key West's airport. Enterprise also has an office in Key Largo. ■TIP→ **Avoid flying into Key West and driving back to Miami; there could be substantial drop-off charges for leaving a Key West car there.**

Contacts **Florida's Turnpike Enterprise** ☎ 800/749-7453 ⊕ www. floridasturnpike.com. **SunPass** ☎ 888/865-5352 ⊕ www.sunpass. com.

MILE MARKERS

Getting lost in the Keys is almost impossible once you understand the unique address system. **Many addresses are simply given as a mile marker (MM) number.** The markers are small, green, rectangular signs along the side of the Overseas Highway (U.S. 1). They begin with MM 126, 1 mile south of Florida City, and end with MM 0, in Key West. **Keys residents use the abbreviation BS for the bay side of Overseas Highway and OS for the ocean side.** From Marathon to Key West, residents may refer to the bay side as the gulf side.

GASOLINE

The deeper you go into the Keys, the higher the pump price goes. Gas stations in Homestead and Florida City have some of the most affordable prices in South Florida, so fill your tank in Miami and top it off in Florida City.

PARKING

The only place in the Keys where parking is a problem is in Old Town in Key West. There are public parking lots that charge by the day (some hotels and B&Bs provide parking or discounts at municipal lots). If you arrive early, you can sometimes find spots on side streets off Duval and Whitehead, where you can park for free—just be sure it's not marked for residential parking only. Your best bet is to bike or take a trolley around town if you don't want to walk. The trolleys allow you to disembark and reboard at will at several different stops. The Conch Tour Train makes only two stops where you can board and disembark.

ROAD CONDITIONS

Most of the Overseas Highway is narrow and crowded (especially on weekends and in high season). Expect delays behind RVs, trucks, cars towing boats, and rubbernecking tourists. The section of highway that travels from the mainland to Key Largo is particularly slow and congested. Occasional passing lanes allow you to get past slow-moving trucks. The quality of local roads in Key West is good, though some side streets are narrow. Traffic in the historic district often becomes congested throughout the day and night.

CAR RENTAL

When you reserve a car, ask about cancellation penalties, taxes, drop-off charges (if you're planning to pick up the car in one city and leave it in another), and surcharges (for being under or over a certain age, for additional drivers, for additional insurance, or for driving across state borders or beyond a specific distance from your point of rental). All these things can add substantially to your costs. Request car seats and extras such as a GPS when you book.

Rates are sometimes—but not always—better if you book in advance or reserve through a rental agency's website. There are other reasons to book ahead, though: for popular destinations, during busy times of the year, or to ensure that you get certain types of cars (vans, SUVs, exotic sports cars).

■ TIP→ **Make sure that a confirmed reservation guarantees you a car. Agencies sometimes overbook, particularly for busy weekends and holiday periods.**

Unless you fly into Key West and decide to stay in Old Town for your entire vacation—perhaps with a bus trip to another Key or some water-sports excursions—you will need a car. Rentals of all makes and models are available at the Miami International Airport, Key West International Airport, and rental agencies throughout the Keys. Reserve your car early during big events such as Homestead Miami Speedway races (Key Largo is often affected), October's FantasyFest in Key West, and the Christmas and Easter holidays.

Alamo ☎ 877/222–9075 ⊕ www.alamo.com. **Budget** ☎ 800/218–7992 ⊕ www.budget.com. **Continental Rent-a-Car**. This service operates in Fort Lauderdale only. ☎ 800/221–4085, 954/332–1125 ⊕ www.continentalcar.com. **Hertz**

800/654-3131 ⊕ www.hertz.com.
National Car Rental ☎ 800/227-
7368 ⊕ www.nationalcar.com. **Sunshine Rent A Car.** Miami and Fort
Lauderdale only. ☎ 888/786-7446,
954/467-8100 ⊕ www.ab-rental.
com.

CAR RENTAL RESOURCES

Local Agencies

Continental (Fort Lauderdale and Orlando)	800/221-4085 or 954/332-1125	www.continentalcar.com
Sunshine Rent A Car (Fort Lauderdale)	888/786-7446 or 954/467-8100	www.sunshinerentacar.com

Major Agencies

Alamo	877/222-9075	www.alamo.com
Avis	800/331-1212	www.avis.com
Budget	800/527-0700	www.budget.com
Hertz	800/654-3131	www.hertz.com
National Car Rental	800/227-7368	www.nationalcar.com

TAXI TRAVEL

Serving the Keys from Ocean Reef
to Marathon, A1 Luxury Limousine has luxury Hummers and
limos that seat up to eight passengers, as well as vans and buses. It'll
pick up from any airport in South
Florida.

Florida Keys Taxi & Group Transportation operates around the
clock in Key West. The fare for two
or more from the Key West airport
to Old Town is $8 per person. Oth-
erwise, meters register $2.75 for
first 1/5 mile, $8 per mile.

Contact A1 Luxury Limousine
☎ 305/382-3035 ⊕ www.a1LimoBus.
com.

ESSENTIALS

▌ ACCOMMODATIONS

The most characteristic type of lodging in the Keys is a small, family-owned place, whether it be a guesthouse in Key West or a dive lodge in Key Largo. The islands do have their share of franchised operations and big destination resorts, but intimate lodging is still quite easy to find throughout the Keys. This is particularly true in Key West's Old Town, where many of the historic Victorian homes have been transformed into B&Bs. Most serve only Continental breakfast (a restaurant license is required to serve hot food).

Most hotels and other lodgings require you to give your credit-card details before they will confirm your reservation. If you don't feel comfortable emailing this information, ask if you can fax it (some places even prefer faxes). However you book, get confirmation in writing, and have a copy of it handy when you check in.

Be sure you understand the hotel's cancellation policy. Some places allow you to cancel without any kind of penalty—even if you pre-paid to secure a discounted rate—if you cancel at least 24 hours in advance. Others require you to cancel a week in advance or penalize you the cost of one night. Small inns and B&Bs are most likely to require you to cancel far in advance. Most hotels allow children under a certain age to stay in their parents' room at no extra charge, but others charge for them as extra adults; find out the cut-off age for discounts. Many of Key West's guesthouses do not allow children under a certain age.

APARTMENT AND HOUSE RENTALS

Although short-term rentals are available throughout the Keys, Key West has the largest inventory, and several rental companies can hook you up. *See Lodging Alternatives in the Key West chapter for local vacation-rental agencies.* National agencies Interhome and Villas International are also good resources for finding a vacation rental in the Keys.

Contacts **Interhome.** Daytona Beach, Miami, Orlando, Sarasota, Florida Keys, Lower Gulf Coast, Tampa Bay Area ☎ 954/791–8282, 800/882–6864 ⊕ *www.interhomeusa.com.* **Villas International.** Miami, Orlando, Broward County, Florida Keys, Lower Gulf Coast, Palm Beach County, Tampa Bay Area ☎ 415/499–9490, 800/221–2260 ⊕ *www.villasintl.com.*

▌ COMMUNICATIONS

INTERNET

Internet access is the norm in smaller guesthouses, lodges, motels, and resorts. Typically, it's Wi-Fi and often free, although not always available in every room, especially in older concrete-block or tin-roof structures. The larger resorts often charge for the service.

EATING OUT

The variety of restaurants in the Keys is vast, but if you were to ask a visitor what is typical, you would probably hear about the colorful seaside fish houses, some with more character than others. Seafood comes so fresh—you'll be spoiled for life. Pay special attention to local catches—especially snapper, mahimahi, grouper, lobster, and stone crab. Florida spiny lobster is local and fresh from August to March, and stone crabs from mid-October to mid-May.

Also keep an eye out for authentic key lime pie. The real McCoy has yellow filling in a graham-cracker crust and tastes pleasantly tart. (If it's green, just say no.) Cuban and Bahamian styles influence local cuisine, so be sure to sample some black beans and rice and conch fritters.

Restaurants may close for a two-to-four-week vacation during the slow season—between mid-September and mid-November.

MEALS AND MEALTIMES
Unless otherwise noted, the restaurants listed in this guide are open daily for lunch and dinner.

PAYING
Most restaurants accept the major credit cards. Some of the small, family-owned operations do not.

WORD OF MOUTH

Was the service stellar or not up to snuff? Did the food give you shivers of delight or leave you cold? Did the prices and portions make you happy or sad? Rate restaurants and write your own reviews or start a discussion about your favorite places in the Travel Talk Forums on ⊕ *www.fodors. com.* Your comments might even appear in our books. Yes, you, too, can be a correspondent!

RESERVATIONS AND DRESS
It's a good idea to make a reservation if you can. We only mention them specifically when reservations are essential or not accepted. For popular restaurants, book as far ahead as you can, and reconfirm as soon as you arrive. (Large parties should always call ahead to check the reservations policy.) Online reservation services make it easy to book a table before you even leave home.

WINE, BEER, AND SPIRITS
If the Keys have a representative tipple, it is the margarita. Kelly's Caribbean Bar & Brewery in Key West is the Keys' only microbrewery, and it sells bottled product.

MONEY

ATMs are common throughout the Keys if you need to get cash, so there's no need to carry a large amount of money on your person.

CREDIT CARDS

We cite information about credit cards only if they aren't accepted at a restaurant or a hotel. Otherwise, assume that most major credit cards are acceptable.

Reporting Lost Cards **American Express** ☎ 800/528-4800 ⊕ www.americanexpress.com. **Diners Club** ☎ 800/234-6377 ⊕ www.dinersclub.com. **Discover** ☎ 800/347-2683 ⊕ www.discovercard.com. **MasterCard** ☎ 800/622-7747 ⊕ www.mastercard.com. **Visa** ☎ 800/847-2911 ⊕ www.visa.com.

▌ TIME

The Florida Keys are in the Eastern Time Zone. The Dry Tortugas lie in the Central Time Zone, but the ferries and seaplanes run according to Eastern time. During daylight saving time, some operations stay open later.

▌ TIPPING

Tip at restaurants (15% is sufficient except at the fanciest, most expensive places, where a larger tip of around 18% is more common). It's common courtesy to leave a dollar or two per night for the housekeeper at your hotel (unless you are staying at a B&B that's run by the owners); leave the money each morning before your room is cleaned.

▌ VISITOR INFORMATION

There are several separate tourism offices in the Florida Keys, or you can try the website of Visit Florida as well for general information and referrals to local agencies.

Contacts **Big Pine and the Lower Keys Chamber of Commerce** ☎ 305/872-2411, 800/872-3722 ⊕ www.lowerkeyschamber.com. **Greater Key West Chamber of Commerce** ☎ 305/294-2587, 800/527-8539 ⊕ www.keywestchamber.org. **Greater Marathon Chamber of Commerce and Visitor Center** ✉ MM 53.5 BS, 12222 Overseas Hwy., Marathon ☎ 305/743-5417, 800/262-7284 ⊕ www.floridakeysmarathon.com. **Islamorada Chamber of Commerce & Visitors Center** ✉ MM 87.1 BS, 87100 Overseas Hwy., Islamorada ☎ 305/664-4503, 800/322-5397 ⊕ www.islamoradachamber.com. **Key Largo Chamber of Commerce.** Stop in for brochures, directions, recommendations, or some colorful Key Largo T-shirts and gifts. ✉ MM 106 BS, 10600 Overseas Hwy., Key Largo ☎ 305/451-4747, 800/822-1088 ⊕ www.keylargochamber.org.

Monroe County Tourist Development Council ☎ 800/352-5397 ⊕ www.Fla-Keys.com. **Tropical Everglades Visitor Association** ☎ 305/245-9180, 800/388-9669 ⊕ www.tropicaleverglades.com. **Visit Florida** ☎ 850/488-5607, 866/972-5280 ⊕ www.visitflorida.com.

INDEX

PHOTO CREDITS

Front cover: Masterfile [Description: Key West]. Spine: PHB.cz (Richard Semik)/ Shutterstock. 1, PBorowka/Shutterstock. 2, John Miller / age fotostock. 3 (top), Michael Dwyer / Alamy. 3 (bottom), Todd Taulman/Shutterstock. 4 (top left), Melissa Schalke/ iStockphoto. 4 (top right), George Burba/Shutterstock. 4 (bottom), Fraser Hall / age fotostock. 5, Stephen Frink/TDC/Visit Florida. 6, Robert J Bennett / age fotostock. 7 (top left), VANILLA FIRE/Shutterstock. 7 (top right), Dave G. Houser / Alamy. 7 (bottom), Danita Delimont / Alamy. 8 (top left), Marcel Pepeira / age fotostock. 8 (top right), Tim Kiusalaas / age fotostock. 8 (bottom), Angelo Cavalli / age fotostock. 11, Visit Florida. 21, Walter Bibikow / age fotostock. 61, Shackleford Photography/Shutterstock. 79, Johnny Stockshooter / age fotostock. 93, Fotoluminate LLC/Shutterstock. 149, Wilson Araujo/Shutterstock.

About Our Writers: All photos are courtesy of the writers except for the following: Lynne Helm, courtesy of John Rude.

ABOUT OUR WRITERS

 After being hired sight unseen by a South Florida newspaper, Fort Lauderdale–based freelance travel writer and editor Lynne Helm arrived from the Midwest anticipating a few years of palm-fringed fun. More than a quarter century later (after covering the state for several newspapers, consumer magazines, and trade publications), she's still enamored of Florida's sun-drenched charms. Lynne updated the Homestead and Florida City sections of the Gateways to the Keys chapter.

 Miami native Jill Martin updated the Upper Keys, the Middle Keys, the Lower Keys, and the Key West chapters. As a freelance writer, she has blogged more than 1,000 articles for the state's tourism website, Visit Florida, and also writes for various travel sites and print magazines. She has appeared on numerous TV and radio shows as a Florida travel expert and is the creator of Sunshine Brain Games, a trivia card game all about Florida. She resides full time in Redland and part-time on Sanibel Island.

 Paul Rubio's quest to discover the world has taken him to 107 countries and counting. Paul graduated from Harvard in 2002 with master's degrees in both public administration and economics, but in 2008 he gave into his passion and became a full-time travel writer. He's won over a dozen national awards for his articles and guidebooks. The prolific writer is the travel editor of *Palm Beach Illustrated, Naples Illustrated,* and *Weddings Illustrated* and regularly contributes to *Ultratravel U.S., Robb Report, Private Clubs,* and the full family of Modern Luxury publications.

Fodor's InFocus FLORIDA KEYS

Publisher: Amanda D'Acierno, *Senior Vice President*

Editorial: Arabella Bowen, *Editor in Chief*; Linda Cabasin, *Editorial Director*

Design: Fabrizio La Rocca, *Vice President, Creative Director*; Tina Malaney, *Associate Art Director*; Chie Ushio, *Senior Designer*; Ann McBride, *Production Designer*

Photography: Jennifer Arnow, *Senior Photo Editor*; Jennifer Romains, *Researcher*

Maps: Rebecca Baer, *Senior Map Editor*; David Lindroth, *Cartographer*

Production: Linda Schmidt, *Managing Editor*; Evangelos Vasilakis, *Associate Managing Editor*; Angela L. McLean, *Senior Production Manager*

Sales: Jacqueline Lebow, *Sales Director*

Marketing & Publicity: Heather Dalton, *Marketing Director*; Katherine Punia, *Senior Publicist*

Business & Operations: Susan Livingston, *Vice President, Strategic Business Planning*; Sue Daulton, *Vice President, Operations*

Fodors.com: Megan Bell, *Executive Director, Revenue & Business Development*; Yasmin Marinaro, *Senior Director, Marketing & Partnerships*

Copyright © 2015 by Fodor's Travel, a division of Random House LLC

Writer: Jill Martin
Editor: Doug Stallings
Editorial Contributors: Lynne Helm, Paul Rubio

Fodor's is a registered trademark of Random House LLC. All rights reserved. Published in the United States by Fodor's Travel, a division of Random House LLC, New York, a Penguin Random House Company, and in Canada by Random House of Canada Limited, Toronto. No maps, illustrations, or other portions of this book may be reproduced in any form without written permission from the publisher.

ISBN 978-0-8041-4354-7

ISSN 1942-7328

All details in this book are based on information supplied to us at press time. Always confirm information when it matters, especially if you're making a detour to visit a specific place. Fodor's expressly disclaims any liability, loss, or risk, personal or otherwise, that is incurred as a consequence of the use of any of the contents of this book.

SPECIAL SALES

This book is available at special discounts for bulk purchases for sales promotions or premiums. For more information, e-mail specialmarkets@penguinrandomhouse.com

PRINTED IN THE UNITED STATES OF AMERICA
10 9 8 7 6 5 4 3 2 1